IN THE DANGER ZONE

Stefan Gates

BBC
BOOKS

This book is published to accompany the BBC television series *Cooking in the Danger Zone*.

Published in 2008 by BBC Books, an imprint of Ebury Publishing.
A Random House Group Company

The Random House Group Limited Reg. No. 954009
Addresses for companies within the Random House Group can be found at www.randomhouse.co.uk

A CIP catalogue record for this book is available from the British Library

ISBN 978 1 84 607264 2

The Random House Group Limited makes every effort to ensure that the papers used in our books are made from trees that have been legally sourced from well-managed and credibly certified forests. Our paper procurement policy can be found at www.randomhouse.co.uk

Commissioning editors: Nicky Ross and Christopher Tinker
Project editor: Gillian Holmes   Designer: Isobel Gillan

Printed and bound in Great Britain by Clays Ltd, St Ives PLC

Endpapers Front (top to bottom, left to right): making dumplings in a factory, Henan Province, China (Ruhi Hamid); making friends with a market stall holder, Gulu, Northern Uganda (RH); milking a camel with the Bedouin, Negev Desert, Southern Israel (Marc Perkins); meeting the Zapatistas, Oventic, Mexico (Alex Mackintosh); holding the tail of a Beluga whale, Igloolik, Canada (MP); taking a break on the way over the Thai–Burmese border (MP); practising Tai Chi, Henan Province, China (RH); eating rat, Paraiya, India (Chris Alcock); target practice with the US army, Kabul, Afghanistan (MP); Harry holding a walrus penis-bone near Igloolik, Canada (Stefan Gates); dogs being sold for meat at an auction, Seoul, South Korea (Alex Mackintosh); sitting on The Pig, Nablus, Occupied West Bank (Alaa T. Badarneh); eating betelnut, Ei Tu Ta refugee camp, Burma (MP). Back: patrolling Cite Soliel with UN MINUSTAH soldiers (Callum McRae); Fatah rally, Nablus, Occupied West Bank (SG); eating camel's hump in Beijing, China (SG); drinking honey wine in Addis Ababa, Ethiopia (Julie Noon); eating humus in the Old City, Jerusalem (MP); milking a goat in Yanun, Occupied West Bank (MP); bushmeat seller, Yaounde, Cameroon (SG); tuk-tuk driving lesson in Mumbai, India (CA); waking up in Yalebo, Ethiopia (JN); preparing civet cat for lunch, Cameroon (Olly Bootle); eating banana tree pupae in Karen village, Burma (MP); Arab members of the Israeli Defence Force on the boundary with Gaza, Israel (SG); eating deep-fried scorpion, Beijing, China (RH); drinking deer penis juice in Beijing, China (Yan Yan).

CONTENTS

HELLO

Bang! An explosion temporarily blinds me. I see a guy sprawled up ahead, covered in blood and screaming hysterically in Arabic, part of his leg blown off. My heart beats out of control as I realize that I'm slap-bang in the middle of a minefield. F**k. There's a place and a time for swearing, and it's here and now. F**k, f**k, f**k.

It hasn't been the best of days: I've already been caught in a mortar bombardment, robbed at gunpoint and administered first aid to two blood-drenched women at the scene of a horrific car crash. To tell the truth, I'm no longer just scared, I'm really f**ked-off and scared, which is a rubbish combination. I'm immobilized by The Fear, an involuntary contraction of both sphincter and brain power. I search my memory for someone to blame for sending me to a place this absurdly dangerous, but it's my own stupid fault. My kids will have to say, 'Daddy died writing a cookery book,' as their mates suppress their giggles. I miss my kids. I miss my wife. I miss my cat. I miss my coffee machine. I despise myself for being here at all. I'm just a weedy, bookish food writer from north London – I wasn't built for war zones.

The adrenalin recedes and I let out a deep sigh. I'm in a pyrotechnic minefield in Herefordshire and the screaming Arab jumps to his feet, right as rain, and berates me in a broad Welsh accent for failing to notice the obvious signs of mines. He watches me go through the motions of sticking my penknife in the ground at an angle as we play-act getting out of this sodding mud. Needless to say, I am now thoroughly humiliated and not a little miserable.

I'm on a gruesome course called 'How to Survive Hostile Environments', which is supposed to prepare me for visiting Category 1 conflict zones like Afghanistan and rebel-held Burma. I've spent the morning with roughty-toughty ex-paras being pistol-whipped and bundled into car boots and watching scratchy videos of people having their fingers cut off by kidnappers. I am now feeling nervous, exhausted, nihilistic and, for some reason, a tad misanthropic. What have I got myself into?

● ● ● ● ●

I am about to embark on the craziest project of my life: two years of travelling to the world's most dangerous and complicated countries, using food to understand a world in crisis. I've always believed that food is a window onto emotion, morality and society, but I suspect that it can also reveal the intimate reality of how big issues like war, disaster, religious conflict and hunger have a tangible effect on *real* people.

We rarely see more than a shallow, macro view of the world and its big issues: we see Afghans on the news, screaming and bloodied in front of burning cars; Palestinians burning flags; refugees mournful and powerless. These people are often stripped of their personality and dignity by the needs of the media. I want to meet, talk and live with ordinary people in extraordinary situations to try to understand the world a little better. Perhaps if I sit down to eat with them I'll find them more like me.

But five days before I leave for Afghanistan, The Fear returns. I'm in the middle of presenting a chirpy TV series called *Food Uncut*, which couldn't be more different from the project I'm about to start. The coming two years will be a cycle of two weeks avoiding bullets in the most godforsaken hellholes of the world, followed by two weeks in this cosy TV studio reading autocues and making cheeky banter, then back to the godforsaken hellholes again. I'm hoping it's a way of staying sane.

Anyway, here I am, about to reveal 'What's Hot and What's Not in the World of Food this Week' (marmalade with gold flakes is in, but Asda wet fish is out), when I get an urgent telephone call from my executive producer Will Daws. His voice is unusually sombre.

'I don't know how to say this, Stef, but the BBC high-risk security team has intelligence that 38 would-be suicide bombers have just entered Afghanistan from Pakistan. On top of that, there's a specific group that's actively looking for a Western hostage and things are pretty hairy. It's entirely up to you. If you want to pull out, you can. Have a think about it and call me back.'

So an already crazy idea has become even crazier, and I stumble through the rest of the day's filming barely paying attention to my script. That night I sit down with my wife Georgia and break the news to her. Actually, I'm ashamed to say that I don't give her all the details – in fact,

I've largely played down the danger of the whole project, so I just say that things are looking a bit rum out in Persia, but not to worry because I'll be fine. I feel terrible. I've only just come to terms with the prospect of spending two weeks of every month away from her and my two daughters. And now this.

Perhaps I'm stupid, cavalier and selfish to even think about flying around the world searching for danger when I've got two beautiful, bright-eyed little girls who need me. Christ, I'm homesick and missing them like crazy, and I haven't even left my front room. And to top that, I'm now enduring a prolonged, involuntary contraction of my sphincter. This is to become a familiar feeling over the next two years: this is The Fear.

But the simple reality is that this project feels important and useful. I'm also an incurable optimist who believes that good things will happen and that somehow or other things will end up fine. And yes, goddammit, the little boy in me who always wanted to explore the world and do dangerous stuff and get trapped on a desert island and use every tool on his penknife is so excited that he can barely think straight.

I call Will and tell him that I'm going.

I visit the BBC Safety Stores – an extraordinary emporium that sells everything from fluorescent tabards to flak jackets. It's run by two young ladies whose sense of humour is generally in inverse proportion to that of their customers, who are always on a last-minute shopping expedition to somewhere awful, looking for odd items that might help them survive.

The ridiculousness and seriousness of the trip hits me as I look at my reflection, wearing a bright blue flak jacket and matching bright blue helmet – on paper it sounds kinda conflict cool, but the reality is I look and feel like a bright blue, dorky tit with a surprised, speccy look on its face.

There's all sorts of other kerfuffle involved with going to war zones: security briefings, visas, endless injections, army accreditation, water sterilization pills, press passes. There's so much stuff to sort out that before I know it, bugger me if I'm not in Kabul, stuck in the most chaotic traffic I've ever seen. I mention to our driver that insurance must be difficult to arrange in this country. He guffaws at my ignorance. 'There's no insurance here,' he says, gunning the engine and mounting the mud kerb. Traffic jams are dangerous for Westerners – high danger of kidnap, so it's best not to get stuck. But our driver says, 'You're safe with me – no one's ever been kidnapped from a car when I've been driving.' Then his brow furrows and he adds, 'Actually, now that I think about it, there was one. But just the one, so far.'

HELLO

My arse cheeks tighten once again as The Fear shivers through me. Welcome to the Danger Zone.

Hang on a minute...

You may or may not be aware that this whole escapade is also a BBC TV series, but it's not like any telly I've ever made before. The crew is just me, a local translator/fixer, plus ONE multi-talented genius who is producer, camera operator, director, sound recordist, health-and-safety officer and drinking buddy all rolled into one. There's a fantastic team back in London who run the production, but on location we are very much alone. We use small cameras, hidden radio mics, and carry a couple of satellite phones, and that's about it.

These lovely telly people don't appear in this book anywhere near as much as they should because I tried to avoid just writing about the making of a TV programme. But the truth is that there are 16 separate trips with seven different producers, all of them long-suffering heroes of documentary film-making.

But here's a thing: whereas the BBC TV series of *Cooking in the Danger Zone* has been subjected to the highest, most rigorous standards of BBC Current Affairs journalism, and subjected to the whip-cracking terror of BBC editorial policy to eradicate any hint of bias, this book...hasn't.

On the contrary, this book tells the story of one man's personal journey around some of the world's most awful places. And that man was often exhausted, terrified, exhilarated, irrational, overly sympathetic, sentimentally attached, homesick, angry and hungry. He was also writing whilst very emotional at the end of a horribly long day.

And he was occasionally a little drunk.

So I hope that you read these essays for what they are: a polemic, unreasonable, emotional reaction to events as they unfolded to a man at the end of his tether. They are biased towards my personal experience, but they are hopefully of a lot more interesting for it.

Stefan Gates
London, October 2007

AFGHANISTAN
Testicles and the Taliban

- **POPULATION:** 27 million
- **PERCENTAGE LIVING ON LESS THAN $2 A DAY:** 53%
- **UNDP HUMAN DEVELOPMENT INDEX:** not available
- **CORRUPTION PERCEPTIONS INDEX POSITION:** 117 out of 159
- **GDP (NOMINAL) PER CAPITA:** $335 (164/179)
- **FOOD AID RECIPIENTS:** WFP aims to provide food aid to 6.6 million Afghans between Jan 2006 and Dec 2008 at a cost of $372 million
- **MALNUTRITION:** 54% of children under five are stunted

I'm nursing a deep-rooted, fear-related nausea, as I toy with my flak jacket, which weighs a ton. I wonder whether I'll be able to walk in it, let alone run from flying bullets if the situation arises.

The flight into Kabul is a peculiar, disconcerting affair. I'm on a UN jet complete with air stewardesses, South African pilot and dark blue leather seats with ample legroom. It's plain and unadorned yet discreetly luxurious. I've hitched a lift using the UN's journalist's arrangement: I pay the full market cost of the flight, and could get bumped up at any time. I sit with my arse muscles tightly clenched, as they will continue to be for the next two weeks, wondering why on earth I didn't get around to writing a will. I glance over at Marc, my producer on this trip, but he's already fast asleep. Bastard.

There's tension in the air, even up here at 35,000 feet. I ponder morbidly on ground-to-air missiles and adventure-versus-idiocy ratios. My misery only increases as we start to descend over Kabul.

I look at some photos of my daughters to distract me, but just then the plane makes a violent lurch and pulls a 90-degree turn. What the hell was that for? My heart pumps like the clappers and I grip the armrests. Suddenly we flatten out just as violently, and I see the runway hurtling towards us. Without pausing to pitch, roll and tickle, or whatever it is those nice cosy BA pilots do, the plane dumps itself with a crash onto a strip of lumpy concrete. My teeth are clamped so tightly together that my gums are about to bleed. I look over at Marc again. He yawns and wakes up before giving me a friendly grin. I'm going to have to work on this relationship.

During my high-risk training I was told that airports are extremely dangerous – I'll be a great kidnap target and I'll be disorientated so I should take the utmost precaution. It's pitch black when I step onto the tarmac at Kabul International airport, and as the other passengers amble off the plane, I stand there trying to wriggle into my flak jacket and helmet. Everyone stares at me. Marc quietly suggests I put the flak jacket away – I'm only going to draw attention from potential kidnappers. Oh God, I'm so confused. I want to go home!

The airport isn't a great advert for Afghanistan. It's crumbling, chaotic, bewildering, filthy and full of angry-looking shouty blokes, closed offices, and people with guns but no obvious affiliation.

We struggle into the car park and throw all our gear into the back of a 4×4. Our driver hoons at breakneck pace through the dark streets – I suppose we're being treated like VIPs, with a special dispensation to flout traffic rules and speed limits in order to avoid kidnappers and Improvised Explosive Devices. Our security is more important than the safety of other road users – we are from the BBC after all. But I soon realize that he just always drives like this, and when I'm finally brave enough to look out of the window I realize that everyone else drives like this too.

There are three places to stay in Kabul. One is the Intercontinental – a vast corporate number to the west of the city, built by the British in 1969, and now in a state of creeping decrepitude. It's perched on a big hill and has a wonderful view across Kabul. And here lies the problem: it sticks out like a fluorescent crucifix on an imam. You couldn't create a better target for missiles in a lawless city if you wrote 'Contents: valuable journalists, diplomats and government ministers' on its side. During the war, all the journalists gathered here to enjoy its bar, pool (women not allowed) and room service, and it remains popular. Every now and then someone bombs it, or casually takes a pot-shot at it with a shoulder-held missile launcher: the last rocket attack was only two weeks before we arrived. A forlorn sign at the entrance says 'No Weapons'. You takes your chances.

The second place is the recently opened, absurdly luxurious Serena. There's nothing wrong with this place, as long as you can get your pretty little head to sleep on those goose-down pillows when outside 6.6 million Afghans go hungry on a daily basis. (I don't mean to sound preachy, but the contrast is a lot to bear.) The Serena has a small army of security guards at the door, bristling with modern weaponry, and inside the prawn cocktail is safe to munch, and the loo roll is of perfect pile. All of which puts it firmly out of the BBC's hotel budget.

I'm booked into the third option: the Gandamack Lodge, a legendary Kabul institution also known as Peter Jouvenal's Place, and the favoured drinking hole of the international press. It used to be the home of Bin Laden's fourth wife and family, but now it's become a small, nicely down-at-heel hotel (although in Kabul terms, it's high luxury) with a colonial feel designed to please grouchy British war correspondents, who enjoy its collection of military souvenirs and antiques.

There are machine gun-toting guards at the low-key entrance, which is both comforting and horrific, but I don't really care any more. I'm exhausted from The Fear, and I'd quite like it to stop.

Marc and I sit down to a bottle of Woolf Blass cabernet sauvignon (didn't expect to see one of those in Kabul) and my first taste of Afghan food: mantu (ravioli-type pasta filled with meat and served in a tomato sauce) and pakaura (deep-fried battered potatoes). It's all bland, but fine – presumably watered down for Western hacks. Marc plumps for chicken breast in a creamy sauce with chips. We chat for the first time, and I begin to warm to him, mainly because he's been to a zillion war zones and I get the feeling he's keen to get me home in one piece.

I'm still nervous, though, so we sink a second bottle of Woolfey and a couple of whiskies before finally going to bed, I'm ashamed to say, thoroughly pissed. It's one way to deal with The Fear. It feels like I've been through a lot already, and we haven't even started.

Good Morning Kabul

A shaft of light pierces my hangover and I drag myself to the window. Ah, yes. Afghanistan. One of the unhappiest, poorest, most heavily-armed and dangerous places on the planet, and a Category A security risk to boot. Added to that, there's no pork, no chicken (bird flu), no fish (no sea), no ovens and no visible women. Why on earth would a food writer want to come here? And what am I doing in a Muslim country with a *hangover*?

● ● ● ● ●

Let's get to grips with Aghanistan. It's a confusing country, so a quick, pub-friendly, 60-second rundown of the major rucks might be useful before we begin.

The Persians started it all back in 500 BC with the Achaemenid Empire, followed by Alexander the Great, and all manner of other imperialists and rogues, including ourselves as far back as 1838, with the First Anglo-Afghan War. We mucked about here with varying degrees of success until finally leaving in 1921. There was a relatively peaceful period from 1933 until it all went to pot again in 1973, when the Russians invaded with terrible consequences.

In 1979 they sent 150,000 soldiers to fight a disastrous ten-year war against the US-funded Mujahideen and gave up only after 15,000 of their soldiers had been killed, and 5 million Afghans had become refugees. As soon as the Russians left, the USA lost interest too, but instead of peace, the country descended into chaos and corruption under the faction-decimated Mujahideen. The Taliban were a politico-religious reaction to the misery, and seized most of the country by 2000, curbing freedoms and violating human rights, especially those of women, but they also imposed order and initially eradicated the opium trade.

Soon after 9/11, however, the USA took umbrage at the Taliban's fondness for terrorists and, alongside the Afghan Northern Alliance, swept through the country with astonishing speed. Since then, cash has poured into Afghanistan from the West, but daily life for most people is still miserable, impoverished and insecure.

I always wondered why people wanted to muck about with Afghanistan. This is one of the poorest countries in the world – it produces little except opium and carpets, it has no substantial resources other than gas, it's a sod of a climate to live in, lurching from arid to freezing with not a lot in between, and it has a feudal system that is almost impossible to crack. So why does everyone want to conquer it? The answer is that it's a *buffer*. Britain invaded because it was on the border with its precious India; Russia because it's a troublesome neighbour; the USA because Russia wanted it, plus it was near the oil-rich Persian Gulf; and Alexander the Great because ... well, he just liked collecting stuff. Trouble is, no one – that's *no one* – has ever managed to control this place without a flagrant disregard for human rights.

There you go – you don't get stuff like this in many food books, do you? Now let's crack on.

● ● ● ● ●

I drive for hours through a thick stew of traffic to find Kabul's central food market. At first glance it appears pretty civilized, with decent stalls and people pottering around, but on closer inspection I can see that it floats on a sea of mud and excrement that smells so bad I want to vomit. I visit a friendly butcher whose lamb carcass displays a vast fatty growth and I get very excited. This is Afghanistan's legendary fat-tailed sheep (it doesn't have a fat tail; the fat actually sits above its bottom), and although I've read about them, I doubted that they really existed. The fat is delicate, light and fluffy, an extraordinary cross between sheepskin and washed tripe. The butcher says it's an aphrodisiac 'worth a thousand Viagra'. It also sports a single, enormous veiny testicle (the other one's already been sold). I wonder if I'll get to eat one of those.

I buy boulani (a kind of vegetable-filled pancake) at a market stall next to an open sewer (all the stalls are next to open sewers), and I shouldn't really eat them on health and sanitation grounds (both the driver and the translator refuse to touch them), but there's no point coming to Afghanistan to find out about food if I'm not prepared to eat it, so I dive in and hope for the best. The boulanis taste great – good thick crêpes covered in searing hot chilli sauce. It's always possible that The Fear has got a grip on my tastebuds and clouded my judgement, but I think I'm going to like Afghan food.

Masr-i-Sharif

Now the adventure really begins. I want to discover how ordinary people suvive day-to-day in extraordinary situations like those here in Afghanistan. Tomorrow is the Afghan New Year, the biggest event in the Afghan calendar, and the biggest celebrations are held in the northern city of Masr-i-Sharif, which is overlooked by the Hindu Kush.

The city was the site of a series of gruesome massacres by both the Taliban and their enemies in 1997–8, and was also the first city to fall to the Afghan Northern Alliance during the most recent of the many Afghan wars. The rout began on 7 October 2001 and ended with John Simpson taking Kabul single-handedly just 37 days later. It is the stronghold of a powerful warlord called Dostum, and it's now relatively safe compared to the insurgency-minded south.

All seats on all flights have been booked out for months, so I've chartered a small plane to fly me to the north. When I call to confirm it the company says that they've decided not to fly – dodgy weather over the Hindu Kush. But if I don't get there today, I'll miss the country's biggest party, so I drive back to the airport to try to blag my way onto another plane. After haggling, wheedling, pestering and whining, I find that there are actually two seats left on a commercial flight to Masr, but I have to wait to see if the last two customers turn up. I pray that they've had an accident. (Not a bad one, you understand, just a stubbed foot or a lost set of house keys, something like that.)

Finally, the booking clerk accepts my bribe. I make a dash for the plane and claim one of the last two seats at the back. Yeehee. The one advantage of a country being this chaotic is that it works both ways – you can get picked up just as easily as you're let down.

On the plane, Marc and I have our first row. I wanted to learn how to slaughter a sheep to discover about halal tradition but according to our research, local custom requires me to have been baptized to be able to do it. I haven't been. The upside is that I've looked into baptism and, apparently, in emergencies, anyone can baptize me, even Marc. I'm not entirely sure that I want my baps tized by Marc, but beggars can't be choosers. Marc, however, finds the whole baptism thing distastefully touchy-feely and not a little weird. He's right, of course.

When we arrive, it's a warm, sunny afternoon. The air is clean and the mountains are beautiful. At last I'm beginning to feel calmer. I'm met by Aleem Agha, my guide for the trip. If you ever go to Afghanistan (and I hope you do), you'll need Aleem. He's like Sallah in *Raiders of the Lost Ark* – a big man with a huge personality, fingers in lots of pies, busting with honour and trustworthiness, and with access to pretty much anyone in the country at the stab of a mobile phone.

We set off, and the driver Basir swiftly finds the biggest traffic jam in the world, en route to the fortified safe house of the World Food

Programme (WFP), where I have kindly been offered a bed for the night. Looking out of the car, I get my first real daytime glimpse of the country and it's quite a shock. There's pretty much no infrastructure – there are no proper roads and most buildings are either half-built or on the verge of collapse. The fact that the country functions at all is little short of a miracle, as the government has little or no control outside Kabul, mainly because it has little or no cash. (This is one of the poorest places on the planet, so it's not surprising that no one pays taxes.)

The car inches its way through the New Year's Eve traffic of cannibalized, filth-farting buses and knackered, dusty jalopies, and people stare at my white Western face peering out of the big 4×4. I can't tell if they look hostile or just interested – either way it adds to the sense of being way out of my depth.

I eventually make it to the WFP safe house on a backstreet. It's not luxurious, but it has decent machine gun-wielding security so it feels safe. The UN runs lots of these places for their staff, and journalists can stay in them for a small fee. There's a cook who makes basic Western foods (shame), there's satellite telly and even a small swimming pool (currently closed for the winter), but if I had to stay for more than a few nights in these siege conditions, I'd be pretty miserable.

Dining with the Taliban

I'm woken by a series of loud explosions from across the city, and The Fear floods back. I creep down to the dining room where the cook tells me it is just some celebratory explosions for the Afghan New Year. It's fair to say that Afghans like their explosions. It's tempting to make a link between that and the fact that they've experienced centuries of war, but that might be cheeky.

Back out on the road, Basir finds a brand new bad-tempered traffic jam and when we do finally arrive at our destination – a huge patch of muddy land grandly called 'the stadium' – we find that around 20,000 people and 300 horses have beaten us to it, and are busy having a massive fight. An enormous, sweaty mêlée of horses is gathered in the middle, pushing and shoving, and being whacked with sticks by their riders. Just to add to the confusion, a sandstorm whips up from nowhere, followed by a rainstorm, and the resulting mud is thick and strong.

This is *buzkashi*, the Afghan national game. The rules are brutally simple – anyone who's got a horse can play – you have to pick up the headless corpse of a goat, and drop it in a chalk circle to score a goal. The problem is that all the other 299 horsemen want to stop you, assault you, then rip the corpse out of your hands and score a goal themselves. That's about it. It's utter mayhem, and no one appears to be having a good time, not even the huge audience, who stand with frowns of confusion on their faces. Nobody seems to know who's winning as factions develop in a bid to ambush whoever's carrying the corpse, and then collapse as soon as someone snatches it. It's violent, incomprehensible, ancient and, to Afghan culture, very important.

The favoured garb is trad-bohemian filth, with Russian tank-commander helmets clearly very popular. An ancient chap sporting a blue nylon wig and riding a frail old Rosinante shouts jokes to the audience. He's obviously the court jester. I get caught in a few stampedes so I take refuge on a tiny seating area with some of the sponsors of the game, where I befriend a man who speaks a little English and says that he owns one of the horses that's competing. I ask him who's winning, and he shrugs 'nobody knows'. Is it always like this? 'Yeah.'

I ask him if the corpse gets eaten at the end of the game.

'What a bizarre idea,' he says, before turning back to watch 300 grown men on horseback beat each other up over a headless goat.

Finally there's a goal: a fearsome-looking fellow, resplendent in a purple velour judo outfit, sporting a vast moustache and quarter of a tonne of mud, manages to drop the goat into the circle. I'm told that this is Shamsull Haq, an important local figure. Eventually the final prize is announced: if anyone can get another goal, they will win themselves a new fridge. The entire horde of frenzied competitors turn ... well ... more frenzied. That poor bloody goat.

After much fighting, it's announced that everyone's knackered, cold, wet and confused, and no one looks likely to win, so the fridge will be up for grabs tomorrow instead. Shamsull Haq pulls his horse up to where I'm sitting and announces that a) he's in charge of the whole shebang, and b) I will be dining as his guest of honour that night. My sponsor friend suggests that it would be wise for me to accept Mr Haq's offer of dinner instead of his. Marc shakes his head. Bad idea, he mouths.

Nonetheless, and probably against our better judgement, later that night Marc and I draw up at Shamsull Haq's place. Aleem has said that I'll be fine, that he knows this man well, he's a powerful local leader, and in any case when you're a guest in an Afghan's house your safety is their responsibility and they must protect you as though you were family. It goes against everything in the hostile regions training manual, but on balance it seems more dangerous not to go – you don't want to go around offending an Afghan's hospitality.

Shamsull Haq lays on a vast spread for us and 25 of his friends. We sit on the floor around a huge red plastic cloth. Lamb is the only food on offer, and on the way Marc drops a bombshell: he can't eat lamb. Well that's just great! Lamb is pretty much the only meat they eat here, and turning down food is tantamount to betrayal around these parts. Hell, I'd probably shoot you in my own house if you turned down my food.

Shamsull chats for half an hour or so before revealing that he is actually Commander Haq, and was a Taliban commander himself a few years ago. I nearly choke on my lamb. I'm dining with the Taliban.

The Fear washes over me again, and I wonder if we ought to quietly leave before anything bad happens. But everyone's very friendly, including Commander Haq, and it would be more foolish to insult them by leaving. So instead we talk about the pros and cons of crushing repression, beards and burkas. I try to do the journalist thing by pushing him to answer some difficult questions, even though I'm woefully underqualified for this kind of thing. He flatly ignores my questions about women's rights under the Taliban and reminds me that the British were just one of many people who tried to conquer Afghanistan. He says it without malice, and when I apologize on behalf of my countrymen (you're not really supposed to do this, are you?) he takes it with good grace.

I ask if he sees me as the enemy. He says no. These days his responsibility is to the people he commands, and he has to try to get along with everyone. 'We can't fight the whole world,' he says ruefully, as though he wouldn't actually mind giving it a bash.

The eating cloth is cleared away and we settle down to play cards. 'Put the camera away,' Haq says, 'betting is *haraam*', (forbidden by God). After playing a few hands we thank everyone for their wonderful hospitality and extremely lamby lamb, and leave. Marc is starving and ready to fall over. I am feeling giddy from this bizarre emotional rollercoaster of a trip, which lurches from terror to comedy without warning. But finally I feel as though I've made a connection with Afghanistan.

On the way back through Masr-i-Sharif we pass the vast, stunning Blue Mosque. Surely a country that can build anything this beautiful can't be beyond hope. On the streets, men are going crazy, dancing and partying – all without the aid of alcohol. I stop occasionally to talk to the

FOOD AND WAR

dancers, but there's a strong sense of hostility, so I don't hang around. It generally takes about an hour to arrange everything required for a decent abduction, so it's best to move on every 40 minutes.

World Food Programme

In contrast to the feast of the previous night, we visit a World Food Programme plant nursery, where women are offered food in return for work. The UN tries to avoid giving food away as this creates a dependency on aid that can be hard to break, so instead they create jobs within their own projects.

I chat to a woman in a beautiful, finely-pleated, Yves Klein blue burka, who says she finds it very difficult to do weeding in her voluminous tent, but she wants to wear it. 'I'm very shy,' she says. 'I have no education, so I don't like talking to people. But I don't mind talking when I wear the burka.'

Her husband was killed by the Taliban, but she's not entirely sure why. I ask her how she feels about his death. 'I'm sad because I have to bring up the children on my own and there's no one to pay for food.' I ask about her emotions several times, but she always answers with facts, as though revealing an emotional response would be as bad as revealing her face. I ask if it's unfair that women suffer so badly, and men seem to have all the power. She doesn't understand the question – even when I rephrase it several different ways. It doesn't occur to her that things can be any different. She says that if she were literate things would be so much better. Her daughter is married but she is young, so doesn't wear the burka, but when she gets older she will.

She says that under the Taliban women weren't allowed to go out and work or tend crops, even if they were widows like her who had no one else to provide for their family.

'But you'd starve without food.'

'Yes. That didn't matter to the Taliban.'

We wander around a few crumbling rural villages, followed everywhere by hordes of excited, beautiful olive-skinned kids. This is how most Afghans live, with no infrastructure, no jobs, living in houses made of mud, and completely reliant on outside help just to get enough food to eat. The trouble is that from the outside, this poverty is mesmerizing. Cherubic kids in rags, simple lives with basic needs, few material possessions and living close to the land.

From the inside, it's very different, and I'm not sure if anyone in the world really has a simple life and basic needs.

I meet Sabra, a widow with six beautiful, mischievous daughters to look after. They are easily some of the poorest people I've ever met, and they live in a single mud room with two small kitchen rooms beside it. Sabra is lively and talkative and doesn't wear a burka. Unusually for an Afghan woman, she's happy to talk openly to me – she's fully aware of how gruesome her life is, she wants her story told and, crucially, she has no male relatives to beat her for talking to an unknown, unrelated man.

For the first time I ask one of the questions I'm here to ask: What does it feel like to be constantly hungry? To be starving? It's a horrible question, and smacks of poverty tourism, but surely it's more dangerous *not* to know.

Sabra is pleased that I've asked her – no one else ever has. It changes, she says, depending on how scarce food is. Today she's got food from the WFP, but when she can't work, the family goes without and she becomes lethargic, irritable, shaky and miserable. She says that she often lashes out at her kids when she's that desperate. When she says this, the kids all laugh and agree. Sabra is very aware of her poverty, and she laughs when I mention that people in the West sometimes romanticize the simple life of rural peasants.

So what *do* the poorest people in the world eat? Often plain starches. Sabra and her family eat a pathetically small amount of WFP split peas that are boiled to maceration into dhal. It tastes surprisingly good, though not, I suspect, if you eat it every day of your life. She also makes unleavened naan bread using WFP flour in a mud-built tandoor oven that reaches a frighteningly high temperature, having been stoked for three hours using anything she can lay her hands on, including carrier bags, twigs and dried turds.

The naans are dampened with a little water before they are slapped onto the side wall of the oven. In a few minutes they are ready and on the verge of burning, at which point they are slipped off the oven and left to cool.

I taste Sabra's food, but can't bring myself to eat the whole portion that she offers me. It seems wrong for a Western journalist to take food from someone this poor. But she tells me off and I realize that I've done the wrong thing – she is offended by my rejection of her hospitality, and if I am to be able to write about the experience of the Afghan poor, I need to get involved.

Sabra finds life tough, filthy, relentless, tiring and bleak. She hates the food that she has to eat, and both she and the kids yearn for rice and meat. I pull some modelling balloons out of my pocket and make some balloon dogs to amuse them, and as we get ready to leave, I ask Sabra if she thinks her daughters will have a better future. She says she just wants them to be able to go to school. I'm told it's not appropriate to shake hands with her, so I thank her profusely and put my hand on my heart in the Afghan custom. As I leave, I'm a bit of a mess: incensed at the desperate unfairness of her life, and wracked with guilt at being able to hop into a car and leave her behind. I tell myself that I'm here to expose and explain things, not to solve them, but my mood has undeniably darkened.

I set off on a two-day drive heading back to Kabul, passing hundreds of burnt-out Russian tanks on the way. They are *everywhere*, constant reminders of Afghanistan's violent history. We stop at the equivalent of a motorway service station – a row of creaky wooden stalls all selling exactly the same foods at exactly the same prices.

A man hears my voice and angrily accuses me of being American. I tell him I'm British and he roars his approval, produces a hellishly out-of-tune guitar and plays an extraordinary version of 'All You Need Is Love'. Or at least I think that's what he's playing. Whatever it is, it's great and about 40 men gather around to listen and cheer.

I try sticky dried watermelon that's surprisingly strong and pleasant, the tart dried yoghurt balls, and the huge, sweet, bright yellow sultanas.

That night myself, Marc and Aleem are guests of an Afghan Aid project. We eat another heady dinner of lamb and qabili rice (lamb, lamb fat and rice with a few sultanas) washed down with Coke. I'm grateful for our hosts' hospitality, although the Afghan custom of keeping the TV on during meals is a little odd.

The Hindu Kush

We wake early and our tiny room smells like a sheep's sweaty crotch, so we're happy to leave it and continue our journey south. We reach the Hindu Kush (rough translation: 'Killer of Hindus' – nice). The mountain scenery is stark, brutal and beautiful. We are stuck behind slow-crawling, smoke-spewing lorries and tiny cars that somehow manage to pack 12 people into the back, with the smallest kid on the rear shelf, head bouncing violently against the window as their car hits the frequent potholes.

Just after the mountains, the road suddenly drops to an open plain, and I spot a vast graveyard of tanks, rocket-launchers, Scud missiles and armoured personnel carriers rotting and rusting into the sand. I'm intrigued, so Aleem talks his way past the small group of soldiers guarding it so that we can wander around. It's mainly old Russian hardware, all the dials and directions written in Cyrillic. They must have been miserable machines to live in and terrible to die in. But it's a strangely peaceful place – maybe because these tanks have been decommissioned and their days of fighting are over. But there's also a ghostly, lingering sense of sorrow.

I look at the Scud missiles – this is the stuff that Iran and Iraq threw at each other during their wars. They've been partially dismantled, and each one has a big red button on its control panel. I've always been tempted to press red buttons so I stare at them. A soldier wanders over to see what we're doing. 'Kaboom', he says, with a warning grin.

The next day I find out that there was a huge explosion at the tank graveyard after we'd left, killing two people, injuring scores more and destroying several buildings. I can't believe I even joked about pushing red buttons.

The Best Kebab Shop in the World

According to international kebab-lovers, the Best Kebab Shop in the World is generally regarded to be Mr Kebabi's in Charekar. I ask around, and am pointed in the direction of a reassuringly ramshackle and grubby building. Inside I meet the jolly and magnificently hirsute Uncle Kebabi (actually the nephew of the original Mr Kebabi, who's now dead), and I ask him why his 'babs are so good.

He swears by lamb tail fat. The kebabs are disarmingly small – just one piece of fat and two pieces of meat – so they are sold in bundles of ten. His lamb is beaten to soften it, then marinated with garlic, onion and salt. I help to cook them over a long, thin charcoal grill, and we go upstairs to his filthy seating area to try them out.

It's all true. These are easily the best kebabs in the world. It's not just the depth of charcoaly flavour and the delicate flesh, but the whole experience: kebabs were designed here, to be eaten sitting cross-legged in Afghanistan, looking out of the window at the Hindu Kush, above a street bristling with armed militia. I'm sure that my sense of low-level terror helps the tastebuds. You just don't get that up Green Lanes.

That night we finally arrive back in Kabul and head straight back to the Gandamack Lodge, where, as luck would have it, the bar has been restocked with Woolf Blass cabernet sauvignon.

The US Army

Disaster. Aleem has been called away. He's desperately sorry and sorts me out with an interpreter called Maghreb (nice lad, fluent English from time spent in Newcastle, but he's no Aleem), and promises to be on the end of the phone for me when I need things organized.

There's nothing I can do to hold onto Aleem, so I crack on, pack Maghreb into the car and head for Camp Eggers, the main US military base in Kabul. It takes a mountain of security checks to get access, but finally I'm in, and I'm here to meet Captain Harraway, a lovely lady from South Carolina.

She's helpful and good-humoured and we wander around the PX (a military supermarket full of Cheerios, Oreos and Sylvester Stallone DVDs) and have a fine latte. I want to convince her to let us cook a meal for the Afghan army. She clearly thinks that the idea is distasteful in the extreme but says she'll see what she can do.

With nothing planned for the afternoon, I visit a market to see what sorts of foods are available. Maghreb takes me to his favourite take-away joint selling something called 'Afghan burgers' – livid pink slivers of matter allegedly containing beef. They look entirely artificial, but when deep-fried in 1000-times-used oil and mixed with the soggiest chips in the world, onions and wrapped in a soft naan, they prove the theory that when you're desperate, any mess of mechanically recovered meat, fat, salt, MSG and carbohydrate will taste divine.

Captain Harraway calls. For some reason beyond her comprehension, the most important generals in the Afghan army, along with the head of the Defence Ministry, want me to cook for them tomorrow at an Afghan army barracks.

Oh, Lord. I'm going to have to make food for 50 VIPs with guns. I've never done this before. In a panic, I decide to do a hands-across-the-water thing and make American-style burgers flavoured with typical Afghan herbs and spices. I should be able to do this in bulk.

I buy a couple of massive fillets from a blood-spattered butcher. He cuts the fillets straight from the carcass – there's no refrigeration, and I guess you don't want to risk more botulism than is strictly necessary by butchering meat before you have a buyer. His mincing machine is a joy to behold. It's an old car engine, complete with accelerator pedal, hooked up to an ancient Polish mincing attachment. To grind the meat, you literally have to turn a key to start the engine, then put your foot on the gas. It belches fumes, but works a treat – and anyway, a little smokiness to the burgers will be welcome. The butcher takes great pride in telling me that the engine came from a 1.6-litre Toyota Corolla.

In the market I find coriander, chillies, onions, garlic, eggs and tomatoes. We visit Supreme, Kabul's famous wholesale store that supplies the army, NGOs and Westerners. You're supposed to have a special pass, but I blag my way in. Mahgreb isn't allowed, which seems a bit off. I buy burger buns, ketchup and that vile mustard the Americans like. Also a bottle of gin and several bottles of tonic. Those are for me.

The Afghan Army

I meet Captain Harraway at Camp Eggers the next morning and she invites me for breakfast in their mess hall (which isn't messy at all, but is strangely futuristic and inflatable). I taste grits for the first time in my life. Interestingly, the only food on the planet that tastes worse than grits is cheese grits. I won't be trying them again.

Captain Harraway and Sergeant Lowery drive ahead of us to the Afghan army base. This is when life gets dangerous – travelling around with the army on streets full of IEDs (Improvised Explosive Devices) designed to kill soldiers. Another US soldier died this morning in the south of Afghanistan. I sit on my flak jacket, and Marc looks at me, daring me to wear it.

At the base I meet an American military trainer who shows me how to assemble a 43-year-old AK47, which I find both distasteful and exciting. I watch a training session and a bit of marching, but I'm stressed about making lunch, so I go to the enormous mess hall and start to prepare the food. I rope in Captain Harraway and Sergeant Lowery, plus two Afghan cooks, and we chop and fry and bump into each other. A sense of camaraderie builds inexorably – it's in no one's interest to see me fail, and somehow we manage to get everything ready in time for lunch.

I start frying burgers and miraculously we produce some edible food. I try one, full of trepidation, but thankfully the burgers are bloody great (and so they ought to be, seeing as they're made with the most expensive cut of beef). They're a bit dry because there's no fat in fillet, but I've thought of that, and brought along a huge slab of neat beef fat so I chop that into the mixture. We're finally ready for the first 20 VIPs, so we march out, cameras and all, and I serve it up. They are sitting on the top table in front of 3,000 of their men. I make a short, cack-handed speech about spreading knowledge and understanding through food, and offer them the finest burgers on the planet.

As they tuck in, I pray that I don't poison them. The reaction is not quite as I'd hoped. They've clearly been herded here as a diplomatic gig and aren't sure what on earth this is all about: they don't know what to do with the flaps of bread, and they seem wary of this sweaty little Englishman. They smile politely and claim that the food is fine, but they're obviously deeply underwhelmed.

The whole exercise is an unmitigated disaster, not only because my customers clearly haven't enjoyed the food, but also because I've slipped into making the gruesome reality show I've been trying to avoid. TV cook Stefan Gates comes to Afghanistan on a mission to cook burgers for Afghan VIPs. What was I thinking?

I just want to forget about the whole experience and the best way to do that is to go and fire some heavy weaponry.

My guides take me out to the firing ranges and teach me how to fire an AK47. This has nothing whatsoever to do with food, but it's certainly an appropriate Afghan experience. Oddly enough, I appear to be a pretty good marksman and really kill the hell out of the bit of paper I am aiming at.

Now look, I'm a lover not a fighter, and I'm possibly even a bleeding heart liberal, but put an AK47 into the hands of any bleeding heart liberal and he instantly turns into an idiotic, kill-crazed, bloodthirsty maniac. Afterwards I try to feel a bit grubby and guilty, but mainly I just want to shoot some more stuff.

When I've calmed down a little, the US army guides show me their MREs: Meals Ready to Eat. These are magical ration packs about the size of a shoebox that contain all the ingredients for a large meal, including Oreo biscuits, chocolate bars and even a stick of chewing gum. The main meal part has a little self-heating pack that's water-activated. Dastardly clever. It heats up the main meal pack to a searing temperature so you can eat it piping hot.

They last for years (if not forever), they're light and portable and pack a great whack of nutritionally balanced calories, so it seems snide to mention that they taste rank. The pasta sauce has been carefully pasteurized, eliminating all bugs and flavour, and the jalapeño cheese sauce is like orange bathroom sealant. Of course, when you're under siege on a barren hillside you just want calories, fast and simple.

I had been expecting to find a bunch of dim, meathead Americans, but everyone I meet is friendly, helpful and funny. I guess they keep the meatheads well away from journalists. I make one interesting observation, though, and it's all about love. The US soldiers are constantly saluting each other to the point of irritation – everyone is assessed for rank and pecking order, and the lower one must salute the higher. It must get very tiring.

The Afghan soldiers, however, just give each other a big hug. I'm not joking; that's all I saw them doing the whole day we were there. It was lovely, and maybe that's where the solution to global conflict lies: get all the armies and militias and warlords to stop saluting each other, and get them to cuddle instead. Perhaps I'll suggest this if ever I get invited to cook for generals.

The Cookery Show

Today is the most important day in my career: I'm about to become a big star on Afghan TV and I'm pretty nervous. But first I visit the Serena, the five-star hotel that exists in a bizarre bubble of MI6-protected luxury amongst the chaos and squalor of Kabul. I'm given a little tour, and I'm desperate to try out the toilets. After the bug-infested drop-squats I've been using up until now, I could sit on these lovely pristine bogs for hours.

Outside the rain starts to fall. Kabul is grim enough, but when the filth and devastation is made liquid, all the rubbish and excrement rises to the surface and vast puddles of stagnant mud appear. Last year it caused a cholera epidemic.

But I have little time to reflect further on the appalling contrasts because I have work to do. I speak to Arn, a Dutchman running the Serena's restaurants. At first I assume that he's just another Westerner soaking up Afghanistan's cash, but this proves unfounded. He accepts that a night at the Serena costs the average yearly wage of most Afghans, but he's genuinely proud to train and employ locals who are learning skills that they might go on to use elsewhere. Frankly, anyone employing people in Afghanistan is to be applauded because these people are desperate for jobs. Arn also has women working in his kitchens, which is no mean feat for an Afghan company. One of these women works as a sushi chef, although she admits she's never tasted raw fish, despite having been preparing it for 12 months. The idea scares the pants off her. Arn seems to be the acceptable face of capitalism, full of talk of reconstruction and training, dissemination of knowledge and filtering down of wealth.

And now comes the high point of my entire trip. Ever since I arrived, I've been angling to get on to the most popular TV programme in Afghanistan, *The Cookery Show* on Tolo TV, which is filmed here at the Serena. After much toing and froing, I've unexpectedly been offered a slot on the upcoming show to make some food and chat with Farzana, a heavily made-up but very friendly female presenter who's Afghanistan's biggest star.

Farzana's producer sits me down before we film and talks in dark tones about the 'circle of respect'. He implies that Farzana is a loaf of bread, and I can make jokes about the dough, but I shouldn't penetrate the crust or I'll be toast (I think that's what he's saying). Of course, what he's really saying is, 'If you pinch Farzana's arse, we will kill you.'

I invented a new recipe last night: 'Stef's Afghan Pesto' made with commonly available coriander and peanuts instead of basil and pine kernels, and I'm going to grill some aubergines to spread it on. I didn't have a clue whether or not it would actually taste good, but I thought I'd take a Western classic dish and make it out of ingredients more common in the Afghan home: coriander, almonds, oil, cardamom seeds, lime juice. The only trouble is that I haven't tried out the recipe – a classic mistake for a TV chef.

For TV shows in the UK we have teams of brilliant cooks known as home economists (much better at cooking than the people who actually appear on telly), who work out the recipe, tell you how to do it, and make the one that you prepared earlier, but when I ask if there's a home economist here, the Afghan TV crew laugh their socks off: 'You're not expecting *help* are you?'

Too late to worry though: it's *showtime*. Woohoo!

The Cookery Show is filmed in a small, drab meeting room in the Serena Hotel, where I wait full of nervous excitement. Farzana walks majestically into the room, all starry haughtiness and disdain. She's wearing what looks like a sparkly fishing net on her head, but I make a mental note not to point this out. Maghreb, along with every other red-blooded man in Afghanistan, has lusted after Farzana for ages, and he'd been beside himself with excitement when he discovered that we'd be filming with her. In the flesh, however, he's disappointed to discover that she sports a thick cake of make-up so the layout of her real face is something of a mystery.

Needless to say, *The Cookery Show* has no visible production values, home economists, structure and, crucially … no grill. In fact, all the programme's resources seem to have been invested in the lovely Farzana's make-up. This is going to be a disaster. I faff around nervously, sorting out my *mise-en-place*. I'm about to humiliate myself on Afghan national TV; I just hope that by the time the show is transmitted, I'll be sat in a smelly aeroplane en route for England.

The cameras start to roll and The Fear returns with a vengeance – more so than when I'd been faced with kidnapping and IEDs. As I chop, toast and mix, I try unsuccessfully to strike up a witty repartee with Farzana without causing a diplomatic incident.

It's all going well until I attempt to use the blender – it's useless. I start jamming the ingredients down with a wooden spoon to get the flipping thing to actually blend my pesto. In frustration I lift the lid off and shove with the spoon at the same time, whereupon the whole thing vomits a geyser of raw sloppy garlic over me, although it largely misses Farzana. She raises one cakey eyelid and I blunder on hoping that no one suggests I'm stoned to death for desecrating the national treasure. After another five minutes of excruciatingly slow chop 'n' chat, I notice the director motioning wildly at me to wipe my nose – I have spent most of the show with a huge green bogey of pesto swinging from the end of my nose. Lovely.

In the event, the pesto is delicious, although Farzana doesn't bother to taste it. After the show I interview her and discover that she's actually lovely and not a little courageous – women are rarely visible on the streets, let alone on the telly, and she and her family get regular threats for being on television. But her profile on the show (coupled with the fact that she wears traditional Afghan fishing nets on her head) is a brave example.

My Testicles

It's my penultimate day in Afghanistan and I'm exhausted, but I feel as though I've spent two weeks taking people's hospitality and giving nothing back. To make up for this one-way love, I decide to invite everyone I've met in Kabul to a picnic. Picnicking is Afghanistan's second national sport after *buzkashi*, and at the weekends, families head for any free patch of land for a bite to eat and some hard-core kite-flying.

On the way to buy the food I pass Kabul stadium, where the Taliban were wont to advertise football matches and then lock the gates and force the crowd to watch mass executions. At the next-door market I meet a sparkly-eyed butcher called Jan, who shows me how to butcher a fat-tailed sheep. I invite him to join me for the picnic tomorrow, and he kindly accepts. He tells me he'll bring a special present.

That night, I meet up with Captain Harraway and a few of her friends who take us for dinner at the airport ISAF (International Security Assistance Force) base, which has several restaurants – we visit a Thai one that serves merrily and comprehensively overcooked Thai food. Although I've become oddly fond of the soldiers, it's the least pleasant meal (other than cheese grits) I've eaten in Afghanistan.

The day of the picnic dawns and Aleem has pulled strings to get us access to President Doud's ruined palace on the outskirts of the city. It's been a shock to see a country with such a proud history reduced to such a desperate, anarchic, confusing, corrupt mess, and it truly feels that Afghanistan is, in its current form, ungovernable. This place isn't given to democracy and paternalism, but instead is ruled by feudal, tribal and religious systems. It seems as though central government rule is almost impossible without the power and infrastructure that a little prosperity might bring, and that's a hard thing to kickstart. Without it, all the lives lost by NATO (over 500 since 2006), the Taliban (3,700 in 2006) and ordinary Afghans (1,000 in 2006) will have been tragically wasted.

But right now the sun has come out and the gloom lifts slightly. It's just a few days before I see my wife and daughters again, and this puts me in a good mood. I feel free and uplifted, like a schoolboy who's finished his exams.

Doud's palace has been looted, but it has stunning views across a devastated and dusty Kabul on one side, and a 180-degree panorama of the Hindu Kush on the other. Military helicopters and cargo planes roar over every now and then. It's guarded by a group of eight ragged and hungry soldiers so I invite them to join us for lunch, too.

I cook Quabili rice, salads and lamb kebabs – cooking always calms me, and I love the solitude of the work. My friends set up a tent with the help of the soldiers then lay down cushions and sit chatting. Aleem has managed to join us, along with Basir the driver, soldiers, translators, drivers, market-stall owners and a bunch of kids (don't know where they came from, but they're welcome). Arn from the posh hotel is here, and we even have an Afghan woman: Fahima, who runs the Kandahar Lodge. Sadly our US army friends couldn't make it as they're busy fighting the good fight.

At the last minute Jan, the butcher, arrives bearing a bloody bag and a huge grin. Inside are ten vast lamb's testicles. Excellent, I will get to taste them after all. I kebab them and get everything grilling. Finally I serve the food with a little speech thanking everyone for their kindness, hoping that Afghanistan will rebuild itself, that things will get better and that discrimination against women will end. We chat about reconstruction and the future. Fahima says that although she hates the way women are treated in Afghanistan, she is proud of her country because it's her home.

An aid package of $4.5 billion has been committed to Afghanistan, yet most people haven't seen real improvement to their lives yet and many live in worse conditions than they did under the Taliban. You can say what you like about how good it feels to be free, but it adds up to bugger all when half the kids here are malnourished.

We try out kite-flying (my main research for this film was to read *The Kite Runner*, so it felt like the right thing to do). In Afghanistan, kite-flying is vicious and competitive: the kite string is covered in ground glass, and the idea is that you tangle your kite with someone else's, then yank it down to cut their string. The downside is that the string rips through your fingers so that within a minute, you're a bloody mess. But it's fun.

As we pack up, two of those vast Chinook helicopters clatter across our view of the Hindu Kush. I look up into the sky and I realize that I'm going home tomorrow, that I've survived my first Category One conflict zone without physical injury or dysentery. But I've seen suffering on a level that took my breath away. Does this make me a real journalist? Does this mean that nothing will ever seem so bad again? I'm about to head off to Uganda to live with refugees fleeing a vicious conflict, but I wonder if I'll slowly become immune to pain and suffering. Will I be able to understand what they are experiencing? Gradually I feel my arse cheeks relaxing and The Fear gently fades away, but I'm not entirely sure if that's a good thing.

UGANDA
Dining with Refugees

- -

POPULATION: 31 million

PERCENTAGE LIVING ON LESS THAN $2 A DAY: 35%

UNDP HUMAN DEVELOPMENT INDEX: 145/177

CORRUPTION PERCEPTIONS INDEX POSITION: 105/163

GDP (NOMINAL) PER CAPITA: $316 (167/179)

FOOD AID RECIPIENTS: 2.9 million in 2006

MALNUTRITION: 19% of the population

- -

Major Nfor is on the verge of pushing my military clearance passes across the table. He hadn't batted an eyelid when I said I wanted to visit war-torn northern Uganda – in fact he isn't too bothered where I go, as long as I pay cash. I've coughed up, as requested, and spent a fair amount of time waiting for his innumerable forms to be filled in. And now, with my pass sitting on the table under his hand, inches from my grasp, he asks the tricky question 'So, what will your story be about?'

'Well ... it's about cooking.'

His hand stops sliding the documents across, and his smile vanishes.

I'm sitting in a dirty little office in Kampala, the capital of Uganda. It's a crumbling, filthy but functioning city that looks as though it was hastily built in the 1950s, after which the builders scarpered, taking all the paint and tools with them, and since then it hasn't crossed anyone's mind to buy any more. The place is bristling with guns; most shops and offices have a bloke slumped on the front steps chatting to passing girls and swinging an AK47 around as if he's the bee's knees. But unlike many central African cities, Kampala works. Overall, Uganda works – you could even say that it's doing pretty well. It's relatively prosperous, with a growing economy, it's more peaceful and democratic than most of its neighbours, and it's blessed with decent natural resources, fertile soil and favourable weather.

So it's all the more tragic that in the north of the country one of the world's greatest forgotten humanitarian disasters has been going on relatively unreported for the last 20 years. A small terrorist paramilitary group called the Lord's Resistance Army (LRA) has waged a pointless war since 1986, forcing somewhere between 1.2 and 1.7 million people to abandon their homes for the safety of IDP camps. An IDP is an Internally Displaced Person (basically, a refugee who hasn't actually left his own country), and the IDPs in northern Uganda survive on subsistence rations provided by the UN's World Food Programme (WFP). I'm going to call them refugees anyway, because 'IDP' sounds even more cold and impersonal than 'refugee'.

Major Nfor's lips curl involuntarily at the thought of me going to one of the world's hungriest regions to talk about cooking. 'It's not like that,' I say, 'it's a film about how people survive.' After a very long pause he pushes my pass over to me. I ask if there are any recent security issues in the north that we need to be aware of. 'No. No problems in the north.' I get up to leave, but just as I'm out of the door he shouts after me: 'Of course, no one is allowed to be outside after 6 p.m. Curfew everywhere.'

On the way to catch a UN flight northwards, my driver casually mentions that the LRA have recently threatened to kill all *mazungus* (whites) they find.

Kitgum

The next morning we touch down in Kitgum, one of the regions worst affected by rebel attacks. It's baking hot as we climb into an enormous 4×4 belonging to the World Food Programme with 'UN' printed on the side. I stick out like a sore thumb, a red-faced *mazungu* peering out of a white car.

I check into the Bomah Hotel – one of the worst hotels in the world. It has a pool full of what looks like snot, some of the filthiest rooms I've ever set foot in, and tap water that's a disturbing light brown colour. But on balance, I'm surprised and grateful that you can even find hotels in places like this.

I make a quick visit to the local market. It stinks, and there are open sewers all around. Most stallholders have only a handful of sweet potatoes or a small sack of flour to sell, and it scares me that there can be so little food available in a town this big. A few traders are doing better: there's a woman who buys and sells fish, standing amidst a cloud of fish scales and flies, and she has a mobile phone, but people like her are few and far between.

The local WFP head, Robert Dekker, takes me to his aid depot where 30-odd bare-chested fellas are loading 140 tonnes of food onto huge, ancient trucks. It's the first time I've seen an aid operation in action and I'm disappointed to see how emotionless it all is. I thought it would be about sympathy, kindness and generosity, but it's actually about logistics. The WFP does a serious job and at this level food aid is about distribution issues, transport, manpower, efficiency, bureaucracy and accountability. Robert knows that he's saving lives but he's not a knight in shining armour – he's doing a job.

Once the food is loaded, a huge army escort of 60 men rocks up to protect the convoy en route. There's an arrogance to these Ugandan army soldiers and I'm not sure I like them, but they've got some big guns, and they should keep us safe from attack by the LRA. I hop onto a Mamba – a rudimentary armoured vehicle – with the commanding officer, Norman, and some of his soldiers and set off for the day's delivery.

I try to talk to Norman on the way, asking some devilishly incisive questions hinting at the army's collusion with the LRA, but he just raises his eyebrows, smiles and stays silent. I haven't got the hang of this journalist thing yet.

We roll into the camp and grind to a halt in clouds of dust. I've been anticipating this moment for months. I had imagined grateful people running and whooping with joy as the convoy arrived, people rushing to grab food, and myself handing out bags of rice to happy, smiling children. The reality is something of a shock. No one comes to meet the trucks when they arrive, and instead there's an eerie silence as the dust settles. Not a soul.

I spot some people milling around the nearby huts, and I can see that the camp stretches for miles. The aid workers get busy with clipboards and signs, organizing distribution points, but I stand there baffled. Where is everyone? These food deliveries happen only once a month, for crying out loud. An hour later a few women start to arrive – the first refugees I've met – and from their resentful expressions and bedraggled appearance I realize how wrong I was about the nature of aid.

See, I thought that people would be *grateful*. I thought that the WFP would feel good about helping the world and saving millions from starvation, and the refugees would in turn give gratitude and thanks for being saved from that starvation. But kindness and gratitude have no place in a humanitarian disaster of this scale, and aid becomes a transaction. These people have lived with extreme deprivation for up to 20 years, and when 1.5 million are this desperate it's the world's duty to resolve it.

In reality, when those aid lorries arrive they aren't dispensing joy. They are a symbol of the refugees' problems, part of their utter dependence on others. We've arrived today, just as aid has arrived every month, and they won't get any more food than before, they won't be any more comfortable, safe or free. If these people have managed to be frugal and no one has stolen their food, last month's rations will have lasted until today, and this month's rations will need to be eked out for another long month all over again.

It's upsetting to see this, and I can't help but feel that we are all complicit to some extent. It's been going on for 20 flipping years, and no one talks about it because northern Uganda isn't a *sexy* conflict. It's long-term, without drama and incident, and with little progress towards resolution. The aid programme doesn't have dramatic, quantifiable results other than keeping people alive. It's an amazing achievement, but you don't get headlines that say 'More than a million people survive for another year'. As a result there's little international pressure or help to resolve the problem, and all we can do is treat its symptoms.

Eventually women, children and a handful of men begin to arrive and queue up, holding their ID cards, and we dispense the rations. It's a sombre affair, and we return to town feeling drained.

Events in town overtake us: the leader of the Ugandan opposition, Dr Kizza Besigye, turns up, and he holds a mass rally on the football pitch. There must be 20,000 people here, so I join the party to film it. There's a general election in a few weeks and tensions are running high.

Besigye is the only realistic contender to the incumbent president, Yoweri Museveni, and he's tremendously popular up here in the northern districts. Museveni has presided over a period of increasing prosperity and stability in most of Uganda, but here in the north, many of the Acholi people feel that he is their enemy. There are rumours that Museveni has failed to act against the LRA because it serves his best interests to disenfranchise and terrorize the Acholi people (they don't vote for him anyway, so they feel dispensable), and to keep this area militarized. It certainly seems odd that such a bizarre conflict with such a small group of protagonists can be sustained for 20 years.

Museveni seems to have become a little dictatorial in recent years, with the abolition of the constitutional limit on presidential terms and the creation of a 10,000-strong Presidential Guard Brigade that is effectively his private army. There seems to be intense intimidation of the opposition, including the arrest of Besigye on a raft of charges such as treason and rape. Yet it's a mark of the state of the country that most Ugandans think Museveni is still the best bet.

That night my career takes another twist: I track Besigye down to the Kitgum radio station and manage to have a short interview with him. I surprise even myself when I step forward with my hand outstretched and say, 'Good evening, Mr Besigye: Stefan Gates, BBC. Can I ask you a few questions?' I ask him why he thinks the LRA conflict has gone on so long and he talks about 'lack of political will' and a need for a renewed offensive. He's calm, direct and doesn't make rash claims, which I find refreshing. We talk for a short while, then he returns to carry on his radio interview.

Aggoro

I am picked up by a UN driver, Richard, who takes me (with three trucks of soldiers for protection) to Aggoro, one of the most remote and dangerous of the camps where I will live for the next few days.

The UN Land Cruisers have air conditioning, VHF radios and cassette recorders, and if you put your bottles of water on the dashboard jammed against the windscreen and put the air con on high, you'll get slightly chilled water. I think if I were a refugee, I might resent these cars. But without this vehicle and protection from the UN and the army, I wouldn't be allowed to travel here.

After three hours bumping along a dirt road, we arrive at the camp. Médecins Sans Frontières have kindly lent me a thatched hut to stay in, but there's no food around, so I pull out my camping stove for the first time and make dinner. Risotto, since you ask, as it's the cheapest, most portable and filling meal I could carry. It's not bad, considering.

Agorro is very isolated and it's been attacked frequently in the past so I go to sleep scared, my fear fed by the sense of terror that spreads across the whole camp at dusk as everyone runs back home and the sun drops like a stone. The LRA attack anywhere, even inside the camps, and usually at night. Throughout the night loud bangs startle me, and I get ready to run. I finally fall asleep just before dawn.

The morning is beautiful and I stroll through the camp accompanied by a small army of children. Wherever I go there are shouts of '*mazungu*', and people stop to stare at the speccy white fella wandering around their camp. I meet Odwa, a gently spoken man of 40 or so, and Doreen, his moon-faced wife. They've kindly agreed to let me see how they and their nine children live for the next few days, and he shows me around the camp.

Agorro is strangely beautiful, a sea of thousands of identical circular mud huts with reed or thatched roofs. They are low and small, about the size of a hatchback car. Families are crammed inside them with pitifully few possessions – usually a few pots and some bags containing their aid rations, some plastic sheeting to lie on, maybe a couple of blankets and a few clothes. On the surface, the dust, the sun and beautiful kids make it seem idyllic. Underneath, though, it's gruesome. Utter poverty, terrible sanitation problems, disease, and almost no education or healthcare.

But (it's a big but – the biggest but of the whole story and our reason for being here) people in these camps shouldn't be defined just by their misery or inability to support themselves, or even their status as refugees. It sounds banal to say it, but until I met refugees and cooked and ate with them, I thought of them as a concept, as a problem that needed solving, rather than as normal, complex people with lives as complicated as my own. Of course, refugees have the same concerns as us: they are falling in and out of love; the kids are playing up; they listen to the news; like me, they can be happy, frustrated, sad, proud, pensive. And the one thing I really never expected: they can be very, very *funny*. Odwa constantly takes the micky out of me, cracking jokes. The revelation is a shock: Odwa and Doreen are just like me, it's just their situation that's so completely different.

The LRA

As I play with the younger kids, Doreen tells me that her son was abducted by the LRA and forced to fight as a boy soldier. 'He was badly beaten and he was forced to undertake training to fight alongside them. I was distraught, I broke down and cried. But I got support from people around me. I had to just keep my head up. Occasionally my heart would stop, but I stayed firm.'

Her son finally escaped and returned home two years later.

The Lord's Resistance Army is a bizarre, brutal and psychotic militia group led by a reclusive man called Joseph Kone, an ex-spirit medium, who has become a perpetrator of self-propagating, aimless spiritually inspired brutality. It's the most evil and destructive organization I've ever come across. The LRA is waging a pointless war against everyone and no one, attacking civilians indiscriminately in their villages. They've never stated any clear political objectives, although they have mentioned that they'd like to rule Uganda according to the Ten Commandments (whatever that means). But the worst bit is yet to come: their tactics.

The leadership of the LRA consists of a relatively small group of adults. The foot-soldiers are children abducted from camps and villages who are brutalized and forced to fight and work. Many girls are kept as sex slaves for the adults. They are often initiated by being forced to kill family members or other children, and those who refuse are killed or mutilated. The children are kept within the LRA using violence and threats, and are told that Kone has a supernatural ability to find and kill them if they leave. The young rebels become both victims and perpetrators of brutality, and this is the LRA's cleverest move because any attack by the army against the LRA is perceived by the public as a massacre of civilian children. The level of brutality is astounding and the rebels have been known to cut off the lips, limbs and breasts of their victims.

The big question is why? The answer is unclear. They live in hiding in the jungle, until recently under the wing of the Sudanese government, who harboured them parimarily to piss off the Ugandan government. They seem to have developed a self-propogating gangster lifestyle, existing by looting, killing and raping. What's most worrying is that they have no discernible aims, which means that they are impossible to negotiate with, except possibly using cash.

That's enough for today. After Doreen tells me the story of her son and about the fractured lives of her friends and neighbours, I go to bed tangled up with anger.

Cooking with Odwa and Doreen

I've arranged to cook breakfast with Doreen, but I get up early to watch the dawn first. The light is always best at 'magic hour' – dawn or dusk – so I walk out to the camp outskirts for a better view. As I leave, a truckload of soldiers chases after me – ostensibly for protection. The army has clearly been watching me all night, and it makes me feel uneasy. I watch the sun breaking across the camp in golden streaks; it is breathtaking.

I arrive at Odwa and Doreen's hut to find that I've missed breakfast; they cook at dawn, and when you've got nine kids clamouring to be fed, you don't need some journalist from London making you late. They have eaten a gruel-like porridge made from flour and water and I try a little that's left over. It's tasteless but filling. Odwa has gone without. 'I can't sleep if they have not had a meal,' he says.

We visit a field outside the main camp where Odwa grows a small amount of food on land he's borrowed. Trouble is, the harvest is over and the food has all gone. This area has millions of fertile acres but they are wasted because the refugees can't walk far from the camp for fear of attack. Odwa points to the mountains towards Sudan, which is just a couple of miles away, and tells me they used to live there on 80,000 square metres (20 acres) of land. I ask if he thinks he'll ever go back there. He's silent for a while, then: 'No, I don't think so.'

We go scavenging for wild food, and chance across some jacka-jacka. It grows like a scrappy shrub and to my eyes looks inedible, but Doreen finds some young shoots and offers one to me. It tastes like young asparagus. After an hour or so of foraging, we have collected enough jacka-jacka for a tiny salad.

Doreen's kitchen is also the hut that she and her daughters sleep in. It is made of mud, and good hygiene is almost impossible. The place is a nightmare when it rains. There are no shelves to keep anything off the floor, but that's fine because she doesn't really have anything. She shows me a handful of dried greens, 'This is what I gathered yesterday from the wilderness. This can is for cooking oil – the oil has completely run out.'

As we're chatting, Odwa arrives to say that the aid convoy has arrived, so we make our way to the collection point. Robert Dekker is here to oversee the aid distribution and, again, no one is excited about the arrival of the food.

Then the bad news: Robert tells me that the WFP has decided to reduce rations from 73 per cent of daily calorie needs to 60 per cent . This is to try to end dependence on aid and to encourage people to grow and forage for food.

Odwa and Doreen are quietly, desperately disappointed. I am worried that there might be a riot, but the whole camp seems resigned to the smaller rations – what would a riot achieve? I ask Odwa if he'd be able to make up the lost food by scavenging or just eat less. 'Eat less,' he says. I say I don't think they could survive on anything less.

'Then what are we going to do when there isn't any alternative?' Odwa says.

They queue up for their rations. I can understand the WFP theory, but the reality around here is that it's not safe for people to leave the camps to forage for more.

Each person is given 1 kg of CSB (Corn Soy Blend), 7 kg maize flour, 1 kg beans or peas and some vegetable oil, and this must last them an entire month.

Food aid also works as currency in the camps, as the refugees don't have anything else to trade. These people don't have any jobs, although once in a blue moon they can get a day's work making bricks near the camp.

The next afternoon I help Doreen to cook dinner. She's bemused and embarrassed at first, but she's flattered by my interest. Odwa has swapped some of his maize flour for tomatoes, some okra and Britannia curry powder – a luxury he can ill afford, but I suspect that he's too embarrassed to let me just eat starch in his home.

During my Surviving Hostile Regions training the medical specialist, Tony, warned me that on no account should I eat in a refugee camp – no sanitation, all sorts of disease, and almost total lack of food hygiene. I would probably come back with an amoeba. But I survived Afghanistan and really should share experiences rather than comment loftily from afar.

We make an okra curry and ugali, Uganda's most ubiquitous foodstuff. It's basically any type of flour mixed with water and stirred until the carbohydrates swell to bursting. It's so smoky in Doreen's tiny hut that I can hardly see and I cry throughout. At one point Doreen casually picks up some burning logs with her bare hands.

I am given the task of stirring the ugali, but, bizarrely, I somehow managed to dislocate my thumb after I fall off my haunches. In the circumstances, it seems wrong to make a fuss about it, and I continue stirring in agony. Finally the food is ready, and I'm shocked at how little there is; this meal will feed about 20 people yet it's probably the amount I'd cook for a Saturday lunch for six.

The men sit in a circle and pass the bowls of food around, each time taking a pinch of the ugali, ensuring a pretty fair distribution. The women (who always eat separately with the young children) don't bother with such social niceties, and just tuck in. Ugali doesn't taste bad – it just tastes of nothing. After the meal I say fond farewells to Doreen, Odwa and their sweet, calm kids. And once again they gently take the mickey out of me. Doreen reckons that my cooking was OK, but I'll never make it in Aggoro camp with my wimpy little white man's hands.

I ask her what she thinks about the LRA and she tells me, 'I wish they would return to their homes.'

I'm shocked. Don't you want them wiped off the face of the earth?

'No. We just want peace.'

Gulu

I'm about to fly out of Kitgum for the notorious town of Gulu. It's a dry, dusty day and the wind kicks up a fierce dust storm. The trip has been an emotional rollercoaster so far – I don't know if I'm miserable for the state of humanity, or elated by the resilience of people. I sit chatting with Robert Dekker in the hut that functions as the airport when he tells me something that almost knocks me off my chair: the WFP have an exit plan ready for when there's a resolution to this whole nightmare, and people are able to go home.

I am shocked – I had begun to see the conflict as being as irresolvable as it is bizarre. Perhaps I've been sucked into the global malaise that has allowed us to ignore this disaster and avoid trying to solve it. But of course, this will end someday. Probably after Herculean international diplomacy and outrageous, undeserved cash deals with the LRA and a great deal more suffering, but one day people might go home and everything will seem like a bad dream.

My spine tingles with excitement at the idea of this misery ending, and I sit in our twin-engine prop plane in a mixture of confusion and epiphanical reverie until we hit an air pocket and my mind returns to turbulent reality.

Gulu is a much bigger, better-functioning town than Kitgum, and has a substantial market where I stock up on food. They sell bo (a leafy, spinach-like plant), dried aubergine, bananas of all shapes and sizes, matoke (cooking bananas), maize oil packed in old Coke bottles, sorghum flour and groundnuts. I chat with the funny, flirtatious women at the market stalls, and they get me to take photos of us together. The meat and fish sections of the market are extraordinary and scary –

obscured by slow, shifting clouds of flies that the stallholders don't bother to swat away. It strikes me that I haven't had a single bout of diarrhoea yet. Odd.

I meet Pedro Amolat, who runs WFP in Gulu. He's an irrepressible, committed guy with a passion for solving problems, and this, combined with what Richard Dekker told me, and the sense of vitality here in Gulu have all helped to lift my spirits. As I set off for the camp at Pabbo I almost have a spring in my step.

Pabbo

That spring disappears the moment I enter Pabbo. This stinking soup of unhappiness is home to 64,000 or so of the most unfortunate humans on the planet. This area is so dangerous that everyone crams as tightly as possible into the centre of the camp, causing a cascade of problems, including appalling sanitation, overcrowding, disease, alcohol abuse, violence and social trauma.

The first thing I see when I enter the camp is a vast sunflower of yellow and orange jerry cans encircling a water pump. There must be 2,000 cans in the queue, and they are surrounded by hordes of bored women and children who have to stand all day next to their cans to make sure no one steals them.

I ask one woman why there's such a big queue. She tells me that it's been like this for two months since the main mechanical pump broke, and no one has arrived with the spare parts to fix it. I ask how long it takes to get water and she tells me, 'If you arrive now, you'll not get water today.'

It's only 11 a.m.

This is the stuff that never makes headlines but which I now realize defines everyday life for refugees: the sheer, grinding *difficulty* of existence, the boredom, simmering fear and lack of control they have over their lives. What we read about in newspapers are the dramatic natural disasters, droughts and wars. One and a half million people enduring crushing boredom for 20 years doesn't sell papers, so this crisis sinks into obscurity.

Pabbo is also mysteriously prone to wildfires, with 200 huts lost the day before I arrived. I've been here only a few hours when there's an inferno near the edge of the camp, so I race over to see if I can help. Of course, there's nothing I can do – there's no water available to put out flames, and once one hut is ablaze the others around it follow pretty quickly. The roofs are made of thin, dry thatch so one tiny spark sends the whole thing up in a few seconds. Around 20 huts go up in flames over the next hour or so. The only upside is that because these people have so few possessions, there's not much to lose.

I speak to Miranda, a woman with seven children, whose hut burnt down yesterday. She tells me that although some people can eventually rebuild their huts, her husband died last year, and she won't be able to do it herself. What upsets her most, however, is that in the mêlée of saving her family and belongings, someone stole her jerry cans. It doesn't bear thinking about.

Pedro tries to explain why this camp is so prone to fires. He says that although the thatch is particularly flammable, it's also possible that the most desperate refugees think they might get more aid if they are seen to suffer more so they sometimes start fires themselves. I am shocked at this suggestion and I wonder if he's just cynical after working too long for the UN, but he says it without malice. And anyway, wouldn't I do the same if I were in their situation? Of course I would: if my kids were hungry, if I felt there was no escape and no one to turn to, I might be tempted to do a lot worse.

Despite the deprivation in Pabbo, there are pockets of optimism along the road that cuts through the camp. This is an important transit route for freight and passengers, and the flow of people has allowed a few enterprising refugees to make money from them. Mostly its just hawkers selling cans of drink, or refugees trying to sell their rations, but there's a mechanic fixing bicycles and cars, and even a few rudimentary restaurants. These are as basic as you can imagine, offering little more than a bowl of stew on a rickety bench, but I'm intrigued to see them at all.

I ask the owner of one of them if I can help her in the kitchen. Her name is Joyce, and she stands, arms akimbo, looking me up and down, clearly unimpressed with what she sees. She agrees and says I can help as long as I buy lunch from her. When you work for the BBC you shouldn't pay for interviews (paying for a bowl of their food is OK). It sounds harsh, but if journalists pay money to people with dramatic stories, then anyone in their right mind will just make up a story in order to earn some cash, and the truth becomes even more elusive than it already is. You can, of course, give your own money away to people you haven't interviewed, but even this can cause bitter resentment when one person gets money and their neighbour doesn't. Better to give to a central organization that can benefit everyone. But I'm only human and

I defy you to go to these places, to look into desperate eyes and not occasionally sneak some of your own cash into people's hands.

Joyce she sets me to work grinding sesame seeds to a fine paste called sim-sim that features in a lot of Ugandan food. We know it as tahini. Without the aid of handy electrical appliances, the grinding is done using a couple of stones, which makes it sound very simple. It's not. It's very difficult, especially with Joyce huffing at my incompetence and a table of hungry customers waiting for their lunch.

We make a stew of goat and another of smoked beef that tastes pretty decent, heavy on bone and light on meat. The whole kitchen carries a hefty patina of mud and muck, although Joyce does her best to keep things clean. There's no power here, so food lies around in the 40-degree heat, and I hope to God that the boiling process has killed as many germs as possible. The stew is served with three different kinds of sweet potato (though they taste identical), and it's a bargain at 30p for a huge bowl.

The men to whom I serve the food are aghast at seeing a weedy *mazungu* bringing their lunch, but they enjoy it – or at least they're too embarrassed to complain. Joyce pronounces herself pleased with my performance. Only then do I realize that I've ground most of my fingernails into the paste, which must have added something interesting to the texture.

As promised, I pay my 30p and eat a bowl of the stew. I've given up worrying about food poisoning and now I'm just hoping for the best. Joyce tells me that she just about makes a living from the restaurant, and at least it's a little more than most people have.

After lunch we look at one of the other restaurants and Pedro introduces me to Atimango, possibly the most beautiful girl in Uganda, with a captivating smile and a wicked sense of humour. She makes fun of our big white UN 4×4 and the laughter is a relief after everything I've seen.

That night I stay at the camp's Catholic Mission run by Sister Mary, an archetypal sweet, birdlike Irish nun. Pedro, his assistant and I sleep together with a cloud of whining mosquitoes in a room as hot as Hades (are you allowed to say that about a Catholic Mission?) and I lie awake quietly fuming with impotent rage about the LRA late into the night. All this suffering, and these rebels aren't even rebelling against anything.

The morning finds us wandering around the tightly packed slum that makes up the centre of Pabbo. It's a dense, apocalyptic vision of a refugee camp, with listless people lying around in the sun, babies playing with turds, and packs of dogs running over everything (what the hell are dogs doing here?). Nowhere is there any water. Pedro is concerned that this place is becoming a dysfunctional city rather than a camp, but it's almost impossible to turn people away.

With so little food to be found here, I decide to cook for all of us tonight. There is a tiny market, and we buy charcoal, bo (the spinach-like leaf), some groundnuts and a charcoal stove made from an old car wheel.

I decide to invite the people I've met here in Pabbo for dinner. I'm worried that it might look like a horribly patronizing gesture, but I want to see them all again, and it would be nice to give them something in return for their hospitality, even if it's only a plate of food. Atimango asks why I want to cook her dinner. This floors me for a while. 'Because I want to see if you like it.' She thinks this is hilarious and agrees to come.

So I cook supper for 12 of us: Joyce, Atimango, the UN team, my producer Ruhi, Sister Mary and a bunch of other people who happen to be hanging around. They are all a little surprised – they aren't used to being invited to eat with the *mazungus*.

It's my emergency risotto again, this time with some blanched bo and perfectly al dente rice. I spend hours preparing the whole thing, with my new friends taking the mickey out of me for being so slow. And when finally I serve it up, they all roll about laughing. This is awful, they say – the rice isn't cooked through and the bo is still crunchy. We thought you were a proper cook.

They hate it so much that I have to take the bowls back and cook it again, and they tease me until they've eaten their fill. Throughout the trip I've felt almost like a poverty tourist, and worried that I wasn't really engaging with the people I was talking to, but this is different. This isn't about cooking risotto for refugees – it's about enjoying the company of friends and sharing what we can. I'm sad when everyone returns home for the camp's curfew.

As I clear up the mess, another three huts burst into flames 200 metres away, an inferno in the dark. All I can do is watch.

In the morning I visit Atimango's parents' restaurant and have a breakfast of chapattis and eggs rolled together – a dish that the Ugandans call rolex (for 'roll-eggs'). Atimango scolds me for being late. When we get ready to leave the camp she looks me straight in the eyes and asks, 'Are you leaving me here? Please don't leave me here.'

I feel terrible – how come I get to leave, but other people don't? But she's bright and intelligent, she works hard and all I can do is hope to God that good things will happen to her.

I meet a lovely old lady who has been a refugee for longer than she can remember. I ask her if she has a message for the LRA and she surprises me.

'Come home and stop this pain,' she says. 'Give us our lives back. Tell the world what you have seen here; tell the world what is happening and help to end this.'

The Night Commuters

I return to Gulu to discover another extraordinary tragedy that the LRA have caused: night commuters. The rebels have abducted and brutalized so many children around this area that every evening thousands of them walk up to 20 km from their homes in villages around Gulu to spend the night in camps set up in the town, guarded by the army. It's an extraordinary scene – thousands of tiny children arrive at dusk, with nothing except the clothes they're wearing. They spend the night in tents, then at dawn they give their names to a register, and leave for their villages all over again. They spend their entire childhood in a state of fear, always running, and never spending a night with their parents.

I talk to one of the commuters, a beautiful, softly spoken little girl of six or seven called Nancy. At registration she is asked why she has come to the shelter, and she says 'to save my life'. She's an orphan and lives with her grandmother in a village 3 km away, less than most. We join her for the return journey.

Nancy's grandmother agrees to let us interview her granddaughters, and it is then that I meet Nancy's sister Coincy, and her story is an even greater shock. She was abducted by the LRA at the age of 14 and spent two years fighting and carrying provisions for the LRA in southern Sudan. She fought battles and killed people. It's the most painful interview of my life as I am effectively forcing her to relive her worst experiences. I fumble with vague questions in an attempt not to upset her and Ruhi begins to get irritated.

'Ask her exactly what happened the night they abducted her,' she tells me.

My inexperience is making this a longer and more agonizing affair, and I'm only *listening*.

Coincy answers in a whispered voice, 'The night I was abducted they came at 4 a.m. and took me away with 40 others. For some reason they let us all go, but as we ran away, some of the officers grabbed me and took me to a base where there were many other abductees. Some of us were told to be "wives" or sex-slaves to the officers; others were killed immediately or used to fight. They indoctrinated us, telling us that the officers were spirit mediums and could kill us if we ever escaped. I was often tortured, beaten and slashed with knives.' She shows me a scar on her back where she was bayoneted when another girl escaped, and they thought that she was planning to follow her.

'I was constantly fighting the government troops, and was always afraid that I'd be killed in the fighting. I finally escaped when there was a big battle with a government helicopter gunship. I threw away my weapon and surrendered to the troops.'

Coincy talks softly throughout and looks at the floor or away to the side. The only time she cries is when she describes how she came back to her village from a rehabilitation centre and the other children were jealous of the bedding she'd been given.

'They said that it should be thrown out because I'd brought the bad spirits of murder with me.' She is quiet and dignified and tells me she would like to continue her education, but doesn't think her grandmother can afford it.

At the end of the day I walk back to Gulu with Nancy and Coincy. Nancy sings us two songs – a Ugandan national song and one she learnt at the children's centre. Both are heartbreakingly beautiful.

As a final gesture, my translator Bitek has suggested that I visit Majo, his mother, in her refugee camp and she can show us her old village. I suggest we take her back there to cook a meal and he agrees.

I visit Gulu market to buy food and chat to the lovely market ladies again. They are surprised when I tell them that I do all the cooking in my house, and shocked when I reveal that I serve the food to my friends too. 'That's just wrong,' they say. 'Why would you do such a thing?' They laugh at me in peeling cackles that go around the entire market. 'This *mazungu* serves food to his wife!'

I buy matoke, more bo, groundnuts, vegetable oil (sold in reused Coke bottles), onions and some potently stinky small fish. We grab charcoal, mats and a couple of cheap saucepans and head for Bitek's mum's house in a small IDP camp 10 km outside Gulu. I am followed, as always, by three truckloads of soldiers laden with all sorts of heavy weaponry. I'm becoming used to this now. Bitek's mum Majo is quiet but friendly, and after we all squeeze into the car, our little charabanc sets off to make an extraordinary Sunday lunch.

When we arrive at Majo's old village both she and Bitek are visibly distressed at the sight of the ruined huts. 'Everything of mine has been destroyed and I have nothing to come back to. It's all gone,' she explains. She talks about the war, the LRA and her suffering, and I suddenly wonder if I've stepped over the line of bad taste. I ask if bringing her here to cook is inappropriate.

'No,' she says. 'I hope this will breathe life into my village. Perhaps it's a sign that soon we will come back here.'

Majo is deeply suspicious of my insistence on helping her cook – she's not really used to this. First we dry-fry some groundnuts and hand them out to the soldiers as a snack. A couple of them burst into laughter. Then Majo shows me how to make aubergine and fish stew. We've been cooking for about half an hour when the commander, Isaac, finally breaks his silence and suggests a slightly different cooking method. It's quite a shock to hear him speak because up until now the soldiers have been a constant but silently aggressive presence, just magically appearing when we drive anywhere. Isaac is a handsome, powerfully built man who carries an aura of importance. It clearly wouldn't be wise to get on the wrong side of him. He has a serious, calm and deliberate voice, and he suggests that we add salt to the frying aubergine. This opens the floodgates, and everyone starts haggling over the recipe – soldiers, Bitek, Isaac, even our driver. The only one who rises above the din is Majo, who calmly carries on cooking.

Isaac turns out to be intelligent and knowledgeable, and deeply proud of his Acholi tribe's heritage. I start to develop a wary affection for him and even Bitek and Majo seem pleasantly surprised at the interaction – refugees have a difficult relationship with soldiers, whom they see as both protectors and aggressors who prolong the conflict with the LRA.

The soldiers become openly friendly, and by the time Majo and I have negotiated the heckling and finished cooking, they are grinning in anticipation of a good lunch. We sit down to eat with as many of Isaac's soldiers as can be spared from guard duty, and everyone declares the meal delicious, even Isaac, who says that it's as good as his mother would make.

Then the most extraordinary thing happens: Majo and Isaac give me and Ruhi Acholi names. Mine is Oriba (Unity) – because Majo says I have brought about a small miracle in bringing together normal villagers, the army, the UN and a small piece of Britain, and this unity is to be celebrated. No one has ever done anything like this for me before and I am deeply touched. Ruhi is called Anyadawe (Beautiful and Moon-faced). We are both glowing with pride.

Before we clear up to leave, Majo asks if she can keep the big saucepan we brought. Of course she can. She says she will call it Stefan to remind her of the day she came back to her village.

As we leave, I ask Bitek if he really wants to come back to live in this wasteland. He's a modern, urban journalist now with a decent standard of urban living. But he says that he'd definitely like to move back to his home village.

'I was born here. I very much long to return.'

● ● ● ● ●

I'm heading for Cameroon now – away from war and brutality, I hope. But it seems that fear and pain are never far away in central Africa, and I have a sneaking suspicion that in Cameroon it might just take another form.

A few months after my visit, the LRA and the Ugandan government announced a ceasefire, but despite my hopes, there's been much talk and little change, and up to 2 million refugees are still in the camps. And, to be honest, most people in Uganda don't expect to see change happening any time soon.

CAMEROON
The Bushmeat Paradox

• •

POPULATION: 19 million

PERCENTAGE LIVING ON LESS THAN $2 A DAY: 50%

UNDP HUMAN DEVELOPMENT INDEX: 144/177

CORRUPTION PERCEPTIONS INDEX POSITION: 138/163

GDP (NOMINAL) PER CAPITA: $1,002 (126/179)

FOOD AID RECIPIENTS: 190,000 to 2007

MALNUTRITION: 25% of the population

• •

I open the door to a *horrible* room in the Meumi Palace Hotel in Yaounde, the capital of Cameroon in central West Africa. There's a thick stench of sweat mixed with something I can't quite put my finger on – possibly blood – and a table covered in empty beer bottles and fag butts. A TV hangs from the wall fizzing static and I can't get rid of the thought that someone has recently been brutalized in here. The smell of mould is overpowering, the shower's bust and there's an entire Natural History Museum of insects scuttling across the floor, including several species as yet unidentified.

Outside my grimy window the rain is coming down like a ballistic power shower. I've just found out that it's the rainy season in Cameroon, and I'm trying to look on the bright side but there doesn't seem to be one. This place is poor, unhappy, sweaty and corrupt.

I've come here to find out about the bushmeat trade, and it looks like being a tricky story. I'm probably going to have to eat all manner of unusual insects and mammals, but it's not that that's worrying me – I believe that we should eat pretty much anything on the planet – the trouble is that in Cameroon it's exactly this belief that's causing an ecological and environmental catastrophe. Cameroonians consume a vast amount of bushmeat, accounting for an estimated 60–80 per cent of all protein eaten (up to 90 per cent in rural areas), and cut swathes through the forest fauna. The meat comes from rodents, forest-dwelling animals and even primates such as highly endangered mandrills, gorillas and chimpanzees. Some scientists warn that the next generation of children will grow up in a world without any great apes at all. If you think you've heard all this before, stick with me because it gets messier. HIV and other diseases originated here in Cameroonian primates, and eating bushmeat is one of the ways animal diseases are transmitted to humans. Many people say that we're so closely related to primates that we shouldn't eat them anyway – it's practically cannibalism.

And here lies my big problem: if I'm presented with a primate and asked if I could eat it, my complex carnivorous rationale is going to be severely tested. I've always based my carnivorousness on the simple idea that we can kill animals for food, but not humans, and I can't start differentiating between species now or my whole carnivorous justification might come tumbling down. And if two sticky weeks of moral and zoological relativity sends me home a vegetarian I'm going to be mighty pissed off.

Yaounde Market

The sky is ominously dark and the clouds are on a rolling boil above us. I curse the series producer, Marc, once again for sending me here in the rainy season, and get into a taxi so knackered that it's an insult to knackered taxis: the windscreen is a mosaic of broken glass and the make and model unidentifiable due to years of being crashed and beaten back into the basic automobile shape.

There is no room in the taxi because there are too many people in it. For some reason we have managed to employ two local guides rather than the usual one. This should make my life easier, especially in a place that's as notoriously difficult to work in as Cameroon, with its high levels of corruption, intransigent bureaucracy and lack of infrastructure, but right now they are having a nasty row about who should sit in the front. The diminutive, intellectual Louis says that he needs to direct our driver so he needs to see better, but the garrulous, assertive Joseph says he's bigger and needs the legroom. It's true – the guy's enormous. In the end it's easily resolved when Joseph gets bored with arguing and physically shoves Louis into the back to join me, and we're off. I wonder why we need both guides with us. Shouldn't one of them at least be off setting up our next meeting? No time to ask – we're bouncing along the roads of a new city and I'm excited.

Yaounde City is sticky, filthy, aggressive and chaotic, but at least it's got roads, electricity, pavements and even working traffic lights. And although Cameroon is poor, for a West African country it isn't doing too badly. It's been stable and peaceful for a long time, which has allowed some development and investment, but it's got its fair share of problems like inequity, a heavy reliance on subsistence farming, and corruption. It's run by an ethnic oligarchy led by a chap called Paul Biya, who's been president for 25 years despite widespread accusations of vote rigging and electoral fraud. But it's the country's insatiable appetite for bushmeat that is causing global concern.

We pick up Mme Pascaline, a proud woman resplendent in flowing African print robes, who makes a living cooking and selling bushmeat. Joseph grumpily makes way for her in the front seat and gets in the back with the rest of us. Holy Mother of God and all the saints, I can't breathe back here! Why can't we get two taxis? They only cost the price of a box of matches. No one can hear me so I sit with my face squashed against the greasy window until we arrive at our destination: a roadside market with several bushmeat stalls. I re-form like a *Tom and Jerry* character that has been briefly and painfully turned into an anvil for comic effect.

Joseph warns me that people are likely to be extremely aggressive towards us. Suddenly I'm pleased that he's big and assertive.

There are some specific licensed markets in Yaounde, but in reality every street in the city is crammed with stalls, including bushmeat stalls. The only difference with the bushmeat is that the stalls are always set back from the road in a half-hearted attempt at hiding, although they are laughably easy to spot.

I follow Mme Pascaline towards the stalls that she normally buys from, with the camera slung low, chatting and smiling as we walk, but the shouts and warnings start as soon as we are spotted: 'No camera! No camera!' It's aggressive and panicky.

There are large piles of blackened monkeys, porcupine, rodents, and limbs, hands and heads of Lord knows what. Many of the monkeys have been spatchcocked and sit in piles with grimacing faces and blackened skin. They've actually just been smoked for preservation but they look gruesome, like they've been tortured in some satanic ritual, grinning because their lips have been burnt off. The stallholders cover the piles with plastic sacking when they realize that we're going to persevere. Joseph tries to talk to them, saying, 'We just want to film our friend buying some meat for lunch,' but the anger and shouting builds to hysteria, so he gives up.

We lower the camera and the shouting calms enough for Mme Pascaline (who is clearly enjoying the attention) to size up a few animals that look like vast guinea pigs. She chooses a small one and bargains the price down to 10,000 francs (about £10), which sounds like a heck of a lot of money. I was expecting bushmeat to be cheap. I make one last attempt to film her buying the meat, but the crowd goes nuts, shouting and pushing, and trying to throw water over the camera. I decide to beat a tactical retreat to the taxi. Joseph follows soon afterwards, whistling with surprise at the reception we got. 'Ooh man, they aren't happy!'

Mme Pascaline giggles in the taxi: 'Ils ont peur' (they're scared), she says. *They're* scared? I was terrified. 'It's illegal to sell bushmeat without a licence.'

'Why don't the stallholders get a licence?' I ask.

'You can't get a licence – they don't give them out because they don't want anyone to sell bushmeat.' Ah. 'The woman is scared that if your footage shows her stall, the authorities will come and arrest her.'

So is it illegal for you to cook and sell the meat? 'Don't be silly,' she laughs.

Joseph says, 'There are many international organizations who are giving money to people fighting against bushmeat hunting. That's why when they see a camera they think you'll take their picture to give it to those people or to the police.'

I'm confused. If I can stumble across bushmeat stalls all over Yaounde, and it's clearly illegal to sell the stuff, why don't the police close them down? And in any case the animals on sale may have looked gruesome, but they weren't endangered species. Louis explains, 'We didn't see gorilla or chimpanzee because the stallholders keep them out of sight. You have to ask for them and they only give if they trust you. Gorilla is very illegal and very expensive.'

There are three legal categories for protected animals: Class A are species threatened with extinction (such as gorillas, chimpanzees and mandrills) and to kill or keep one requires signed authorization from the minister in charge of wildlife. Class B species (such as buffalo, parrots and African civet) are not necessarily threatened, but may become so, and you need a permit to hunt or sell them legally.

The tricky bit comes in the last category: Class C, which is wide-ranging and contains blue duiker (a small antelope), porcupine, cane rat and all manner of other bushmeat. There can be many reasons why animals are in category C, but certainly these three species are far from endangered (all listed as 'Least concern' in the IUCN Red List, a register compiled by the International Union for Conservation of Nature and Natural Resources). The meat on the stalls all appears to be in this third category and by all accounts it's very popular.

A terrifying problem that's been looming in recent years is zoonosis: diseases jumping from wildlife to humans. The origins of HIV-1 lie in the central common chimpanzee right here in southern Cameroon, and almost certainly transferred to humans through hunting or butchery of bushmeat. Ebola and the glamorous-sounding simian foamy virus are also known to have made the jump.

But if it's illegal to sell them and extremely dangerous to butcher them, why don't Cameroonians just eat something else? Louis explains that 'Cameroon doesn't have a tradition of animal husbandry, mainly because it's always been so easy to catch animals in the forest. Why would anyone go to all the effort and expense of keeping animals when you can just go and lay a trap?'

Mme Pascaline has a simpler line: 'People like bushmeat. It reminds them of living in the forest.'

Delicious Little Porcupine

We drive to Mme Pascaline's house in the slum area of Yaounde called Moloko. It's notoriously dangerous here, but she is well respected (and our guide is the size of a small, semi-detached house), so it feels safe. She has a little shack to serve food from, and behind it, in a rubbish-strewn alley, is her kitchen – really just a place where she leans a fire against a rock.

It turns out that the cute furry creature I thought was a vast guinea pig is actually a 'porc-epic' – porcupine. I don't think I've ever even seen one of these before, but I thought they were covered in vicious quills rather than fur, so I stroke it. I scream with agony as the thick fur turns out to be vicious quills indeed, several of which are now protruding from my hand. Must check my rabies jab is up to date when I get back to the hotel. I dig out *Kingdon's Field Guide to African Mammals* (essential reading for anyone planning to eat out in Cameroon) and identify our little friend as a bush-tailed porcupine. Apparently he's a type of rodent and he's far from endangered.

I help to de-quill the porc-epic by pouring boiling water over it to loosen the quills, then scraping them off with a knife. Around its legs and head the quills seem to be so small as to resemble fur, but they are still angry little things that attack me at will. Underneath the quills the skin is thick, pinky-white and rubbery. It now looks like a huge bald guinea pig.

I ask Mme Pascaline if she's concerned about some types of bushmeat becoming extinct, but she says, 'I know they can never disappear, no matter the amount that we eat.'

I say that there's been a lot of research that says many of the popular species will be locally extinct in Cameroon unless people change their eating and hunting habits.

'Hmm?' she says. She really doesn't care.

'What about gorilla?'

'I've eaten it, and I serve it here, but I need the help of another person – I can't do it all by myself,' she shrugs. 'My favourite is porcupine. And chimp.' Blimey.

'Why's chimp so good?'

'Because it almost smells like human flesh.' Her brother tries to stop her talking, scared that she's taking things too far, but she insists, 'Yes, it's true.'

I ponder her frame of reference, but she hurries me along so that we don't miss the afternoon trade. We chop the porc-epic up into small pieces and lay it in a pot with a few fragrant leaves that I've never seen before. They smell of the best bits of Cameroon: sweet, flowery and dungy. I add a few onions and a little water and the pot goes on the fire for 45 minutes. Meanwhile, Mme Pascaline puts me to work peeling plantain (like bananas, but taste like sweet potatoes).

She unties little wraps of white peppercorns, cloves, fennel seeds, chillies and chick peas, and I grind them to a paste using a large, flat stone. The pot's beginning to smell delicious.

Mme Pascaline lifts a little hatch and declares her restaurant open. It's got bench seats for about ten people, and in a few minutes the place is full. I have to reserve a portion for fear of lunch running out. It's the first time I've eaten porcupine, and I'm very excited. It has a thick layer of tough, fatty skin marked like a honeycomb from where the quills were pulled, but then: tragedy! It's disgusting, like chewing a gamy mouse-mat. The meat is pretty hard to get off the bones, and it's tough and pungent, like … like … I'm eating engine oil. This doesn't seem to bother the punters, who can't seem to get enough of it.

The customers are all boisterous blokes, dropping in on their way back from work. They sing a little song about the porc-epic for me: 'Hey delicious little porcupine, be kind and don't injure me with your little thorns.'

One of the men says, 'Bushmeat is important. It's what we grew up with. In villages and even cities some people can't afford beef, so you just go in the bush and catch whatever and eat it.' They admit that it's very expensive but 'It's a treat – although it's not just rich man's food, we can't afford to eat it every day.'

I'm joined by Ofir Drori who runs the Last Great Ape (LAGA) organization. LAGA tries to encourage the Cameroon authorities to prosecute people who trade or traffic Class A endangered species, filming undercover footage to incriminate traders. Ofir is really an ape man, and doesn't care so much about Class C bushmeat, but he mentions that eating it 'does create a problem of harming the overall biodiversity in several areas'. More importantly, because Class C animals are now considered contraband, the price of bushmeat has risen, and traders are often linked to Class A animals, drugs and people trafficking, so even porcupine is inevitably part of the wider problem.

I worry that making bushmeat illegal when it's clearly enormously popular in Cameroon just pushes the industry underground and creates a new world of criminality – as with Prohibition in 1930s' USA. Ofir throws his hands up in the air and says, 'I don't care. It's illegal and people shouldn't do it.' However, he says that there's a world of difference between the illegal commercial bushmeat trade in the city and legal subsistence hunting and eating of bushmeat in rural communities. But he adds that, 'The most important problem is corruption, no doubt about it. And again it is not [only] Cameroon; Central West Africa is all the same.'

Snake-oil massages and other miracle cures

Louis takes us to meet Bobu, a traditional healer who uses extraneous bits and bobs of endangered animals to heal all manner of ailments from gammy legs to rows with the missus. He's got gorilla legs, leopard skulls, various horns and tusks, and a wide array of wood shavings 'from very rare trees', all of which look spookily like the same bit of wood that's been ground to a dust.

'I'm a doctor and I can cure any kind of problem. People often come to me when hospital medicine has failed. I have lots: all the mystical medicines. For instance, if someone has mental problems, or if you fall out with your boyfriend, I can help you and put you back together,' he claims.

He is also the most magnificently smelly man I've ever met.

He shows me around his wares – gorilla bones, lion limbs, panther skulls and all manner of bird bits. 'That's the panther's skull, it's an antidote against poison. That's the arm of a lion. It's to heal fractures. This is gorilla bone, which is for mystical illness that they can't cure in a hospital.' He offers to make me an aphrodisiac that will keep me going at it for a day and a half. I tell him that Mrs Gates is more into tenderness than competition-level endurance pounding, but he waves away my objections and lazily throws several handfuls of sawdust into a scrap of paper and demands that I pay him 15,000 francs.

He's obviously a total and utter charlatan, which would be fine, but I prefer my charlatans to have a bit of charm or grace. Worst of all, he has a gammy leg of his own, which you'd have thought he'd have been able to cure himself. When I ask why he hasn't, he laughs uproariously and swiftly changes the subject. He asks me to suggest an ailment to cure, so I confess that I've had a dodgy shoulder from too much swimming, and he prescribes a three-week course of python-fat massages. I tell him I've only got an hour, so he thinks for a moment and says, 'That'll do fine.'

He takes me back to his shack in a nearby slum to perform massage on my gammy shoulder. It's one of the sweatiest, smelliest, seediest rooms I've ever been in, and I'm not very keen on the idea of this snake-oil salesman laying his hands on my flesh. But it might be interesting and, to be honest, if he does cure my gammy shoulder with his pseudo-spiritual claptrap I'll be enormously grateful. You see, I'm falling into his smelly trap – these holistic therapists are crafty buggers, aren't they?

He shows me around the tricks of his trade, including his mystic telephone – a gourd in the shape of a 1970s' trimphone that he uses to summon the spirits. I promise I'm *not* making this stuff up. He says he's going to use python fat to rub into my shoulder, which is priceless – a snake-oil salesman actively selling me snake oil. He gets a little fire going, then rubs the python fat on his hands. It *stinks* – like rancid butter mixed with week-old BO, then mixed with skunk juice. I'm almost certain that it's chicken fat, which would be great because python is a Class B 'slightly endangered' animal. He also has sand on his hands, which makes the whole experience utterly, utterly unpleasant. He rubs it in with a great deal of force, taking my breath away.

I wonder why he doesn't use more commonly available animals, but he says, 'People want rare animal cures because they are powerful, symbolic, exotic, and you just don't get that with a chicken. The chicken isn't important at all, it's only good for eating, and the bones aren't mystical.' It's all part of the bushmeat jigsaw – this stuff has a greater resonance here in Cameroon.

Monkey Business

Joseph finds me an area with a bushmeat stall, but the woman who owns it is angry and covers the monkeys and pangolins with a tarpaulin, so I walk away. I spot a woman sitting behind a bowl of enormous wriggling grubs and I ask her what they are. 'Palm weevils,' she says. 'They live in the palm oil tree, and we collect them by cutting palms down and inside you find the weevils.' They look as aggressive as an insect could look. I have to try them. The stallholder advises me to 'Boil them for a few minutes, then grill them over charcoal. They are delicious.' They are also pretty expensive, so I buy a small bag, enough for a snack for all of us, and set off to find a stallholder who can help me cook them.

The central Yaounde railway station is a major hub for the capital, milling with people. It also has endless stalls fronted by charcoal stoves where you can buy freshly chargrilled fish. I ask several stallholders if they will help me out but most refuse. Finally I convince a woman to help me in return for a few thousand francs.

I get out my bag of weevils and take a closer look at them. They are the size of my thumb, with large pincer-like mouths, black faces and hairy chins and they wriggle like frenetic sex toys. I must get that thought out of my head.

She helps me boil and grill them, after which they become a little shrunken, but the grill-marks make them look oddly appetizing – as though they've been photographed for an aspirational food-and-interiors magazine. Joseph and I tuck in. They are crunchy yet sloppy on the inside, and taste slightly sweet and meaty, with a texture very much like shrimps. The heads are gritty, and the overall effect is, I'm sorry to say, quite repulsive. I keep eating them, hoping that my reaction is just fear and prejudice, but after twenty or so, I still can't enjoy them. Joseph, needless to say, can't get enough of them.

Suddenly a man in a uniform barges in on us and starts shouting. Apparently we haven't asked permission to film here. Joseph squares up to him like a fighting cockerel and starts shouting straight back, which doesn't seem to me to be the cleverest approach, especially as the other guy has a gun. After much shouting and gesticulation, the uniformed man drags Joseph away to inspect our filming permit. Another man demands my passport. This has suddenly become very messy. The only person who looks happy about the situation is Louis, who clearly blames Joseph for the mess and wears an 'I told you so' expression.

We look around and spot a group of angry policemen sitting drinking beer a few stalls down from us, and Louis explains, 'They think you have filmed them drinking beer while they are on duty.' The head of the railway station's police department is there, and he looks furious.

All of a sudden we are arrested and told to drive to the police station. Oh dear. We follow the police cars to their compound, and while we're in the car, Joseph hurriedly calls his chief-of-police friend to see if he can pull a few strings. When we get out, we are made to wait for two hours until the railway police chief calls us into his office. He has been bullied into letting us go, and he hates us more than ever. He wishes us luck through gritted teeth, gives me back my passport and tells us to go on our way. It's very odd, an exercise in bullying and low-level corruption. Luckily we came out on top this time. I hope our luck continues.

● ● ● ● ●

Louis takes me off to meet some bushmeat sellers who've agreed to set up their stalls away from their normal location so that I can talk to them and see their meat. When we get there, however, chaos ensues with women grabbing the meat, yelling and threatening us, and pushing each other. We persevere and eventually manage to speak to a stall owner while everyone harangues us. 'The bushmeat ban is just white men meddling in African affairs: leave us alone,' he says.

He's selling python, blue duiker, porcupine and rats, plus several breeds of monkey and one live but terrified, hissing pangolin curled into a ball that he constantly prods. He says that none of them is endangered (although python is actually a Class B endangered species) and that he doesn't know or care what the classification is anyway.

I ask why everyone is so aggressive and he says, 'People are shouting because when you come and film like this it can make the forest guard come and arrest us.' Then he himself threatens me: 'I don't want to get arrested for appearing on TV. If that happens, then next time you're here, I'll just take a machete and cut you down, and break the camera.' Time to leave.

Into the Bush

I get up at 3.30 a.m. and pick up a very grumpy, arrogant gendarme called Albert. I know you shouldn't judge people on first impressions, but this bloke definitely eats babies. I have paid for him to join me on a trip to the rural forest areas because he should be able to avert potential violence and extortion and head off any difficulties I might have with local bureaucracy. He clearly isn't happy about babysitting me, but he's had no choice in the matter. Despite his grumpiness and my misgivings, he works wonders: on our way we get stopped at endless checkpoints by obscure officials, and it's not clear what they are looking for, but as soon as Albert grimaces at them, they wave us past. You don't mess with a bloke who eats babies.

As dawn breaks we arrive at a small collection of huts to meet Andre, a local hunter and his wife, Estelle. People like him are the poorest in Cameroon, and in rural areas there's a great deal of poverty, but of course, there's also an abundance of wild animals.

Andre takes us out hunting in the forest immediately behind his house. Only five or ten minutes into our hike we discover a cane rat lying dead in one of Andre's traps. Half an hour on, another of Andre's traps has caught a 'chat-tigre': a palm civet cat according to *Kingdon's Field Guide*. It looks like a small leopard crossed with my own tabby, Tom Gates. We return to Andre's hut and I help Estelle cook the civet cat. Defurring it is one of the more horrific experiences of my life – not because it's gruesome, but because I keep imagining that I'm skinning Tom, who's been a faithful friend to me for years.

We eat the cat sitting outside their mud and lathe hut and chat about bushmeat. The cat's good, but dry like rabbit and with a strange, catty skin. As we chat, the Baby-Eater comes over and demands a bowl – he's a serious fan of bushmeat, despite being a policeman, but Andre is terrified of him. I ask the Baby-Eater to sit away from us so that Andre can speak openly and he harrumphs off.

Andre admits to having hunted and killed gorillas and chimpanzees, but he has to hide it from everyone in the village for fear of being grassed-up to the authorities 'When I kill a gorilla by myself, I hide it because if news is out that I killed a gorilla, they'll try to catch me.'

He's a little unsure about whether he feels guilty about hunting gorillas – he's clearly well aware that they are endangered and that it's illegal, but he points to his small, grimy hut. 'Look, I'm not a rich man,' he says. 'I'm just making some money for my family. If I had caught more than the cat today, I would have called a woman I know who buys the meat from hunters and sends it to the city for sale.'

Few activists say that people like Andre shouldn't hunt to feed their family. But it's in the commercial hunting – when Andre sends his bushmeat to town for sale – that the burden on forest biodiversity becomes a problem. Hunters lay extensive traps and hunt the more valuable endangered species, which traders then buy and transport to places like Yaounde where they can get a higher price. And from what I've seen in Yaounde, it's happening on a huge scale.

So who's to blame? From where I'm standing, Andre is a man who's struggling to feed, house and clothe his family, he lives a poor and difficult life, and I can entirely understand why he hunts and sells bushmeat without a licence. How else is he going to get by? You could lecture him until you're blue in the face about biodiversity and ecological responsibility, but like you or I he'll need money tomorrow, and in the absence of any other means, he'll nip back into the forest behind his hut, thanks very much.

It's often claimed that the logging companies are at the root of the trade. First, they cut roads deep into formerly impenetrable forest, which destroys the habitat for animals, and at the same time opens up new areas to commercial hunting. Second, they provide the transportation for bushmeat when it's smuggled on their trucks.

I say goodbye to Andre and Estelle and drive a few miles east to the disingenuously glamorous-sounding Auberge de Moins Coin hotel in the sleepy village of Ayos. It's got a rudimentary bathroom but no running water and no electricity (although the smiling owner says that he's hopeful that both the power and water might return later). I take a look at the sink, and there are a couple of huge black, hairy feelers waving out of the overflow hole – they clearly belong to some enormous hidden insect that is right now laying plans to visit me tonight and tear me limb from limb. I smile at the friendly owner and say that I'll take it. I've stayed in worse places, and in any case, there's no other option.

At about 9 p.m. the power suddenly kicks in, and a small but harsh fluorescent tube that I hadn't noticed before flickers into life, revealing the cloud of mosquitoes that I also hadn't noticed. I put up my mosquito net. But then the power spreads to the rest of Ayos, and the sleepy village starts to party. Pumping, banging, yelping Congolese and Cameroonian music fills the air. Ollie (producer and cameraman) and I grab Louis, our driver Nfor and the Baby-Eater, and wander out in search of beer and food.

The night is hot and sticky and the streets are now full of people strutting their stuff. Girls arm-in-arm flirting with the boys, groups of men arguing ferociously, women declaiming gossip and laughing like bassoons, bars blaring music far louder than their sound systems can really handle, plumes of hearty fishy smoke pouring from all the fish-grillers lining the road. It's Hollywood Africa, and it's thoroughly uplifting. Ollie and I find the only quiet bar, with gentle lilting Cameroonian music, couples chatting, and three fish-grillers set up outside, so we take a seat.

We order some local beers, whereupon the owner turns his stereo up to supersonic volume and puts on some screeching, shouty music. Louis orders a bottle of Guinness (oddly enough, Cameroon is the fifth largest market for Guinness and Nigeria is second only to the UK). After a few beers, the Auberge de Moins Coin seems eminently acceptable, and I hum in tune with the mosquito cloud until I sink into a deep sleep.

The Sanaga-Yong Chimp Sanctuary

We stop off at the Sanaga-Yong Chimp Sanctuary the next day. I have mixed feelings about this: it's great to save an animal from unnecessary pain, but these places rescue a tiny percentage of vulnerable animals, and spend a lot of money on giving them a strange, if safe, domestic life spent accompanying their handlers. If I was being harsh, I'd say that sanctuaries are sentimental places where the cutest animals in the world are cared for by rather wet animal lovers, but they do try to highlight the problems of the bushmeat trade. I had asked Andre what he thought about chimp sanctuaries, and he just laughed. A waste of money for white people to play with animals, he thought, although, as a dedicated hunter, he perhaps isn't their target market. Often the overall intention is to return animals to the wild, but it doesn't always work.

I'm shown around the sanctuary by a gorgeous young French lady called Agnes, who shows me the baby chimp pen full of cheeky little chimplets rolling around, laughing and whacking each other with sticks, in much the same way that my daughters do. I let out an involuntary paternal 'aaah'. Then we go out to the forest to play with an older, but just as gorgeous chimp called Sambe, who is attended by a ridiculously gorgeous Cameroonian volunteer called Sophia. The wall-to-wall gorgeousness of the place is making me go all soft around the edges.

I ask Agnes if Cameroonians are really aware of chimps and how endangered they are. 'No, they're not aware at all. Chimps and gorillas have been eaten for centuries, throughout central Africa. We have to make them aware that they're eating their cousins, and we have to stop them. Scientists predict that in 15–20 years they'll be gone.'

I like Agnes, but that emotive phrase 'eating their cousins' clangs horribly, like the common assertion that we share 98 per cent of our DNA with chimps. We also share around 50 per cent of our DNA with bananas, so does that make soft fruit our second cousin?

I wonder if people who work in sanctuaries have their heads in a lovely but sentimental cloud, so I ask Agnes if it's realistic to stop people eating bushmeat when it's such a core part of Cameroonian culture and there's no realistic alternative. She says, 'At least we can start with great apes. I'm pretty optimistic for great apes. If the population doesn't stop growing, and people continue to burn the forest to make fields, there'll be nothing left, so it has to be sustainable. Also, it's illegal, but most people are ignorant of the law. To give you the whole picture, there were 1–2 million chimps at the beginning of the last century, and now there are only 100–200,000 left in the whole of Africa.'

Sambe does somersaults over me, and climbs up on my head. She is remarkably child-like in her facial expressions, her teasing and playing, and she really does remind me of my kids. I have to wear a surgical mask so that Sambe and I don't swap diseases, but Sambe has decided that her main task in life is to pull it off. Then she manages to get her finger in my mouth, and even Agnes curls her lips up and says, 'I wouldn't let her do that. Chimps have a habit of putting their fingers up their bottoms.' I gag.

Hunting, Shooting ...

After a final night in the Auberge de Moins Coin, today is one of those grin-and-bear-it days. We drive flat out for seven hours at a breakneck pace on dreadful dirt roads to try to get to a remote town called Bilabo before sunset. Our driver Nfor insists on keeping up a ridiculous speed in order to fly over the potholes. I toy with the idea of asking him to slow down, but think better of it, and instead try to muffle my involuntary gasps as we skid around blind corners. It's painful, boring and relentless, and made worse by the fact that there are now four of us in the back seat, three of whom (I don't want to point fingers) smell awful. The Auberge de Moins Coin may have been rudimentary, but it offered a bucket to wash in, and it seems a little selfish not to avail yourself of it when you're going to spend an entire day squeezed in the back of the car.

By the time we get to Bilabo I smell as bad as the rest of the back seat and my arse has taken a fearful battering. We find a dodgy bar that a passer-by thinks may have rooms. I get out of the car but stand curled over like an old man for about 15 minutes until I can finally creak my spine back into shape. Nfor has to prise his hands off the steering wheel and he looks to be in as much pain as me. The barman tells us that he has one room available, but it's big, so we could all fit in it. We take a look at each other and imagine the combined stench of our fetid bodies. Without a word, we shuffle back to the car, creak our bodies back into a sitting position and drive off.

Eventually we find Le Giraffe, an extensive but entirely empty warren of filthy rooms attended by a taciturn fella who'd rather not have the bother of us staying, thanks all the same. But we are desperate men, and the light is going so we insist he shows us a few rooms. Ye gods, I didn't know a bed could sustain that much fungi. It's like an out-of-control Petri-dish experiment. Resigned to our fate, the Baby-Eater negotiates the price of the rooms down to £2 a pop. In the circumstances, it's a rip-off.

We drop our kit amidst the mildew and wander into town where loads of women are cooking fresh fish. We all order some, along with some wrapped cassava, and settle down in a bar opposite to wait for it as the heat of the day wanes ever so slightly. The bar is full and happy, and the beer is a welcome relief after the day's low-level agony. The fish arrives, and I swear that a Michelin-starred chef couldn't have cooked it better. The combination of charcoal, fresh whole fish, warm sticky air and strong cold beer is a magical thing, and there's not much you can add to it. The bar owner cranks up the stereo and we listen to Makossa music by Petit Pays – a mixture of salsa, funk and African harmonizing that's a bit '80s, but none the worse for it. It's another wonderful, sticky African evening that makes me feel alive and glad.

I don't sleep a wink during the night, despite going to bed on a headful of beer. It might be the smelly, damp bed but whatever it is, the last thing I need now is to get back in that flipping car again. Nfor guns the throttle and once again we're tanking along the dreadful dirt roads at 100 reckless km/h. After three long hours we get to Deng-Deng, a village of 3,000 people deep in the Cameroonian forest.

The village is a muddy, sprawling, higgledy-piggledy collection of tiny mud-and-wood shacks. At a distance, the place looks wretched and impoverished, but on closer inspection, it's not so bad – it's just the mud that makes it look so grim. The village kids are bright-eyed, happy and healthy, pointing and yelling at us as we walk past.

I meet Philippe, a hunter who has agreed to let me live with him for a few days, and he takes me straight off to pay my respects to the village chief. The chief seems like a nice guy and we chat for a while about the mosque he's planning for the village and his hope that Deng-Deng will receive some development help in the near future from a nearby dam project, but he's actually more excited to talk about a football match planned for this afternoon when Deng-Deng take on another local village. 'Make sure you're back in time for that!' He tells me that Philippe is one of the best hunters around and then gives me his blessing to film and stay overnight in his village, and to eat with Philippe.

Back at Philippe's mud hut, though, everything has started to go wrong. The Baby Eater has been throwing his weight around, and has demanded that the villagers bring him some food. He sits in the shade with a big smile on his face, spitting the bones of a small rodent onto the floor and ordering Philippe's wife Eli around. I sigh: I can't help thinking that the petty abuse of authority is as ugly a problem in Cameroon as it was in Uganda. This isn't just an irritation for us – Phillippe is so freaked out by Albert that he has said that he can't go hunting with me for fear that Albert will arrest him. Louis takes him aside to reassure him, whilst I send Albert off to finish his lunch on the other side of the village.

Eventually, after calming Philippe down and staying and chatting with the villagers for a few hours to let them get used to us, Philippe agrees to go hunting, but claims that he doesn't have a gun. Louis says he's not telling the truth – he's got a gun, but he thinks that the Baby Eater will try to confiscate it from him. Eventually Louis has a brilliant idea. Let's borrow a gun from the village chief – that way no one can fret about getting into trouble.

We head down the road that bisects Deng-Deng, and a few miles out of the village a track veers off to the left. Phillippe tells me that this is an old illegal logging road, and he's grateful for it because it allows him to get deep into the forest where the animals are. Like most people I've met in Cameroon, he is sceptical that bushmeat hunting is harming the ecosystem – 'Look at this forest,' he says, 'it's full of animals and plants. This isn't dying out just because I hunt a few animals.' We pass an abandoned camp used by the illegal loggers, littered with rubbish and old fires. It looks as though it has recently been used.

We hike through the jungle for five long hours in search of animals, checking traps and stalking birds, but we're out of luck. Frustrated, Philippe decides to teach me the distress call of the blue duiker: a nasal warble that sounds like 'neep, neep' squeaked by Roadrunner in a fluster. I'm pretty good at a range of strange animal sounds, including paranoid sheep, neurotic cows, horny frogs and bored ducks, so Philippe is surprised at the quality of my duiker impersonation. He puts me to work, neeping away, while he waits for a charitable duiker to come to my aid. Eventually, one creeps through the undergrowth and Philippe takes a shot at it with no success. It's the nearest we get to catching anything – the traps are all empty, and the birds are all perched so high in the jungle canopy that it would be a waste of bullets trying to hit them. This hunting business is clearly a lot harder than I imagined.

... Football ...

Back at the village there's an extraordinary football match going on – Deng-Deng are playing a local team, but it's far from Sunday football back home, where a few overweight blokes bluster around trying not to snap their Achilles tendons. These guys run around like greyhounds, flying into tackles and generally playing as though their lives depend on it. They are encouraged by the fact that every single woman in Deng-Deng has turned out to watch the match, cooing, cheering and jeering in equal measure. The match is markedly better and more exciting than the last time I went to see Arsenal play (not much of a surprise, really), and I can see why Cameroon have done so well in the World Cup.

Deng-Deng lose the match 5–4, but no one seems too upset. I go back to Philippe's hut where Eli shows me how to make their version of couscous. It's nothing like our couscous, which is a type of pasta (most people think that it's a grain like bulgur wheat, but they're wrong). Instead it's processed cassava, a root vegetable a little like sweet potato.

We pound the boiled cassava into a dry porridge the consistency and colour of crumbled feta cheese, and lay it out on a basket. This will be dried on the roof of the hut and used to make a starchy paste to accompany bushmeat. At this stage, it tastes slightly chalky, slightly vomity and extremely sour.

As soon as dusk arrives, a nearby hut throws open its doors and bursts into raucous life. It turns out that this is one of two bars in the village. I buy a round of beers from the bar and we settle down outside to eat a meal of yesterday's leftover porcupine stew and the prepared couscous (less sour, but still nicely vomity). Almost as soon as we have started to eat, a furious row breaks out. A very drunken bloke from the visiting football team accosts Philippe and tells him that as we are visitors, we should be eating with the village chief rather than with him. He tries to explain that the chief has given us his blessing to eat here but drunkie has got his beerphones on and won't have any of it. There's a horrible scene of pushing and shoving for a while then, as if by magic, the chief appears to join us for supper, and the troublemaker hops onto a motorbike and hoons off into the dark. I pity anyone out on the roads tonight.

The chief apologizes for the kerfuffle, and tucks into a spot of porcupine with us, then takes me off to the other bar in the village, which has power, and so serves cold beer. He reminds me that he isn't allowed to drink alcohol because he's a Muslim, then orders a beer anyway, but in a whispering voice (I guess that makes it all right). We have a rare old time chatting about hunting and village life over our cold beers, then the chief's friend asks if I fancy having sex with any of the village ladies tonight, because he knows several who'd be happy to oblige. I thank him for the kind offer but say that I'm too tired from our jungle trekking for that sort of thing. He shrugs and tells me I don't know what I'm missing, before the Baby Eater takes him aside to find out a little more about what's on offer.

We get back to Philippe's place, and the bar nearby is pumping out some good ol' Congolese soul music. My room for the night is a few yards away from their speakers, so I'm blessed with all the elements of a drunken, slightly aggressive African village party in my room, but with none of the fun. Sometime after 3 a.m. the bar calls it a morning, and I get a couple of hours' blissful sleep.

In the middle of the village I find the referee from yesterday's football match, who also happens to be the village representative of the local logging company. I visit him on the off-chance that we can see the logging operations. He makes a couple of calls using my satellite phone and, miraculously, he manages to get permission from someone for us to visit. The logging companies *hate* the BBC and are usually very wary of letting anyone see what's happening on their plots, so I'm amazed that we've been given access.

... and Logging

We drive to the logging concession with one of Philippe's hunting friends who works there driving trucks. Like many of the locals he is very much in favour of logging because it brings much-needed jobs to poor villages like Deng-Deng, and he rarely if ever thinks about the long-term consequences. He does, however, admit that, 'None of the money paid by the logging company to the government ends up in the hands of the people who live in the forest.'

The statistics are terrifying: between 1990 and 2000 some 90,000 sq km of forest were cleared in Cameroon, and logging concessions covered 76 per cent of all protected and unprotected forests. Forest products generate around 20 per cent of Cameroon's export revenue.

The companies all want *ventes de coupe* (freedom to cut) licences, which entitle them to log an area of 25 sq km of permanent forest over a short three-year period with no management plan to limit environmental damage, so there's high potential for destructive logging methods. There are many reports that the companies actually use the licences as cover to illegally cut a much larger area.

We drive deep into the forest through roads cut specifically for logging. These go for miles, deep through the trees, passing impenetrable flora and fauna that, by rights, we shouldn't be able to see. We drive for an hour through this logging concession, passing vast tree-moving trucks and piles of massive tree trunks ready for shipping. I find the sight deeply unsettling.

We come across a team of two men who let me watch them chop down an enormous red-brown tree. They make deep cuts into the trunk and stick branches in the cuts. Call me a lily-livered, hand-wringing liberal, but the whole operation makes me feel sick. They tell us that the tree is going to fall due south, but at the last minute it starts to creak and the loggers panic. It's falling north instead. We scamper around the tree and back off as it begins a slow-motion fall. It takes a long time to come down – maybe 30 seconds of rumbling earthquake noises building up to a huge crashing crescendo as it hits the forest floor, bringing down scores of other trees and vines as it falls. Then an eerie silence.

I ask the loggers if they worry that they are doing lasting damage to the forest, but they don't want to talk about it. I persevere until they finally say, 'There are millions of other trees here. If we cut one down, it makes way for more.' I should be clear: this logging isn't a scorched-earth concept that leaves behind a ragged field – they cut down only the most valuable trees, which are often hundreds of metres apart, so the place doesn't look particularly less forest-like to my eyes, but it's lacking in mature hardwood trees. I'd say that the tree they've cut down is probably at least a hundred years old. The loggers move on because they have a quota to fill – twelve trees have to be cut down today.

Midnight Train to Yaounde

We drive back to Bilabo and wait for a train that's due at midnight. Thankfully we are avoiding the gruesome drive all the way back to Yaounde, and instead we are going to go out with the forestry soldiers who inspect the train for bushmeat smugglers. This train used to be the main smuggling route into the capital, so in an attempt to restrict the trade, bushmeat has been entirely banned. It's not just a conscientious move – the World Bank has provided funding to help Cameroon railways and it's partly contingent upon halting the bushmeat traffic.

Just before we get to the station the Baby Eater stops a man on a motorbike who has a porcupine strapped to the pillion. He wants to buy it to take home to Yaounde – the man is a bushmeat maniac – and this porcupine is half the price he'd pay in town. But we're travelling on the train, I tell him. It's *illegal* to carry bushmeat.

'Yes, but no one will search me – I'm a gendarme,' says the Baby Eater.

'Exactly. We're making a film about *bushmeat* and about people smuggling it. You can't drag us into this.'

The Baby Eater is furious, but lets the man on the motorbike go.

The station is crammed with people on the platform selling all manner of foods from baskets carried on their heads. At around 2 a.m. the train finally arrives, jam-packed with people. Louis has to bribe the conductor of the train to get us four berths so that we can leave our kit with the Baby Eater and head off with the forestry soldiers searching the train for bushmeat.

The train is extremely smelly, with people lying over the floor in several layers. The soldiers tiptoe through the carriage trying to avoid treading on feet and hands. The passengers are all resentful, and reluctantly let the soldiers go through their luggage, but they shout and heckle me, saying that I should take my colonial attitudes back to the UK. At one point we pass a high-ranking army officer who argues with the forestry soldiers, asking why they are bothering to criminalize ordinary Cameroonians.

The soldiers search some lively-looking bags and everyone seems to have food of some description, especially smoked fish, in their luggage. That's why the train smells so bad. After a few carriages, however, they discover an abandoned sack of monkeys and cane rats, all blackened with smoke. No one claims the sack (funnily enough). Then, a few seats along, we find a woman who has a large bag of bushmeat crammed next to her on the seat. But when challenged, she just denies that it's hers, and no one around her is willing to say different. The soldier says that it's obviously hers, but of course they can't prove it, and if she admits to owning it, she'd face prison, so we'll never know. The woman is, however, very unhappy. If it was hers, she's probably just lost several weeks of potential income, and may now be in serious debt. I don't know if she deserves my sympathy or not.

We finally collapse in our cabin and manage a couple of hours kip as the train crawls painfully slowly towards Yaounde. When we arrive, I feel a sense of relief tinged with sadness. The bushmeat problems seem as complex and unresolvable in the countryside as they are in the city, and the laws seem to be punishing poor and vulnerable people who have few other opportunities.

The Chicken of Love

We drive a little way out of Yaounde to visit a cane rat farm where they breed rats of James Herbert proportions – they are the size of small dogs, but infinitely more aggressive, like psychotic Jack Russells. It's actually a nascent training and research centre for breeders, and they have only 50 or so rats at the moment. It's a commercial centre, set up in the hope that there'll be a big cultural shift and people will turn to setting up their own cane rat farms. I'm sceptical to begin with – these vicious little rodents are armed with industrial-strength incisors so they need immensely strong (and expensive) concrete-and-steel cages that look way beyond the means of an average Cameroonian.

Paul, the boss, says that cane rats could be one of the solutions to the bushmeat problem, especially as a 6-kg rat fetches 20,000 francs at market – that's about £20, a huge amount of money around here. Maybe Paul's onto something. We find a particularly well-fed specimen and take it to Paul's house where his wife, Louisette, shows me how to prepare it. First knock it over the head to render it unconscious, then cut its throat and bleed it. After this, the process is similar to the porcupine, and I prepare myself for another meal that tastes like engine oil. We douse it in hot water, after which the fur comes off surprisingly easily, then butcher the little fella into 12 or so pieces, and fry it briefly, then boil for half an hour with onions, spring onions, chilli, garlic, green pepper and salt. She serves it with a sauce made by simmering tomatoes with onions, chilli, garlic and peanut oil, and beautiful wraps of manioc (cassava) paste that's been wrapped into thin bundles and boiled.

But here's the lightning bolt: cane rat tastes *absolutely* fantastic, one of the best meats I've ever tasted: unutterably succulent, moist yet with a full, fragrant flavour – like the best Label Anglais free-range chicken thighs money can buy. I've tried a lot of strange and unusual foods on my travels, but the cane rat is far and away the best meat I've ever found. I tell Louisette (known to everyone here as 'Mami') that it's fantastic, and she's rightly proud.

Raising cane rats is one possible way of shifting from a reliance on bushmeat hunted in the forest regions, but it's currently a drop in the ocean, and the industry is tiny. Paul says, 'My dream is that this will be one of the international meats that could be eaten in Europe, on the plane when people are travelling.' I agree, but tell him that he has a marketing problem. I can't ever see supermarkets in the UK stocking their shelves with meat that has the word 'rat' in the label (more's the pity). But there are some horrendous substances that they do manage to sell by the million simply by giving them different names: take crabsticks, for example. So I suggest renaming cane rat as 'heaven toad', 'dream horse' or 'the chicken of love'. Paul tells me he'll think about it and get back to me.

The Dangers of Bushmeat

The next morning I set off for one last interview before leaving Cameroon. On the way I chat with Joseph about the anti-colonial feeling in the country, and the sense I got on the train that Cameroonians think that Europeans are making a fuss over nothing, that we can't stop meddling with a place we don't really understand.

Joseph explains, 'We tend to hate the French, but we quite like the English.' The country was governed as two separate entities – as League of Nations mandates – from 1919 until independence in 1960. 'Most of us think that the French clung onto power to take as much – they could from the country, and to retain a bit of influence. And they come back here now with the Italians to run logging companies, and they know that the money they pay for licences goes straight into the pockets of the politicians, and they don't care.'

As we drive through Yaounde, I spot a bus with two live goats tied to the roof. They look surprisingly calm about it.

Matt LeBreton works in possibly the cleanest place in Cameroon. Admittedly it's a laboratory, but even so, it's difficult getting somewhere to be this spick and span in a place like Yaounde. Matt researches wild animal ecology and disease in Cameroon, and he's at the really scary end of the bushmeat trail: species-jumping diseases that evolve in animals and mutate to infect humans. We're talking about the really nasty stuff: Ebola, Aids, anthrax and that one I really hope I never get – simian foamy virus.

He makes big claims about what his research might be capable of: 'There's a whole world of pain waiting to be prevented … we like to think we could've stopped HIV if we'd been doing this a while ago. It's a big problem, but what you have in Cameroon is people having contact with all sorts of animals that people don't mix with elsewhere.'

I mention that I had squirrel for lunch, so I ask if that's likely to be a problem. Matt says, 'The thing to remember is that preparation is what causes the trouble … the most viruses are killed by cooking, although diseases particularly associated with squirrels and other types of rodents are things like monkey pox. Maybe call me to tell me how you are in a few months' time.'

Gulp.

●　●　●　●　●

I wonder if there aren't better ways to solve the bushmeat problem because whatever's being tried ain't working, and instead there's a climate of fear, resentment and confusion. Perhaps the government should be stricter about applying the laws they already have, but there may be a more radical solution. Rather than criminalizing bushmeat and driving it underground (and away from the authorities and researchers who can keep an eye on it), perhaps it would be more effective if the government *legalized* bushmeat and taxed it. That would provide income and a market that's open and therefore easier to regulate. The trouble is that Cameroon isn't the squeakiest-clean of countries – languishing at 138 out of 163 in Transparency International's Corruption Perceptions Index – and maybe more bureaucracy, tax and income offers more potential for gerrymandering and corruption. But it could be said that the bushmeat trade couldn't be much worse than it is already. And it's not just a problem bubbling away on another continent: officials estimate that 7,500 tonnes of illegal bushmeat are smuggled into the UK every year, too.

What has affected me more is the anthropomorphic connection I felt with that sodding chimp, Sambe. I didn't expect to be carried away so much by her sweetness, her playfulness, her … there's no way of getting around this … her humanness. My carnivorousness has been based on a clear moral line, where I feel able to kill (or at least take responsibility for the death of) and eat anything that isn't human. But Sambe has blurred the line for me. It's not just that it's illegal and immoral to eat an endangered species: those issues aside, I wouldn't have been able to eat her anyway because she reminds me so much of my kids. And the trouble is that once that line is blurred, the whole specious edifice of a carnivore's moral justification is in doubt. I'll just have to extend the moral fence to include primates and stick my fingers in my ears and hope it doesn't get any more complicated and start including pigs. Oh, God, am I going soft? Perhaps I'm going to have to cook my cat just to keep me on the right side of the tracks.

● ● ● ● ●

Cameroon has a complex story, but my next destination has a simple history writ large. Twenty-five years ago the Ethiopian famines were, quite simply, the biggest food event of my lifetime. A grand-scale tale of human destruction, a story of global guilt, global redemption and back to global guilt again. I am terrified at the idea of going there, of trying to do justice to the gravity of the subject, and of trying to understand the human impact of such horror. Is it really appropriate to sit down for lunch with someone who's lived through a *famine*?

ETHIOPIA
Famines and Feasts

POPULATION: 77 million

PERCENTAGE LIVING ON LESS THAN $2 A DAY: 78%

UNDP HUMAN DEVELOPMENT INDEX: 170/177

CORRUPTION PERCEPTIONS INDEX POSITION: 130/163

GDP (NOMINAL) PER CAPITA: $177 (176/179)

FOOD AID RECIPIENTS: 5.6 million

MALNUTRITION: 46% of the population

'Hello Addis ABABA!' [25,000 people cheer.]
'I've heard people say that Ethiopia is a poor country. Ethiopia isn't a
   poor country!' [25,000 people roar.]
'Because Ethiopians have LOVE in their hearts!' [25,000 people
go wild.]

● ● ● ● ●

I t's the last day of my trip to Ethiopia and I'm standing in an
extraordinary place at an extraordinary time. In a few seconds it will
be the dawn of the second millennium, which is weird because
according to my calendar it's 11 September 2007, but Ethiopia is a little
different. You see, back in the 16th century Pope Gregory brought in a
new calendar that shifted the date of Jesus' birth (according to the old
Julian calendar) by seven years, nine months and 11 days. The
Ethiopians, being an orthodox bunch, and historically never particularly
keen on embracing the modern world, decided to ignore Greg and stick

with what they had. After all, who wants to go around replacing the stationery and resetting the video recorder?

And this extraordinary place is a vast warehouse built especially for a party in the centre of Addis Ababa. A warehouse party might not sound extraordinary, but this one has been financed to the tune of $10 million (plus whatever else the government has added – rumoured to be another $10 million) by Ethiopian-Saudi billionaire Sheikh al-Amoudi, and it's crammed with 25,000 people who've paid around $160 a ticket to be there. It seems a little snide to mention that the average Ethiopian annual income is only $177, but I'm currently feeling a little … conflicted. And the big shocker is that this warehouse is temporary, to be dismantled in a few months' time to make way for another building project.

I don't want to piss on anyone's millennium parade here, but $10 million is a lot of money, and when you're in one of the poorest countries on the planet, you can't expect to shell out that kind of cash on a warehouse, some nibbles, beer and a half-decent band and not get me asking a few difficult questions.

But there's no time for that now: the bloke up on the stage is only Will.i.am of the popular beat combo the Black-Eyed Peas! Hoh yes! And he's counting us down to the Ethiopian millennium and giving up the love, and there are 25,000 of us down here who've cast our reservations aside to party like it's 1999, and hey, if there's one thing Ethiopia needs, it's a thick, meaty slice of optimism to get the country back on its feet. So we all shout: Five! Four! Three! Two! One…

Mekele. Two Weeks Earlier

The flies. No one warned me about the flies. Persistent, fizzing, ticklish, swarming, disgusting. They crawl over my face, my eyes, lips, ears and hair. I spend the first couple of hours angrily swatting them away, but my skin slowly gets used to the sensation, and I eventually give up and let them wander over me, more irritated by my own swatting than their tickling.

I'm in Mekele in northern Ethiopia, one of the notorious dustbowl fields of death in 1984 where over 1 million people died. The names Korem, Bati and Mekele have had a diabolical, holocaustic resonance for me ever since I saw the famous footage of the Ethiopian famines on BBC news. These were the three worst camps where Michael Buerk uncovered a horrific scene of mass starvation and aid workers tearing their hair out with nothing to feed millions of desperate people and few medicines available to treat any who had enough strength to make them worth saving.

But from the ashes of death, misery and torment grew an unlikely hero: the world. Television made the world stand to attention, and for once the world proved ready and willing to take responsibility for an isolated nation it barely knew anything about, staging the biggest single peacetime mobilization of the international community in the 20th century. The outpouring of shock, sympathy and cash was remarkable because it came from individuals as much as from governments and politicians. Kids were mobilized, rock stars got recording, trucks were driven across the world, and people dug deeply into their pockets. Food started flying through the air, dropping in bundles from planes, thrown out of the back of trucks, and millions of people's lives were saved.

And yet ... and yet. Despite the good that was done and the heartfelt sympathy and the vast donations, Ethiopia's luck didn't change. Despite everything Ethiopia is still a broken country today, and I can't understand why, in the 21st century, nearly 25 years after those great famines, there is such widespread chronic food insecurity, why there are twice as many hungry Ethiopians as there were in '84. Why today over 37 million Ethiopians are malnourished and why the country *still* needs $1.6 billion of aid every year.

There are legions of statistics declaiming Ethiopia's poverty and desperation, but the one that really sticks out is Ethiopia's ranking in the UN Human Development Index (I call it the Happiness Index): 170 out of 177. When you're that low down, being one place higher or lower means little. Basically, life in Ethiopia is, for most people, bloody awful.

So I'm in Mekele to find out what the hell is going on. I must admit that I was apprehensive at the idea of coming here, where the ghosts of a million starved souls haunt the land. But of course our nightmares invariably disappear when we confront them, and so it is with Mekele. This place is nothing like I imagined. There's no dustbowl, no bony lethargic cattle; instead the undulating hills and fields are a lush carpet of vegetation so green that it looks like Devon in spring, a sensation only strengthened by the light but persistent drizzle that's falling and the flowers that seem to blossom everywhere.

I had heard that this year the rains didn't fail, as they have so catastrophically five times in the last 20 years. But even so, I wasn't prepared for this place to look quite so fertile – not when the World Food Programme is expecting to feed 5,640,794 Ethiopians this year.

But there's another side to this: my guide Dawit points out that it's green now because we're here just after the rains. Underneath that greenery lies poor, infertile soil. The reality is that much of Ethiopia suffers from soil erosion and soil exhaustion, unsustainable farming practices and wildly erratic rainfall that brings floods and droughts. Yet despite this, 85 per cent of the country's labour force works in agriculture, and they are often locked into a vicious cycle of poverty brought about by low-return agriculture causing food insecurity, and a consequent lack of access to the education that might break the cycle.

Gebru and Yalezmer

The next day I arrive in a remote village to stay with Gebru Abera and his wife Yalezmer who live in a rural Mekele village and grow their own food. Most Ethiopians are subsistence farmers who raise a few animals or plant staple crops and sometimes sell anything that's left over after they've fed their families. Gebru is famous around these parts for staying put in the village in 1984. 'I stayed here to look after our last cows while my wife and children left for the camp to look for food.' It's a measure of how important cattle are that he took such an extreme risk. Gebru made it through, although they've never managed to restore their herd and they constantly struggle to make ends meet.

I've brought the family a gift of coffee and sugar, and Mama Yalezmer insists on using it to perform the traditional elaborate two-hour-long Ethiopian coffee ceremony. The beans are roasted over a charcoal stove, filling the house with a delicious acrid-sweet smell. At the same time, Mama throws a handful of incense on the charcoal, which belches thickly-scented smoke. 'It's to clear the flies,' she says, although with my eyes streaming, I'm not sure if I don't prefer the flies.

Three separate rounds of coffee are made from one handful of beans, and before we taste it, Gebru intones a prayer for us. The coffee, when I finally get to taste it, is fantastic: deeper, richer and fresher than any coffee I have ever tasted in my life. Extensive slurping is expected, and I enthusiastically oblige, to Gebru's amusement. He's enormously proud of his house – it's made of rocks and mud, but it's beautiful, with benches built into the walls. It could be a rustic romantic hideaway straight out of *Vogue*, if it wasn't for the cloud of flies. Gebru points to a small room hanging up high. 'That's my food store,' he says. 'I had to put it up there so the rats stopped eating everything. It's empty now.'

Gebru takes me on a long walk to the highest point in the village, from where we can see 40 or 50 km of green countryside stretching out beneath us. He tells me about the big droughts: 'This is all like sand – all our crops fail and there's nothing for the cattle to eat. So many of my friends and family in the village have died. But then sometimes the rains come in floods, and the crops are all ruined again.'

'Why do you think that Ethiopia still needs so much aid?'

'Because people are lazy.'

Wow! I wasn't expecting that one. But Gebru is adamant. 'People get aid, and they don't have to work their fields, so they sit and do nothing. And the next year, when the aid doesn't come, they complain and blame the government.'

On the way back to the village Gebru shows me a large, swampy pond. 'This was built by the villagers as part of the government's Productive Safety Net Programme [whereby the needy work on government projects in return for food or money]. It's pointless – nobody wanted it, nobody uses it, it's a breeding ground for mosquitoes and as soon as there's a drought it dries out anyway. What a waste of time! The problems for farmers like me are drought, flooding and aid. We are all farmers in Ethiopia, and when the aid arrives, I can't sell my spare food – who would pay for my grain when people are given it for free? And when there's a good harvest, the price drops and I don't earn enough money to buy seed to plant for the next year.'

One of the big problems in Ethiopia is the lack of storage facilities for grain, so even if there is a good harvest, the food can't be put away for the following year, and the market fluctuates wildly.

Back at her house, Yalezmer refuses to let me walk off around the rest of the village without eating some food, so she shows me how to cook injera – a sort of pancake that has the texture of tripe crossed with crumpets, and a heady yeasty flavour. If Ethiopia has a national dish, it's injera – every family has a bucket of the watery dough fermenting at the back of their hut ready to be cooked. Yalezmer's is the popular traditional version made from a tiny indigenous Ethiopian grain called tef, mixed with water and left to brew. She whips off a lid made of dried cow dung and shows me her hotplate made from dried mud, under which she has stoked a ferocious fire. She takes a cup and pours the injera mixture in a spiral to make a beautifully even pancake. The heat bubbles through the mixture, creating the tripe texture, and after a couple of minutes with the lid on, it's done.

Now it's my turn. I try to pour the mixture but my spiral becomes a cack-handed splodge, thick in places and thin in others. Yalezmer raises an eyebrow, but remembers that I'm a guest, so declares my efforts 'wonderful'. Outside the door, her beautiful daughters are pissing themselves with laughter. I put the lid on and my injera cooks, the thin bits swiftly burning and the thick bits remaining wet and doughy. I apologize and slide the pancake off, whereupon it boils my skin and I jump up with a yelp. We both try a little, and, despite its unconventional shape, it tastes great. I sit down to eat with the whole family, plus a few neighbours who have wandered in to take a look. We eat yoghurt and chilli powder with the injera, which turns out to be a startlingly good mop for sauces.

Just one warning: don't put your fingers in your mouth. It's extremely rude to do this in Ethiopia – you are inevitably manhandling a communal blanket of injera so if you lick your fingers, everyone else is liable to get a taste of your spit. It's agony for me because I love licking food off my fingers and right now my fingers are covered in yoghurt so the temptation is strong. I catch myself licking them unawares every now and then, to disappointed looks from Mama.

I take a wander around the village. It's a ramshackle and crumbling collection of mud huts and scrubland surrounded by fields, and most of the kids are half-naked or in rags, and they are all strangely small (around half of children in Ethiopia are stunted).

I speak to some of the other families and a whole new set of problems becomes apparent: land and population. Zoferi Woldetensae shows me his hut and small yard. 'Look at me,' he says, plucking at his shredded shirt. 'Do I look like a rich man? I have no land and only five goats. I have nothing to rely on and nobody to help me. Sometimes I get work on the Safety Net Programme and that keeps me alive.'

The problem is this: the Ethiopian population is growing at a phenomenal rate, according to UN figures, and at 77 million it's already double what it was during the '84 famines. Well, that makes it much clearer – no wonder there's such a problem in Ethiopia. The resulting pressure on land here is immense, with the distribution of land amongst extended families creating smaller and smaller plots.

Zoferi's friend Asseba Addis is in more difficulty: 'I can't work because I have a bad leg, so I don't even get aid. A few years ago I agreed to join a relocation programme and the government took many of us to a new area and gave us land.'

The Ethiopian government decided to move 2.2 million people living on barren land to more fertile lowland areas around the country. Resettlement has an inauspicious history here: Haile Selassie tried it in 1974, but many died and others fled the country. Many in the aid community see the idea as badly planned, poorly executed and problematic, and they refuse to contribute to the programme.

Asseba's experience seems to bear this out: 'We got a government grant and cleared the land and made it into a farm, but we started to get ill with malaria. And then, when the farm was finally running, we were kicked off by a man who said the land was his. The courts agreed, and we had to come back here, where we have nothing, and now the government want their money back.' He is terribly bitter about the whole experience, and there seems to be nothing he can do about it.

The village is dirt poor, and I ask how many of the fields belong to Zoferi. 'None,' Asseba replies. 'The priest owns all of this.' And as if by magic, the priest appears – a tall and angry man sporting what looks like a woollen blanket on his head. He yells at Zoferi to keep the goats out of his field.

Before we leave I ask Gebru and Yalezmer what they think about the millennium celebrations. 'Great stuff,' they say. 'Just what Ethiopia needs – a way to look forward to a wonderful future.' I ask if they resent the fact that tens of millions of dollars are to be spent on the celebrations, but they look at me as if I'm mad: 'Sounds wonderful. I hope you have a great time. It is such an auspicious event for our beautiful country.'

Addis again

After losing a whole day to Ethiopian Airlines, we are back on track to travel 800 km south to Addis Ababa. I'm beginning to appreciate being here a little more now. To be honest, I'm very much on probation here in Ethiopia. When we applied for our visas and filming permits we were told that on no account were we to mention the famines. Now, I can understand a country wanting to look to a bright future rather than a miserable past, but to skip over the greatest food crisis of recent times in a food and current affairs programme sounds a little unreasonable. In fact, it sounds ridiculous.

However, to show willing, we take a look at the two wealthiest bits of the capital: the airport and the Sheraton Hotel. Unlike almost everything else in Africa – such as cars, books, houses, banks – which tend to look about 50 years old, the airport is very new and sparkly. It's also quite controversial, having displaced a slum of 10,000 residents, and cost a reported $123 million to build. It's like a small Stansted, and it has attracted widespread criticism as a vanity project. I'm not so sure that it's as simple as that. I hate to sound like a capitalism apologist, but I think that vanity projects sometimes have an inordinate impression on a poor country's diaspora and investors, who for better or worse like to see that money can be spent and big projects can be realized.

And I suspect that totems as idiotic as this can bring money into a country, and that this encourages more investment. OK, $123 million is a lot of money, but how much should an international airport cost to build in a country desperate for growth? Is $100 million all right? Fifty million? While we were there the airport was pretty busy (presumably employing hundreds of people and bringing in visitors and their cash). Could $123 million have been spent by the WFP feeding millions of people? Maybe. Would that have made a *long-term* improvement to Ethiopia? Well, it hasn't so far.

Next, we take a look at the palatial Addis Ababa Sheraton where, as journalists never fail to point out, rooms cost up to $5,000 a night (although they skip over the fact that you can also get one for $280). I'm sure UN employees love this place, as do foreign dignitaries. In fact, I know that big BBC news correspondents are quite fond of it too, even as they intone to the camera about the fat cats that frequent it (sadly, little ones like me don't get to stay there, although I manage to get a couple of nights in the Hilton – nice lobby, no water in the rooms – to offset the grimmer nights out in the villages). The opulence of this place makes me feel a bit grubby, so I leave, but again I suspect that these places bring employment for hundreds of people, and draw visiting richos to stay and spend their cash in the country.

The World Food Programme

The World Food Programme office in Addis Ababa is a large and relatively shiny building, surrounded by lots of their big white Land Cruisers. I head off south, following one of the Land Cruisers on the first leg of a four-day trip, another 800 km south, to deliver food aid. First, we visit the pick-up point, and this is where my sympathetic view of the World Food Programme starts to falter. About 12 WFP officials stand around watching us film a small truck being loaded by around 20 porters. It's all a bit weird, a rather cheesy PR display. Perhaps we are complicit in this: we asked if we could film the food being loaded, but I didn't realize it was being set up especially for me, or that so many people really needed to watch.

Then events take a funny turn: I tell Melese, the assistant press officer for the WFP, that I'd like to ask him about aid, and he goes *nuts*. 'That isn't what we had arranged. That was never agreed.' Well, who is going to explain to us what's going on? I ask. 'I don't know. That was not the understanding. I don't have the authority.'

This is very odd. 'Melese, you are a press officer – surely, if there's anyone who can talk to the press, it's you?'

'No, I can't. That wasn't the understanding.'

I suddenly develop a dislike for this man. I am planning to spend four days on a food distribution trip, and if the WFP can't tell me what's going on, what food aid is and what its pitfalls are, I've wasted a lot of the BBC's time and money. And, more to the point, the WFP is going to come across as a strange, paranoid and shabby organization. We call the head of press, who says, 'We never agreed to an interview.' What? What is *wrong* with these people? They're the effing World Food Programme, not the Chinese Communist Party. What could they possibly have to hide? The head of press says she'll think about it (what is there to *think* about?), so we have no choice but to push on, following our lone food truck and the irritating Melese south.

Aid is a tricky thing. There's no doubt that emergency aid measures saved millions of lives in 1984, but as the aid agencies say, 'If you see an airlift, somebody's screwed up.' And this opens up a whole world of complications. Aid can also be a destructive force, ruining the long-term ability of a country to feed itself and fracturing the self-determination and self-sufficiency of a country when delivered badly. And the aid world is a multi-billion-dollar industry where big salaries can be earned and life can be very good.

The WFP gets a lot of bad press – in the gloriously angry book *Lords of Poverty* by Graham Handcock, for example, which rails at the fat cats, failed projects, unaccountability and bureaucratic inefficiency of the UN and the big NGOs. I don't know if this is fair or not: I've met a fair amount of decent World Food Programme people and I always think that the phrase 'fat cat' is a signpost of lazy journalism. Are these people fat? Bad? Wealthy? Perhaps they are just wealthier than most journalists?

Whatever the definition, if I'm honest, you'd probably have to pay me pretty decently to run a food distribution project thousands of miles from my family, in a poor, dangerous and difficult region, with no home comforts. And yes, you'd probably have to give me one of those big comfy white 4×4 cars with air con so in case I get stuck out after dark. I can rough it like anyone else for a few weeks, and I can offer my time, love and sympathy for a while. But there are relatively few people (wonderful though they are) who are in a position to give up their lives to voluntary work. So although I'm sure there are inefficiencies and bad people around, I'm generally glad that my money goes to pay people to work for the UN. But this is Ethiopia – the biggest aid story in the world. I wonder if this is where all my understanding and reasonable attitude falls apart.

As we drive, I mull on the issues. The WFP in Ethiopia gets most of its donations from the USA – $504 million ('over recent years to end of January 2007'). However, that's actually a little misleading because the USA has to, by law, spend all that money on buying goods from US agribusiness and shipping them on US-owned transport, whereupon the recipient either distributes the (now very expensive) food or flogs it to get cash for its projects. Weird, huh? It's all good news for US farmers, shipping companies and the politicians who get their cash and votes. But, as I've seen over and over again on my travels, dropping food into a market destroys farmers' livelihoods and over a couple of seasons makes communities less able to support themselves.

In 2004 the US government provided $500 million of food aid, but only $4 million of long-term development aid. Something's wrong there. It's so damaging that CARE International, one of the big aid groups here, took the extraordinary step of rejecting a donation of $45 million this year – and a rejection like that is a big deal for an NGO. The EU abandoned food aid in kind in 1999, and all but 2 per cent now goes in cash.

We pass through the Great African Rift Valley and watch the landscape change from green and lush to rocky and barren. We are travelling on Ethiopia's main north-south road – their M1, if you will. It is a decent, straight, two-lane road that rolls over hills and past lakes, although away from the city the traffic is minimal – there's only one vehicle every 15 minutes or so. We pass the huge central lakes – beside one is an enormous flower-growing greenhouse – probably about 1.5 km square. Tens of thousands work in the flower industry, but there have been concerns about working conditions, including contact with pesticides and ecological damage. Workers earn about 40p a day, but at least they have a job. And the industry is growing fast: some say that flowers may soon rival coffee as an export crop.

We arrive at the food distribution centre in Yalebo a couple of days later. Around 100 women have been selected from the local community to receive aid because their children are badly malnourished. Before they are given anything, though, they have to sit through a nutrition talk. I sit in the middle of them and chat to a few women at random. Our WFP officials get extremely agitated about this. They have chosen an aid recipient for us to talk to, and they are worried that I will get the wrong message if I just talk to anyone willy-nilly. The woman I sit next to proves their point. She says, 'I don't know why they suddenly told me to come here – I've never been before. I'm not going to turn down free food. I don't know why they suddenly decided to do this.' Oh dear.

I meet Faté Gilo, another aid recipient, who invites us to her hut. Her village is on a barren hillside, and is nothing more than a scattering of temporary-looking huts. Faté shares two tiny huts with her husband and eight children. The huts are extraordinary tiny structures the shape and size of a VW Beetle, made of sticks bent over for strength, and covered in a patchwork of cardboard boxes and bits of plastic. She has brought home 25 kg of WFP flour and 3 litres of oil. Normally it takes her two hours to carry this load home, but today some English bloke has offered her a lift in his car, and she's not going to turn that down.

Faté has no land and no cattle. She does, however, have a donkey, and she uses it to carry out a job right at the bottom of the employment heap: collecting firewood. 'When you have nothing else, you can earn money by foraging in the fields for dead wood to sell.' She's bitterly angry that it's her only lifeline. It's exhausting, backbreaking work, and as we travel around the south we see thousands upon thousands of people doing it because there's simply nothing else. Most people – from tiny children to the elderly – walk with huge bundles balanced on their heads and in their arms. Faté is, in relative terms, extremely lucky to have a donkey to help her, and her income from firewood is much higher than most – 50p per day.

She shows me how to cook the aid rations. It's not hard – we boil some water, add some flour and oil and keep stirring until it looks like porridge. That's it, really. But this WFP stuff is good – the starch absorbs a huge amount of water so a couple of handfuls make a massive pot of nutritious sludge. It tastes of nothing, but Faté isn't concerned, as long as she can get her kids to eat it.

I like Faté – she has a sparkle in her eye – but she has lived a terribly difficult life, surviving on food aid for the last ten years. 'We eat whatever God gives us, but generally we eat once a day.' I ask her what it feels like to be chronically hungry.

'I have a churning pain in my stomach and a pressure on my heart which makes me breathless.'

I ask if she's trapped in a reliance on aid, and she explains that she has no land, no cattle and no job, so there's no way out. 'Why can't they give me a goat?' she asks. She'd have her own milk and might even be able to breed them. Well, let's ask the WFP.

We have managed to get them to agree to an interview. Annoyingly, Melese is the nominated interviewee, and his face is a picture of irritation, fear and hatred as we sit down on the bonnet of a car to chat.

'Aid can sometimes be a negative thing, can't it? Can you explain what aid dependency is?' I ask.

'No, I can't.'

'Eh?'

'The WFP doesn't make people dependent on aid, so we don't know what it is.'

'Come on, you work for the world's biggest aid organization – you must know what aid dependency is.'

'No, I don't.'

'Well, you must be the only person in Africa who doesn't know. We all know – it's a cyclical reliance on aid, isn't it? When aid causes problems in local markets, and people's lives revolve around aid rather than growing their own food?'

'I couldn't tell you.'

The temptation to push this bloke backwards over the bonnet is overwhelming.

'OK. The WFP spends only half of its budget on food and the rest goes on transport, storage and other operating costs. That seems a little high – can you explain why this is?'

'No, I can't answer that.'

Oh, for the love of God.

'Melese, I'm not trying to trick you. I want to know what the WFP's line is on these issues – it's not as though I'm asking unusual questions. I'm sure there are good reasons for WFP expenditure. I just want you to tell me what they are.'

'Oh.'

'I spoke to Faté just now and she said that it would be much better to buy her a goat rather than give her regular food aid. I'm sure that it's more complicated to hand out goats than to hand out sacks of flour, but why doesn't the WFP do something like that?'

'Because we are only allowed to deal in food. A goat isn't food.'

'Yes it is.'

'No it isn't.'

'Yes it is.'

'No it isn't.'

'In what way is a goat not food?'

'It's just not. Have you got any more questions, because I really should be getting on?'

I detest this man. The people around here need tools, cattle, irrigation, education and infrastructure for storage of food, animal feed and water, and they need access to markets where they can sell their produce. Africa has received $1 trillion in aid in the past 50 years. Perhaps if more of that had been spent on long-term projects (like goats?), the world wouldn't have to continue to pour good money after bad to keep people dangling at the end of the aid string. Whether the WFP can't do these things here in Ethiopia, or it is doing them and I just haven't seen it, I may never know.

Moyale

We visit another village of VW Beetle huts to speak to a woman we met yesterday who said we could stay overnight in her village. Abedia is out collecting water when we arrive, so we go to find her at the water hole with some of her kids. She's stunningly beautiful – in fact Ethiopians are probably the most beautiful people I've ever met: tall with fine features, kind eyes and an aura of poise and dignity. The children are invariably absurdly cute, with beautiful eyes and enormous smiles. I shouldn't get sentimental about this – you don't have to be gorgeous to deserve sympathy – but hey, all kids make me weak at the knees.

I expect to see a bucket being dropped into a large hole to pull out water, but we find a small ditch a few feet deep, at the bottom of which is a tiny, muddy, sandy puddle. This is the main water supply for the village, and Abedia scoops the water into a couple of containers. Only 35 per cent of Ethiopia's rural population has access to safe water, and this slurry most certainly isn't it.

Abedia came to Moyale last year to escape fighting between her tribe, the Guji, and the Gabra Ormo tribe over water and land. The situation is worsening for Ethiopia's 6 million cattle-raising pastoralists, especially in the eastern lowlands where a shortage of grazing land and floodplain land for cultivation has caused a great deal of tribal conflict. Abedia says that it starts with cattle rustling, and quickly escalates to violence. 'I walked for seven days to reach this village after my house was burnt down. It happened when they looted our cattle and killed our people. It wouldn't have been so bad if they looted the cattle and spared our lives. But they took our property and killed us too. Life is unbearably cruel. We have lost all our cattle and camels, and we survive by selling firewood.'

At the height of a drought last year 90,000 people were displaced during tribal conflict in southern Ethiopia and in cross-border conflict with Kenyans. Abedia and her brother-in-law, Ibrahim, don't know if they'll be able to return home, so they are stuck here, landless and reliant on aid like everyone else.

We have put up some small tents next to Abedia's hut to stay in overnight, but as the night draws in we get a call from one of the WFP drivers who says that there have been reports of gunfire and rockets being launched nearby. This place is pretty dangerous for Westerners right now, and our car will mark us out as a perfect robbery or kidnap and ransom target. He says we shouldn't stay here for the night. I ponder the situation but can't quite make up my mind what we should do – I'm eager to stay here in the village and find out more. Then Dawit (best guide in Africa) tells us to be quiet and listen. It's the unmistakable howl of a hyena. Abedia says, 'Hyenas attack people where they sleep. Leopards can attack people fetching water, and snakes bite people. There are so many problems that God is the only guardian we trust.'

We pack up our flimsy tents and say fond farewells to Abedia before heading to the nearby town. I hope she's going to be OK.

A Little Cup of Blood

We head further south. On the way, I spot someone selling bundles of qat, a local stimulant. I stop and buy some and try a little. It's extraordinarily bitter, so the seller's friend offers me some sugar to eat with it. It's still not particularly pleasant. Dawit explains to me that all the local truck-drivers chew it so they can stay awake to drive through the night. The only downside is that the vehicles crash rather a lot, which is why they are known locally as 'al-Qaeda trucks' for their suicidal devastation. Seeing as I won't be driving, I tuck into the bundle to see what happens, but within five minutes my hands become unbearably itchy, followed by my legs and feet. I'm having some kind of violent adverse reaction to whatever the stimulant compound is. Oh Christ, this is agony! I want to rip my skin off. I sit on my hands, but then my legs get itchy. I press them against each other but it doesn't do any good. It isn't helped by the fact that everyone else in the car finds this side-splittingly funny.

Eventually the sensation fades, but slowly, so bloody slowly. Perhaps I wasn't built for qat, which is a shame because I was quite looking forward to it.

Eventually we reach Yalebo, a community of the Borena tribe who've herded cattle around here for 2,000 years. There's a main central village with a few mud and concrete huts, but most people live in little satellite hamlets further into the hills. They are the closest thing I've ever seen to the traditional African village as shown in the pages of *National Geographic*, and they are built specifically for pastoralists. A circular fence of thorns the size of a football pitch protects each group of about 20 small, round mud-and-thatch huts from hyenas. There's a large entrance-cum-holding pen for cattle, and another for people. Like the other ethnic villages I've visited, it's idyllic, yet brutally poor. There's no cultivated land nearby, and people have practically no possessions whatsoever in their huts.

We meet Dora who has five cows and a few goats. He had twice as many until the last drought ripped through his herd. He lives a precarious existence, constantly on the verge of hunger and disaster and vulnerable to the cycle of floods and droughts. In recent years, he's noticed the cycle getting worse. The one thing that kept him alive when all his animals died is a small patch where he plants maize (a grain that's relatively easy to store).

Last year saw the worst drought in a decade across their lands and it's estimated that at least two-thirds of the Borena's cattle died.

'Are you able to store food to last through droughts?' I ask him.

'Yes, if you have oxen and it rains, you can produce enough and even keep some grain for the next year and beyond. If you don't have oxen and you have to plough by hand, you are not able to produce enough, even for one season – at best it will last you six or seven months.'

'And what about food aid?'

'When the drought destroyed our cattle, they gave us a little amount of food for two months. Things like lentils and a mixture of food that we didn't even know what it was, but we ate it.'

Even when the Borena are really hungry, they don't kill weak cattle as they believe it curses the land. And they don't eat cattle that have died, as they think the meat will be bad. However, they have developed a practice of drinking the blood of their live animals to provide extra nutrition, and Dora is keen for me to try it. He brings one of his goats, ties its neck with a strap to create pressure and pierces the vein in the neck with a shallow arrow shot. I hold the cup to the goat's neck. After the initial flinch at the arrow, the goat seems strangely calm as it gives up half a cup of blood that trickles out. It's quite a gruesome way to get a meal, but skills like this are essential when you're so often on the verge of desperation.

When the strap is untied, the blood stops and the relieved goat wanders off. The blood is stirred to prevent it from clotting, then I take out the clotted matter and drink the liquid. It's a bizarre sensation drinking the fresh, warm blood of an animal I can see chewing grass next to me. It doesn't really taste of anything at first, but then I can sense a simultaneous sweetness and saltiness, like when you taste your own blood. It's quite nice, although I'd prefer it less warm.

I meet Golicha and Hule, another couple who used to have over a hundred cattle. Now they have just five cows and five goats to support a family of 12. I help Hule strip corn nibs from some cobs she's bought, enough to fill a small bowl. This is all there is for supper tonight.

'There are times when we don't get anything. It badly affects the growth of the children; it makes them skinny. I get headaches and I don't have healthy teeth so I find it hard to chew this.'

I ask why, when there is so much pressure on the land to provide for so few people, do people have such big families

'Family is a gift of God. We didn't have the knowledge to plan our family, so we just went on having children.'

The reality is that this is an economic necessity, and Hule is hoping that their ten kids will bring in money and help to look after them in their old age, as she did for her parents.

I look at the bowl of food. It's extraordinary – this is half a bowl of corn to feed the seven people who will be here tonight (the other children are away from the village). It's a tiny amount of food, a tiny amount of calories.

I am still trying to get to the bottom of why the deprivation here continues. Golicha explains that during droughts, 'Ignorance is the main problem. If we had the necessary knowledge, we wouldn't have lost our property like that and become helpless. Since we didn't have knowledge we just lay next to our cattle and watched them perish.' His talk of tragedy and hunger is made all the more intense because he's been caning qat and his pupils are vast. He looks pretty scary – intense yet vacant at the same time. It's a weird combination.

I go to bed troubled. Mankind's ability to survive is extraordinary. Even in the most inhospitable jungles amidst vicious conflict and frozen tundra people manage to squeeze, tease and nurture food from the ground, air and water. Yet in my darker moments I have begun to wonder if our ability to survive has been the source of such widespread misery. If we weren't so good at surviving, if humans didn't thrive in the grimmest places, fewer people would have to endure so much misery. But the thing is this: there are many aspects of human life that the UN's Human Development Index (the Happiness Index) can't quantify: love, family bonds, faith, hope, patriotism, pride, traditions, sense of home and sheer bloody-minded endurance. And it's these things that can keep people going when everything else in their lives is a stinking heap of shit.

Back to Addis

CrackadoodleDOOOOOOOOOOOOO!

What in the name of all that's holy is THAT? I jump out of bed, shouting 'Aaargh!' then swiftly jump back in again when I realize that I am wearing no clothes, and I'm a guest in Golicha and Hule's hut. Guests aren't supposed to behave like that. I find the culprit, sitting proudly on the floor beside my bed. A cockerel whose neck I would have broken if it hadn't been the only livestock left to my kind hosts. It's fine that we are up absurdly early, though, because we have a big day ahead of us – we have to get back to Addis Ababa.

On the way back we are stopped and searched regularly – the authorities are concerned about terrorists trying to capitalize on the millennium celebrations. There's a violent insurgency in the Ogaden region, thousands of Ethiopian troops in Somalia, and tensions rising again with Eritrea over the two countries' disputed border, so the soldiers give us a theatrical but hapless search.

I take a look around the slums of Addis – the capital is said to have the highest percentage of slums of all the capital cities of Africa. About 80 per cent of the city's population are living in them – that's nearly 2.5 million people.

I've met up with a guy called Zelalem who's taking me to see his mum, Mulu. Their home is in the middle of the slums and although Zelalem calls it a nice middle-class area, it's actually a network of muddy tracks that cut between rows of squalid corrugated-iron shacks. Their home is a tiny airless room that fits a bed, a pile of cooking tools and a wall of fantastic old family pictures. Mulu makes a living selling injera and other foods around the city. She's cooking a special chicken stew as a treat for the millennium holiday, an Ethiopian favourite called doro wat. It smells delicious, and despite the fact that it's not quite ready, she lets me try a little. It has the unmistakable flavour of the Ethiopian staple chilli called ber-beri, which sounds like a vicious tropical disease but is actually a very specific, very hot chilli, it tastes great.

Mama Mulu tries to describe the slums for me: 'Life is difficult. We have to work very hard. When I get food I eat, but when there is no food my family spends the night with empty stomachs. In the past, when I was raising my children, I used to buy wheat and maize with 10 bir and that would be enough for a week; now that money wouldn't buy enough food for one day.'

Bizarrely, she remembers the big famines of 1984 as a time of plenty: 'It was better at that time. Then it was accepted that there was famine so aid flowed in. Now there is no aid coming in and people are crushed in silence. Here in the slums the thing that kills us is not famine, but inflation. The prices go up so high but we can never earn more money, so we can't afford to buy food.' Food prices in Addis rose 27 per cent last year, making life extremely difficult.

Street Children

Muuehabto and Atersaw are two of the 150,000 kids living on the streets of Addis. They are 13 and 14 years old, although they look much younger. They never smile.

The boys live with a handful of others in a disused shop doorway beside a busy street, having moved here from the countryside when their families couldn't manage to feed them. They survive by begging and eating handouts or (for the more enterprising ones) selling cigarettes and sweets to buy leftovers from restaurants. Street kids are an embarrassment to the government so they are often forcibly removed. Many were reportedly rounded up in advance of the millennium celebrations, before being dumped out in the countryside. 'The police or sometimes civilians and security guards shout at us when something is stolen and accuse us of collaborating with the thieves. They beat us up. It's forbidden to sleep, play or beg around here. Sometimes officials are expected to pass this way, so they clear the area. They sometimes round us up and dump us in a forest where no one can see us.'

It's very difficult to film around here as locals are often hostile to foreign journalists so I try to talk to them as quickly as possible. They take me to sample a typical lunch of leftovers from a local restaurant. They collect their food in a plastic bag and settle down to eat it on the roadside, but our camera has already attracted attention and a crowd gathers.

We start to walk away with the kids, but suddenly the mood turns ugly and a crowd of 20 men are jostling and arguing with us. A man grabs one of the kids, and I try to step between them. The crowd are becoming mob-like. Some of them are clearly drunk and don't seem very sure what they're angry about, but get involved with the pushing and shoving all the same.

Someone asks why we are filming poor people when they show Ethiopia in such a bad light. This is not what you should be filming, they say. A policeman joins in the muddle, accusing us of filming without a permit. We get our permit out to prove him wrong, but there's no point persevering, so we leave and meet the kids in a nearby square.

They didn't want us to show a negative picture of Ethiopia? Quite what they want us to show instead, I'm not entirely sure. The Sheraton? The airport?

Millennium

Anyway, there's no time for being snide because I'm back in Ethiopia's most expensive, shortest-lived warehouse. Up in the gallery area sit a variety of heads of states, including the Sudanese president, Omar al-Beshir (blimey – who invited him?). The prime minister, Meles Zenawi, makes a speech admitting what Ethiopia has been through: 'After undelivered promises and dashed hopes, this generation has started to break the cycle and we are at the dawn of a new era.' He's not enormously clear on what the new millennium will specifically achieve, but I decide it's best not to heckle.

Outside the warehouse are catering areas where free food and drink are handed out – as much as you can eat. The difference between this and what I've seen in the countryside is overwhelming. I chat to some of the party-goers, about half of whom seem to have paid for their tickets, while the other half are on the blag. One smart young chap says to me: 'As an Ethiopian, even living abroad, millennium is a new start for our country. A promise, a new beginning.'

This building has cost $10 million. Is that a good use of money in a country like Ethiopia?

'Well, first of all, it's a guy's private money, so he should spend it however he likes. But let me ask you this: have you been to an Ethiopian wedding? Oh boy, they're mad. As a nation, we love to throw parties. We will sell everything we own to put on a fantastic party, even people who have very little will manage to do something spectacular. It's in our blood.'

I stand outside the warehouse and consider whether this whole shindig is just a big, gruesome waste of money. As ever, it's not that simple. On an economic level, the millennium has brought tens of thousands of the Ethiopian diaspora back to the country, and it's these people who are the most likely to invest here, create jobs and help move the country forwards. If this party has encouraged them back, it could be worth way more than $20 million.

On an emotional level, it's the country's millennium, for crying out loud. Of course they should celebrate it, and if that involves someone spending $10 million, well it doesn't sound like the best use of cash to me, but who knows what a few weeks of optimism might do for a country? Perhaps a few people will be inspired to solve problems, to help their countrymen, to think about long-term solutions to the country's crises. Heaven knows, perhaps some wealth might even filter down from these people to the millions at the bottom of the pile … eventually.

Anyway, Will.i.am from the Black-Eyed Peas is on stage and he's quite excited.

'I've heard people say that Ethiopia is a poor country. Ethiopia isn't a poor country!' [25,000 people roar.]

'Because Ethiopians have LOVE in their hearts!' [25,000 people go wild.]

'Five! Four! Three! Two! One! HAPPY MILLENNIUUUUUUM!'

So finally, seven years, nine months and 11 days late, it's the year 2000. Around 25,000 people (including me) get down to some serious hugging, loving and smiling. We're all beside ourselves with excitement.

I want this outpouring of optimism and patriotism to turn into something solid, so despite my journalistic desire to wag fingers, I'm determined to end this on a positive note. Here goes …

The Ethiopian economy has grown by 10 per cent for the last few years. Now 10 per cent of very little isn't very much, but at least things are getting better. This place is one of the great cradles of civilization, so if there's any truth in history repeating itself, these people might one day be back at the top of the wheel. And, of course, they have a nice shiny airport and a nice shiny hotel. The WFP is talking more and more about long-term aid projects rather than short-term emergency distribution, and this is really what Ethiopians need. So many problems remain, but for one night most people are going to look to the future, full of hope.

I walk slowly away from the stage and as I pass the toilets, I see that they are swamped with inebriated party-goers. Some of them are unconscious, others look like they won't be standing for much longer. One girl vomits copiously over her boyfriend's lap but he's too drunk to be annoyed, so he just stares down blankly at the mess. There's quite a lot of vomit sprayed around, now that I look more closely. One man is lying flat out on the road, weeping with joy or sorrow – it's hard to tell.

I try to push the memory of horrific scenes of rural poverty out of my head. Thoughts of Dora, Gebru Abera and his wife Yalezmer, Faté and her kids and the street children Muuehabto and Atersaw. But it's impossible, so I breathe deeply and hope to God that this optimism reaches them, that somehow this filthy excess turns into something good.

Good luck Ethiopia. I hope things get better for you.

● ● ● ● ●

I must admit that I'm feeling a guilty relief that it's my last African adventure. I've begun to see misery and unimaginable poverty as some cracked, bastard version of normality, and it's time to go home – or at least back to my own continent: Europe.

CHERNOBYL
Cooking with Radiation

POPULATION: 46 million

PERCENTAGE LIVING ON LESS THAN $2 A DAY: 19.5%

UNDP HUMAN DEVELOPMENT INDEX: 77/177

CORRUPTION PERCEPTIONS INDEX POSITION: 99/163

GDP (NOMINAL) PER CAPITA: $2,275 (104/179)

FOOD AID RECIPIENTS: n/a

MALNUTRITION: 3% of the population

At 1.26 a.m. on 26 April 1986 an experiment went horribly wrong in Reactor 4 of the Chernobyl Nuclear Power Plant and a massive explosion blew the top off the building. The world's worst nuclear accident unfolded, spewing radioactive material across much of Europe, including the UK. Twenty years on, millions of square kilometres of land are still badly contaminated and radioactive particles are still making their way into food.

Following the break-up of the Soviet Union, Ukraine became an independent state, but it's still coping with the Chernobyl legacy.

Reactor 4

I'm travelling with Marc again and we check into the gruesome but affordable Hotel Rus in central Kiev. I immediately want to leave the country. People are rude and unpleasant here, the place is harsh and unwelcoming and everyone looks depressed. It's as though the city is enveloped in a cloud of misery and pain.

I meet up with Helen, who works for the BBC in Kiev. She's actively scared of radiation (which seems strange for someone who has chosen to live three hours from Chernobyl): she keeps a Geiger counter on all the time in her apartment, and refuses to go anywhere near the Chernobyl plant. Despite this, she has reluctantly, but kindly, agreed to lend me her Geiger counter for the duration of my trip.

Later, she takes me for some classic Ukrainian food to celebrate my arrival. We visit Tsarska Selo (the Tsar's Place). The clientele seems to be largely gangster/moll, and it advertises 'Guarded free parking' on its literature. It's an ersatz, fibreglass version of a Ukrainian peasant cottage, and they serve us classic peasant cuisine with a flashy gangster twist: cabbage and potato ravioli, pork fat with raw garlic, mince wrapped in cabbage, sturgeon with cauliflower sauce and green borscht, made with sorrel.

It all sounds a lot worse than it tastes, but by the end of the meal, I am already oozing flatulence, a feeling that is destined to stay with me for the next two weeks. We try out various beers, firewaters and vodkas and suddenly Ukraine seems to become an altogether nicer place.

I stagger out of the restaurant and head for home, but on the way I spot a supermarket and decide to pick up supplies for the next few days. Marc and I have been banned from eating any food grown in the exclusion zone around the nuclear reactor, so we need to bring some of our own. I've heard it said that you should never go shopping when you're hungry for fear of buying too much food. I'd like to add to that: never go shopping when you're flying off your nuts on vodka because you'll wake up the next day with all sorts of bizarre and useless foodstuffs.

So when I wake with a thumping vodka head the next morning and get up to take my head to the sink, I stumble over four large carrier bags full of dried fish, flat sausages, smoked stringy cheeses, and an assortment of arcane breads, a dozen packets of instant borscht and a variety of bottles of fine vodka. All pretty much useless in the field.

At 8.30 a man knocks on the door and delivers breakfast. I'm so viciously hung-over that I forget to mention that I haven't ordered any. I sit in my underpants looking at a plate bearing three unadorned hardboiled eggs. The perfect post-Soviet austerity breakfast. I try to eat a dry boiled egg, but can't get it down. Then I realize that breakfast must have been delivered to me by mistake. Someone else must be sitting in his underpants in another room like a guy in a Tarkovsky film, waiting for his boiled eggs, and getting angrier and angrier.

Never mind, there are more important issues to deal with: my few remaining brain cells for a start. I feel dizzy and a little bit disgusted with myself and decide to make a pact with Marc that we shouldn't egg each other on to down shots of vodka any more.

I meet him in the lobby half an hour later, but he claims to feel fine. The swine.

I get into the world's smelliest minibus for the journey from Kiev to Chernobyl, and as soon as we leave the city the roads become spookily deserted and the bulk of the traffic is bovine. The landscape is hideously flat, a mixture of grassland savannah and wheat fields – Ukraine used to be called the breadbasket of Europe, and wheat is even featured on the national flag.

Three hours later we arrive at the Chernobyl 30-km exclusion zone checkpoint, a decrepit jumble of huts and barriers plonked on the road to the nuclear power plant. This exclusion zone is also called the Zone of Alienation, but for many Ukrainians and Belarussians it's the entrance to hell.

I'm suddenly consumed with anxiety about the entire trip. My wife had shaken her head in disbelief when I told her where I was going. 'I don't want you bringing any radioactive particles into this house,' she warned. Quite so. But I'd read that the radioactivity that's left here is very low-level stuff. Not much to fear. So why is there still a 30-km exclusion zone 20 years after the accident? And why do I feel such a strong sense of foreboding? Even the weather has turned ominous: bright sunshine giving way to torrential rain, then gales, and back to sun again. It all adds to the sense of apocalypse.

I finally meet my guide, Denis, who works for the snappily titled Ministry of Emergencies and Affairs of Population Protection from the Consequences of Chernobyl Catastrophe. He's been assigned to me for the entire trip within the zone – a mixture of guide, minder and chaperone – and I mustn't travel anywhere without him.

How can I describe Denis? I've never met anyone who cast more of a cloud of glumness than he does. He's miserable, monosyllabic and unexcitable. His answers to questions are abrupt and unhelpful, his explanations obscure and disinterested, and he chain-smokes the entire time. He answers my questions with a single word, after which I expect him to add something or qualify it, but the rest of the sentence never comes.

'Can we visit the laboratory that tests food?' I ask.

'No,' he says.

'Can we ask someone for permission to visit?'

'Maybe.'

'Well, can you then?'

'OK.'

Marc and I look at each other with raised eyebrows: we're stuck with this guy for a whole week. But there's no time to argue – my one and only opportunity to visit Reactor 4, the site of the accident, is this very afternoon so I have to get on with it. As we drive on, the Geiger counters begin crackling ferociously. The radiation levels here are already .100 μSv (microSieverts, a measurement othat aims to reflect the biological effects of radiation as opposed to the physical aspects) three times the normal level – and Denis says, disparagingly, 'If they had .50 in Kiev they would panic.'

Inside the Zone of Alienation is a second security cordon the 10-km exclusion zone, which is the original area that was evacuated soon after the accident. A tingle of fear creeps down my back as we get nearer. The road is potholed and scraggy – no one bothers to maintain a road that has no future. We pass empty buildings and farms, and I see that wildlife has begun to reclaim the land. It's eerie: the roads are peppered with bus shelters at which buses never stop; signs that shout propaganda slogans to no one; and an extraordinary network of knackered steel pipes snakes its way around roads, paths and houses like something out of Terry Gilliam's *Brazil*. After the accident, the earth could not be dug up because it would disturb the radiation particles in the topsoil, so all pipes have had to be laid above ground.

We pass Reactors 5 and 6, which had been under construction at the time of the accident. The cranes that were working on them have never been removed. They just stand, ghostly and apocalyptic, workers frozen in mid-toil.

Finally we arrive at Reactor 4. The building itself looks like any huge industrial plant, but it's covered in a vast metal and concrete casing – called 'the sarcophagus' – that was built swiftly after the accident to encase the reactor and its remaining fuel and components. It's a horrible, gruesomely fascinating sight. I stand gazing at it, speechless and appalled. Massive though it is, it's hard to comprehend the scale of misery and destruction that has been caused by a simple broken machine. It's a temple to hubris.

I ask Denis how he feels about Chernobyl, and disturbingly he tells me that he loves it. This guy is very odd. We compare Geiger counters. They read 7.00 μSv – that's 23 times normal background radiation.

We are about 200 metres from the nuclear reactor and I'm beginning to suffer from a disconcerting physical tingle. I'm also starting to feel dizzy and anxious, but surely it has more to do with the power of suggestion than with radiation (odd, though, because I'm not particularly prone to anxiety or phantom ailments, and I'm not big on holistic psycho-spiritual diagnoses).

I mention it to Denis and say that it must be psychosomatic, but he says that he's had physical symptoms of radiation several times: 'Headaches, very bad headache, you feel thirsty, you feel dizzy.' I ask if that scares him, but he says, 'Not much.' Despite this, he says it's too dangerous to stay here any longer so we head off.

One of the strangest things about the power plant is that, in spite of the devastation, the other three Chernobyl reactors were restarted less than six months after the accident and continued to operate until December 2000. The plant produced 10 per cent of Ukraine's entire electricity needs at the time, and regardless of objections from other European countries, the Soviet Union was willing to take the risk. Were these people insane?

We drive to Chernobyl town itself. Another eerie sight. Although it's decaying, overgrown and bleak, it does have some facilities to cater for the scientists and support staff who are still here decommissioning the plant, and I'm surprised to see people walking the streets. There are even a couple of shabby stores selling processed food, biscuits, fags and booze. Marc and I stop off to buy some vodka and beer – it's going to be a long week – and then make our way to our hotel. Yes, Chernobyl even has a hotel, although it's not like any hotel you might have stayed in. This is a prefab slum of damp, mouldy rooms built for foreign workers staying on site, and it's utterly, marvellously miserable.

Marc and I drink beer in my room and despair about how on earth we'll make it through the week with only Denis to talk to. Then we turn on the telly to find *Carry on Camping*. It's been dubbed, but they haven't bothered to turn the original soundtrack down. The Ukrainian translators just talk over the English actors. Marc goes to bed, but I'm fixated by it, trying to hear the English original in the background. I spend an hour glued to the box. Chernobyl does weird things to a man.

Our hotel has a restaurant designed in the glorious mould of Soviet utilitarianism: dour, damp, depressing. It's not a place for smiles, which is fine because no one seems to smile much anyway. In designing this building it seems the authorities knew that Chernobyl was never going to be home to much joy.

I sit down to breakfast, which is spookily similar to the other meals I've had so far: a plate of fatty salami, garlic sausage, shredded beetroot and shredded cabbage covered in mayonnaise. My meal finishes with what I'm told is egg and noodle broth. It's really just hot water with a bit of fat floating on it. Marc admits that he was told before we arrived that this is the worst restaurant in Ukraine, but he didn't want to tell me until we got here.

All the food in the restaurant is imported from the furthest reaches of Ukraine. I drop into the kitchen to talk to the chef, a large lady who presides over a roomful of grim-faced girls and crusty pans, all of them covered in a thick coating of caked-on fat. She roars at me when I ask if she'd eat any food grown on the land around here: 'Niet, niet. Good God no. We don't eat fish, meat, fruit. We don't eat anything. It's all contaminated. You can't. You can't.'

Later I meet the head of the ecological testing labs who proudly shows me around his dilapidated and crumbling building. His instruments all look like antiques from the 1960s' space programme – all very pretty but very clunky.

At the labs the breakfast I ate a few hours before starts to threaten another toxic disaster, so I run to the loo. There's no loo roll, so I have to break apart some cardboard to use instead. Deeply unpleasant.

When I return, the head scientist agrees to lend me a few of his inspectors to visit some of the radiation hot spots tomorrow.

The Red Forest

Strangely enough, the area right outside the reactor where I'd stood isn't the most dangerous place in the Chernobyl exclusion zone. We load the van full of soil and flora inspectors and head off for the Red Forest, a huge area of trees that turned red and died immediately after the accident. It's renowned as the most radioactive place in the region.

I have to put on my contamination suit and disposable boots, as instructed by BBC Health and Safety experts back in White City. Needless to say, all the inspectors and guides in Chernobyl laugh their pants off at the sight of my bright white suit and bright blue foot-bags. I'm glad to offer them something to laugh about. My only comfort is that Marc has to wear the same.

There's not much to see at the Red Forest – it's just an unhealthy mass of trees with a crumbly road running through it. I watch the scientists taking soil samples and I try to talk to them, but my Geiger counters start to crackle with a panicky fizzing noise. I have a dosimeter attached to my boots that warns me when I'm exceeding the safe accumulated dose over a period of time, and the alarm on that trips too, adding to the racket. Our counters peak at 70 µSv – the highest we record on the whole trip, and 2,300 times higher than normal background radiation. Denis says that he's suffering from a radiation headache so we'd better go. We kick the earth off our boots, dispose of our disposable suits and quietly leave.

I wonder if I'm becoming irresponsibly relaxed about spending time in dangerous environments. It's not big or clever. I've done my hostile environments training course, faced The Fear in Afghanistan, and stumbled through war-torn northern Uganda, so is it possible that I've become numbed to the danger? I need to be wary of this creeping sense of immortality, not to mention the self-importance that comes with being a journalist investigating stories of pain and suffering. I mustn't forget that I'm just a speccy little food writer.

Pripyat

Later I visit the cooling lakes opposite the reactor and see the extraordinary monster catfish that live in it – the most radioactive fish on the planet. They are the size of small whales, but also terrifyingly prehistoric. With no natural predators (would you eat a fish from the Chernobyl cooling lakes?) these fellas just keep on growing. I throw huge loaves of bread into the water and the largest one lazily rises to the surface and slurps them down.

I head for Pripyat, the town that lies in the shadow of the power plant (Chernobyl itself is actually 15 km from the reactor) where old buildings are being consumed by trees and bushes, and flourishing woodlands and wildlife. The exclusion zone has been reclaimed by nature, and nature is doing very well without mankind thanks very much. The populations of deer, boar, elk and beaver are expanding fast, and even extremely rare lynx have been spotted. The fact that the area is polluted with radioactive isotopes bothers them not a jot.

It wasn't until two days after the Chernobyl accident that Pripyat was evacuated, and 50,000 people were hurried onto buses. They were told that they'd be away for three days, and they were allowed to take only a single suitcase of possessions. But they never came back.

It's a ghostly, tragic place that looks like a set from *Planet of the Apes*, abandoned in a hurry 20 years ago: fairground rides swinging in the wind; shop hoardings crumbling away from buildings; bushes growing inside houses; and trees bursting through the concrete. Nature is re-invading everywhere.

In the apartment blocks, books and pictures flutter in the wind. In the 1990s, looters began to sneak in and ransack the place, taking everything they could find, from personal possessions to toilet seats. Everywhere there are reminders of the young families that used to live here – bits of old dolls lying around, abandoned toys rotting in car parks – I find this especially distressing. No one knows how long it will be before humans can return, but most agree that it will take at least 300 years for the worst radioactive isotope (caesium-137) to decay to 1000th of its current potency.

I wander around in a daze and discover a building full of old Soviet posters and props, presumably used for propaganda plays and marches. Outside I stumble across an inexplicable radiation hot spot above an eviscerated doll, its arms stretched out to the sky. You couldn't think of a more gruesome symbol.

One of the radiation inspectors used to live here in Pripyat, and it's only his job that's brought him back. Andri was 18 when the accident happened, and he says, 'When I first got the job it was very difficult. But I've been working here for 13 years and I'm used to the fact that the town is no longer here. I used to dream at night that the town still existed. Everything was nice and clean, new, beautiful … it's all ruined.'

This whole place could have been thought up by a cheap thriller writer, especially the ghostly fairground that was due to open a week after the accident. There's a Ferris wheel, dodgems and toddlers' rides, but the children who were meant to enjoy all this have instead had to deal with thyroid cancer.

As we're about to leave, our inspectors, Denis and the driver stop for a quick picnic of smoked pork fat on dry bread. They offer some to me, saying that this is the best food you can eat – like Ukrainian drugs. It might not sound like high gastronomy, but I love smoked meats and I haven't eaten all day and it looks and smells heavenly. However, I have been warned that I'm not allowed to eat it, otherwise I'll get in trouble with BBC Health and Safety. So I sit and watch as they laugh at how pathetic I am. These guys ought to know what's safe for them – they're nuclear inspectors for crying out loud – but the trouble is that Ukraine is such a butch, macho culture that they would probably eat plutonium if they were egged on and fuelled by enough vodka.

I spot a couple of huge wild boar – it's the first time I've ever seen them – and I'm properly excited at the sight. The problem with these animals is that they eat all the foods that absorb radiation, and are free to roam in all the most radioactive areas of the exclusion zone, so they are extremely unsafe to eat. This doesn't seem to bother one ancient but dapper old man whom we spot cycling nonchalantly through Pripyat without a care in the world, an axe strapped to his bicycle. I ask him what the axe is for and he says it's for walloping wild boar. 'I made it specially with this long handle.' I ask if he eats the ones he catches. 'Why not?' he says before wobbling off, narrowly missing a tree growing though the tarmac.

I return to the Hotel Chernobyl for more borscht, shredded cabbage and beetroot and a slab of sausage. I'm becoming oddly fond of the brutishly smoked sausage and pork fillet I get with every meal. It's strong enough to put hairs on your nipples.

Marc and I retire with an armful of beers and talk late into the night about radiation and social disintegration.

Anna and Michael

I rise early, nursing another vicious hangover – a beer one, which makes me feel particularly unpleasant and bloated – and I top it with a coffee and a fried egg, leaving all the cabbage, much to the annoyance of the kitchen staff.

I pick up another truckload of radiation inspectors and head for Iliana, a village to the east of Chernobyl. One of the most extraordinary things about the exclusion zone is that about 300 people have moved back here despite the contamination.

The returnees are mainly elderly, and mainly women, and they moved back a year after the disaster when the authorities hadn't really made up any rules to administer the exclusion zone. Returning is highly illegal but anyone who's been to rural Ukraine knows that it doesn't pay to mess with an elderly babushka. These old biddies are ferocious.

Anna (83) and Michael (82) are your classic, beautiful, noble, gnarled peasants straight out of Chekhov. They live in a romantic idyll

BAD FOOD

of a cottage scattered with farmyard tools, a deep well in the front yard, flowers bursting from the garden, plum tree heavy with fruit – the works. They never stop talking and arguing, and make their presence felt by bellowing everything at the top of their voices (they claim to be deaf, but I don't believe a word of it). When I say that I can't get a word in edgeways, Anna says, 'That's just the way I am. I can't whisper. I have to talk a lot!' I fall in love with her instantly. If I have one ounce of her vigour and stubbornness when I'm 80, I'll be a happy old man.

The couple moved back to the exclusion zone when their temporary accommodation was damaged by storms. They live in their old house with a cow, pigs and chickens and a large plot of land for potatoes, beets and cabbages. They don't feel poor, they don't worry that the land is contaminated, but they mourn the loss of their community and friends. Anna bursts into tears when she talks about losing all her possessions back in 1986.

She begins cooking lunch so I join her in her filthy, flyblown, outdoor kitchen. She's boiling water with chopped potato and a couple of bay leaves, and fries some pork fat, a few little onions and salt, which she pours into the water. She adds a pack of noodles and we chat whilst it all simmers. Denis mentions to her that I'm not allowed to eat anything from inside the Zone of Alienation, and she cackles with scornful laughter.

'What's wrong with you?' she asks. 'There's nothing to fear from my food – God will protect you.' I ask her if she thinks it's crazy that I'm not allowed to eat anything and she says, 'If it were contaminated, we would have died long ago! But we've been eating it for 20 years already!'

Inside their cottage the flies are terrible. A couple of fly-stick rolls hang down forlornly from the ceiling, covered in a fuzz of corpses. The swarm of remaining live ones wanders over my hands and head, making me feel grubby and sticky. Marc reminds me again that I'm not to eat anything. He's beginning to sound like a scratched record, bless him.

But with four burly Ukrainians egging me on, and the honour of a gorgeous 83-year-old babushka and her husband at stake, directives from west London seem a long way away. Anna's tactics turn to simple bullying: 'Why not? Why aren't you allowed? Eat! You have to eat it. You won't die, don't be afraid! Just eat it! You won't die! God will protect you! We eat it and we're alive – and you'll be all right too!'

It's lunchtime. I'm hungry. The most adorable little bully in the former Soviet Union has cooked lunch for me and a group of teasing radiation inspectors from the most radioactive place on the planet has said it's safe to eat. Marc's voice gets a little louder now he can see that I'm being tempted. 'You're *not* allowed to eat it.'

I linger and look. Anna brings out a plate of homemade smoked pork fat and homemade butter. Ahhhh. Our driver cracks a raw egg straight into his mouth and swallows it to a cheer from his compatriots. Anna lays the soup on the table. Mmmmmmm.

Suddenly, I can bear it no more and I reach out to snatch some butter, bread and pork fat. I scoff like a gastronaut possessed whilst Marc shouts from behind my back. It's too late now: I tuck into the soup and stuff hunks of bread into my mouth. It's like a blessed release, a riot of raw, rural flavours, and I pause only when Anna puts a glass of vicious, rocket fuel-strength plum brandy in my hands. I make the mistake of pausing for a second so she forcibly lifts the glass to my lips and upends its contents into my mouth. Oooooh.

The misery of Chernobyl, the lingering paranoia about radioactivity, the malignancy of nuclear power, the dark shadow cast by Denis – all of it evaporates for a few seconds. I sit down, spent. This must be what it feels like to cheat on your wife: a flash of orgasmic bliss followed by a slow-building sense of guilt and panic. I look shamefaced at Marc, but it's clear that he's washed his hands of my safety. He's imagining the inquest: 'I'm sorry, Georgia. I did everything I could to stop him.'

The inspectors and our driver all tuck into the plum brandy, and eventually we stagger out to take some soil and water samples. After pottering in the garden for a while I start to sober up and wonder if I've done something terribly, terribly stupid.

We take our soil samples back to the research lab to get them tested. The head of the lab says that paranoia about radioactivity had been fuelled by journalists looking for a panic story. Much of the land around Chernobyl has returned to safe levels. He also says that nuclear power will soon be the only option for us, seeing as fossil fuels will run out sooner or later. Although Chernobyl was a terrible disaster, nuclear reactor design is much safer now, and we'll have little choice but to embrace it when the oil runs out.

I'm in two minds about this: of course we have to come up with some solutions, but we still haven't worked out any safe or permanent ways of disposing of spent radioactive fuel, despite the fact that nuclear power has been around since 1938.

On the way back from Pripyat I spot the Chernobyl fire service helicopter and ask Denis if we can arrange a flight in it.

'No.'

I push him to try and finally he goes to ask his superior just to get me off his back.

'Maybe,' he says. 'Five hundred dollars, no guarantees.'

'Fine,' I say, 'but no flight, no $500.'

'Hmm,' he says.

Hanging Around

I'm missing my kids enormously. Perhaps it's the thought of all those devastated families from Pripyat broken up by evacuation. I phone home and tell Daisy that we're going up in a helicopter soon and she asks if she can come. Of course you can. 'Can I take my shoes off and are there lots of chairs?' Yes, sweets, or course there are.

Ukraine is a little like Norfolk, only more miserable. Endless stretches of flat or, at best, gently undulating landscape. Much of it is unfarmed scrubland – sheep would have a field day (literally), although Ukrainians, unlike Afghans, don't seem particularly fond of lamb. Other than that, there are miles and miles of forest, which are fine in mountainous regions where you can marvel at the beauty of nature from atop a craggy peak, but when the land is flat as a pancake, all you can see are the first few trees and nothing else; it's all a bit claustrophobic. Still, makes for simple driving tests. Start this car and drive straight for 30 km.

At last I am told to make my way to the helipad. Denis actually pulled it off! I'm staggered. When I get there, the ancient Sikorsky helicopter is waiting for me, looking like it was built to one of Da Vinci's original designs. I swear I can smell vodka in the cabin, but it may just be the gently rotting interior. The pilot says that he's very experienced and that the helicopter is quite reliable. Quite? I have to count out $500 in grubby notes before we go anywhere.

This whole shebang doesn't fit in very well with the BBC's safety policy, which clearly states that all helicopter firms must be checked for their safety record. But there's no time for that, and I'm wearing my immortal specs, so we press on. As a nod to health and safety, I ask the pilot for a quick safety briefing, but he looks at me like I'm mad. 'Don't touch anything, and don't be too scared,' he says, and flicks a switch. The vast hulk of rotting steel begins shaking like a washing machine full of logs. After an age, he steps on the gas and we rise miraculously from the ground. I'm sure I can hear a choir of angels singing, but then I realize it's the sound of a thousand rivets whining and straining.

We head off over Chernobyl town, and I can see the reality of the devastation. It looks even more grim and desolate from above. We fly north towards the power station, and pass thousands of clumps of foliage where houses used to be. The way that nature has moved back in once again reminds me of the set of a cheap horror flick.

We circle the plant, a vast monolithic monstrosity that spreads across the land like a concrete rash, then Pripyat, which looks even more haunting and lifeless from overhead. Then over Anna's house and village (I wave but I can't spot her waving back) and back home via a ship graveyard – rotting steel ships and barges that were involved in the clean-up operation sit scuppered in a huge lake.

The pilot looks over at me. 'Enough?' We finally thump onto the landing spot with the elegance of an elephant ballerina, but it's a relief to get down in one piece, and I thank our pilot effusively.

Slavutych

At last I leave Chernobyl and head for Slavutych – the town that was hurriedly built to house the workers needed to keep Chernobyl going after the accident. I can't wait to go – I've felt weighed down by the tragedy of this place and the relentless symbols of loss and pain. Trouble is, the 20-minute route to the town cuts through Belarus, and they won't give us a visa, so we have to take the five-hour round journey via Kiev, still in the agonizingly stifling company of Denis.

The relief I feel when I arrive in Slavutych almost overwhelms me and to celebrate our escape from Denis, Marc and I go out to the nearest bar to ease our stress in a lake of cheap vodka.

Later I meet my new guide, Ilyena, who talks with a classic Bond-movie spy-villain Russian accent. She's fun, opinionated and eloquent – everything Denis wasn't. She takes me to the town market and although it's surprisingly small for a town of 25,000 people, it's lively. Most stallholders seem to be Anna-alikes: tiny, elderly babushkas with wizened faces and beautiful smiles, selling a few peppers, aubergines, lots of dill, parsley and basil, tomatoes and loads and loads of tiny sweet cucumbers for nibbling and pickling.

I get chatting to a woman who sells meat and wishes she could turn the clock back to Soviet times. She had been part of a collectivized state farm, and the collapse of communism had ruined agriculture and her lifestyle. I suggest that collectivized farming has been blamed for widespread misery and environmental damage, not to mention the death of millions under Stalin, but she angrily insists that she doesn't care about the others – her life was better before the fall of the USSR. I buy some of her pork to cheer her up a bit.

Because this market is so close to Chernobyl, every stall has to have its food checked at an on-site radiation-testing lab. I take my pork along to be checked – I'm done with the devil-may-care approach. I chat with the friendly lab supervisor who sports startlingly yellow hair and thickly applied make-up in the traditional Ukrainian style. Her nails are like a baroque masterpiece. She says that she rarely, if ever, sees high radioactivity levels from food in the market – perhaps only five instances in the last year and ten the year before.

That evening we meet up with some of Ilyena's friends for a riverside barbecue. Amongst others, there's Anatoly, a lovely but slightly ear-bending ex-'liquidator' (the name given to the people who worked as part of the clearing-up operation after the accident); Denis, a wild-living 20-year-old; and Denis's friend, who has a fashion-busting ponytail-through-baseball-cap thing going on at the back of his head.

Everyone's a little wary at first, but after I reveal the stash of beer and vodka I've brought to oil the wheels of love, they quickly become my best friends.

Denis's mother Natasha has banned him from drinking vodka in front of us as a way of keeping him on the straight and narrow – vodka does seem to be an enormous problem for Ukrainians, especially among young men like Denis who've had to live through extreme social upheavals and have few job opportunities. I feel ashamed for bringing the booze along, but Natasha says, 'It's fine, he has to learn to deal with it.' His desperation for vodka is manic and obsessive, and his mum follows him everywhere shouting and chastising him for constantly trying to get his hands on it.

Oddly enough, there's lots of beer available for him to drink, and his mum doesn't mind him necking that, but he isn't interested. Ukrainians see beer as a soft drink.

'Do you worry about radioactivity in food?' I ask. None of them does. Ilyena's elderly friend Nadia says that they appreciate the lifestyle in Slavutych – it's better than most towns in Ukraine because there's good healthcare and housing, and if the food is contaminated with a little radiation, it's a small price to pay.

This astounds me, but everyone agrees with her. Denis and his mate couldn't care less; it's as though he's never thought about it. 'Nothing's happened yet,' he says.

His mother explains, 'Why are we so tolerant? We have another reason. It feeds us. They built this town and we live here only because of the Chernobyl power plant.'

Nadia tells me about the day of the accident: she had to battle with the authorities to keep custody of her kids because a bus driver had gone off with their ID documents. She had gone to her *dacha* (a cross between a country cottage and an allotment shed that many Ukrainians own) with a friend but they suddenly started getting terrible headaches and raced home to Pripyat to see the tragedy unfolding. She cries as she remembers everything she lost.

Yuri – a wonderful, smiling bear of a man – cooks huge pork kebabs marinated in his top-secret recipe (which he readily reveals after a couple of vodkas: soak the pork in a mixture of vodka, dill, basil, parsley and onions). The pork's a little raw, but I reason that you can't grill away radiation-like germs, and anyway, it tastes great.

Anatoly talks about his experiences as a liquidator. He says that Ukraine has been vilified as a polluter of the world, but in fact, the Ukrainian people were the heroes who gave their lives to stop the disaster getting any worse and killing millions more.

Magic Mushrooms

The mayor of Slavutych has agreed to take me out for the day. Trouble is, all he's really interested in is getting the BBC to film his horse at a local stable, whilst all I want to do, given we're slap bang in the middle of the season, is go mushroom picking. Mushrooms are one of the foods that absorb radioactive particles most readily and foraging is hugely important to Ukrainians. I want to see if the land around Chernobyl really is as safe as the authorities claim, but the mayor isn't ready to play ball.

The mayor is a tall, imposing, balding fellow of 60 and he's been in charge for 15 years. He is relatively popular, although there are dark mutterings about him spending a lot of time shaking hands, and precious little improving the lot of the townsfolk. After watching his horse trotting around the stables for hours on end, I finally manage to drag him away to some nearby woods to search for mushrooms.

He turns out to be a dull, political animal, sticking to stock phrases about opportunities for entrepreneurs in his wonderful town and how it's a marvellous centre for technology (there's little evidence for this, but I nod sagely). He's deeply reluctant to talk about radioactivity, and although I force him to admit that food issues are of crucial importance, he won't elaborate. 'None of this land around here is dangerous,' he says. 'It's not a problem we have.'

I suggest that local people are remarkably accepting of such a terrifying idea as radioactive food, and ask him whether their attitude has been shaped by Stalin's enforced famines in the 1930s (Stalin took revenge on the rebellious Ukrainians by starving them in a shameful episode that killed 2.5–4.8 million people). He skips over the issue, saying, 'Actually, there is some debate about that.'

What? Is he really denying that the famines happened? But he waves the question away. Many Ukrainians see themselves as ethnic Russians and he doesn't want to be seen to take sides. Well, what're 4 million murders between friends?

I eventually give up and go looking for mushrooms, much to the mayor's relief. He's already carrying a large bag of mushrooms that he says he picked with his wife earlier that morning (I find out later that his stable girl actually picked them for him). In this endeavour we are more successful, finding masses of ceps and chanterelles. I'm overjoyed – I've never seen such an embarrassment of fungal riches, and it makes up for the disastrous interview.

After bidding the mayor goodbye, I take some of the mayor's mushrooms to be tested at the market lab, just in case something interesting crops up. I wander in and our lovely shocking blonde chops them up and drops them into her strange radiation contraption. We chat for a few minutes until the machine goes 'ding' and I notice her jaw drop. Suddenly there's a palpable tension in the air.

The lab technician is a very worried woman. She taps her calculator and shows it to us. It reads 2,300 becquerel (another unit of radioactivity), and she points to her table of safe levels. My mushrooms are eight times too radioactive. 'Sorry? Say that again?'

Eight times the safe levels.

Is she surprised? 'Yes.'

'But it can't be true: I picked these with the mayor.'

'That's all very well – I'm glad you had a nice walk. But you'll have to throw the mushrooms away.'

This is the woman who, just yesterday, had told me that they had found only five cases of radioactive food in the last year, and ten the previous one.

I get straight on the phone to the mayor. 'We took the mushrooms to be tested and I have to warn you that they were eight times over the safe levels.'

'So it doesn't matter. So it cannot be that they are seriously high.'

'Are you still going to eat them?'

'No problem, I will.'

His cavalier approach astonishes me, but then he's a politician: I shouldn't be surprised at all. Did he really go and eat them? Who knows?

I'm flabbergasted – not by the mayor, but by finding mushrooms that weren't just radioactive, but extraordinarily radioactive. Everywhere we go people say, 'There's no problem, nothing around here is contaminated, you journalists just try to stir things up.' I had begun to believe them, although I did wonder if a desperately poor country would really keep expensive radiation labs in the town if it didn't need them.

I ask Ilyena what she thinks about all this, and she's genuinely surprised that we've found such a high level of contamination. Is she worried about the mayor?

'Ah,' she sighs. 'He is a fatalist maybe. And he tries to transfer his belief to other people of his town. So we live with radiation and we know there are a lot of people eager to come to Slavutych to work. And we pay this price of not paying attention to radiation.'

Across the former Soviet Union, this is people's prime concern: a bit of money, housing and a functioning infrastructure. If that means they have to cope with a bit of radioactivity … well hey, they are willing to put their fingers in their ears and hum gently to avoid thinking about the potential horrors.

Is this a kind of blackmail, I wonder, seeing as the Chernobyl Power Plant and its shutdown still needs thousands of workers? She doesn't think so. People here are happier than everywhere else in Ukraine. I don't get it: why aren't people worried or angry? Is it something to do with the Ukrainian national character?

'Ah,' Ilyena's eyes light up. 'Yes, we are used to suffering, in taking burdens, shouldering disasters, absorbing pain and trudging on. Because no one's going to help you, and you have to keep on living.' She explains why no one smiles in the shops and restaurants: they see it as insincere – what is there to smile about? All these Americans who come over here are always smiling about nothing – what is wrong with them? There's nothing to smile about.

On our last day in Slavutych we are spotted in the bar and invited to a drinks party by the Slavutych English-speaking ex-pat community, lorded over by Mavis, a Little England curtain-twitcher from Sunderland. The weirdness of being at a Chernobyl nuclear drinks party is trumped only by my conversation with Paul, a US radiation expert whose job is to analyse the risks of people's contact with radiation in order to assess the likely financial fall-out in insurance terms – i.e. how much radioactivity can the staff endure before the resulting medical and legal bills make it financially unbearable for their company? It's a strange and shameful extrapolation of the financial from the human costs, and the conversation leaves me feeling grubby.

I've become increasingly confused about the moral/economic/ political/medical/radioactive web of misery that the Chernobyl disaster has thrown over this area of the world and it's hard to draw conclusions. Maybe I'm confusing the Chernobyl that is an event in time with the Chernobyl that is a place full of people and lives. These people have consumed radioactivity and sighed deeply, and got on with their lives. On one level it's extraordinary, and on another it's inevitable and unremarkable.

Ilyena tackles all of this in the way that Ukrainians know best: we retreat to a *dacha* and drink obscene, brain-numbing quantities of moonshine. Many Ukrainians genuinely believe that vodka flushes radiation out of their system. There's no medical evidence to support this ... but that's not really the point.

● ● ● ● ●

Just before I leave Kiev for London I go for a final radiation check. I'm terrified. If I've picked up radionuclides, I might take radioactive contamination into my house, harming my kids and myself. I wonder if I've been reckless and stupid to eat food grown in the exclusion zone. A stern medic tells me to strip to my pants and enter a radiation chamber that looks like a turn-of-the-century relic from the Imperial War Museum. The door grinds shut, and a probe travels up and down a rickety track above me.

When I emerge, Marc looks a little worried. They did see something, he says, and my nervous smile fades. The woman tells me that I have raised levels of radioactivity in my stomach. Oh. Shit.

After letting me stew for a while she says that *luckily* it's within safe limits, the results aren't so bad and should return to normal in time. That's the last time I wear my immortal specs. What was I thinking?

There is possibly one last twist to this story, and it's called 'radiation hormesis'. It's a controversial theory that ionizing radiation can actually be *good* for you at low doses, activating genes that repair radiation damage, which then also reduce damage from other causes. It's a radical theory with many detractors, but it would be a glorious twist if there was some truth in it.

Ukrainians appear to be digging their heels into the ground to avoid being dragged back to the dark ages, and this has created a tough people who don't care much for insincere smiles. But I'm off to South Korea next, where I suspect they are primed for grinning, strapped into corporate joy-seats on a stellar economic trajectory that has taken the world by surprise for the last 50 years.

SOUTH KOREA
The Dog Eaters

POPULATION: 49 million

PERCENTAGE LIVING ON LESS THAN $2 A DAY: 50%

UNDP HUMAN DEVELOPMENT INDEX: 26/177

CORRUPTION PERCEPTIONS INDEX POSITION: 42/163

GDP (NOMINAL) PER CAPITA: $18,392 (34/179)

FOOD AID RECIPIENTS: n/a

MALNUTRITION: n/a

South Korea is one of the great economic miracles of the 20th century. It leapt from being a dirt-poor, inward-looking, Chinese-dominated and war-ravaged wasteland in the 1950s to becoming one of the leading tiger economies of Asia. But underneath this extraordinary progress lie endless mucky secrets: dodgy corporate governance; some tricksy accounting (spectacularly revealed during the Asian financial crisis of 1997–9); and a comprehensive sweeping aside of barriers to industrial progress, such as democracy and human rights. During the middle of the 20th century corruption festered, and military rulers crushed opposition and ran the country for their own ends until 1992, when a semblance of genuine democracy began to creep in.

It's a better place now, but whilst corruption is still a huge problem, most modern Koreans are reluctant to criticize. Perhaps this is due to the power of Confucian hierarchical systems and the obsessive respect shown to elders. Or perhaps they're just easily embarrassed (Koreans do seem to have a debilitating fear of embarrassment). Either way, there are some problems they'd rather tuck under the carpet …

I'm going to South Korea to find out about dogmeat. Not the strange meatesque compound we feed to dogs, but meat that has come from dogs raised for human consumption. I know, I know, it's an emotive subject, but it's one that the UK media has generally used only for hysterical and unedifying journalism. Most reporters, including some from my own beloved BBC, have seen fit to file copy essentially declaiming: OH, MY GOD, THEY EAT DOGS!

So here's what's under the Korean carpet: in the run-up to the Seoul Olympics in 1988, dog restaurants were banned in order to deflect national embarrassment over 'unsightly food' (heaven forfend). As soon as the Olympics were over, the restaurants swiftly reappeared without opposition. When the football World Cup came along in 2002, there was another furore. The FIFA president himself urged South Koreans to stop eating dogmeat. (Quite why a bunch of football executives installed themselves as arbiters of carnivorous relativism is unclear, and certainly declamations of morality are pretty laughable coming from either FIFA or the IOC.)

Whatever their reasons, it was enough to embarrass the Koreans, and despite the fact that dog is a popular national dish, embarrassment is the one thing they can't handle. The dogmeat dealers were all swept off the streets again. By this time, though, the government had already removed all legislation from the industry, thereby officially ignoring its existence, so now they can't be said to sanction it (and the international community is assuaged), yet they haven't lost face at home to nationalistic dog-eating voters. Brilliant!

As a result, dog farmers can do what they want to the 1–3 million dogs raised each year for human consumption.

I'm hoping that this visit will provoke a thoughtful and dignified moral exploration of food taboos, rather than an ethical bun fight. I'm going to try to keep an open mind, take a look at the whole industry, try to understand the Korean national character, do a bit of moral cogitation and, as long as it's been raised decently, at the end of the trip I'd like to eat dog.

When I first told my wife about this plan she was wearily appalled (she's yet to match my enthusiasm for eclectic foods, but I'm working on her), but she later became genuinely worried about the reaction from the public – people who might target me for eating dog. I told her, 'I'm not doing this in a gung-ho, look-how-hard-I-am extreme eating kind of way,' but she was still nervous. 'There are weird people out there,' she said. And she was to be proved right.

Let's get one thing out of the way: I don't see anything particularly wrong with eating dog. I don't think I'm a nasty person. I certainly haven't set out to upset animal-lovers and I won't steal your schnauzer if you invite me for supper – I just think that if you've resolved the moral and emotional complexities of carnivorousness to eat cows, pigs and chickens (and I think I have), then you *should* be able to eat pretty much anything, as long as it's lived a decent life.

I may differ from the vast majority of people in Britain on this one, but it seems odd that one intelligent, cute, loving animal that has stood by man's side and sustained him in his hours of need (I'm talking about the noble pig here) is somehow less valuable than another. At the same time I'm not blind to emotion: I know that people see dogs as companions, and there's a powerful bond between people and their pets. But what about when they're *not* raised as pets? I'm not eating *your* dog, after all.

I believe a lot of other things about carnivorousness, namely that we shouldn't cause unnecessary pain to animals we eat, and that we have a responsibility of care towards all those animals that give their lives for our stomachs. I'd like to think that we have an unspoken contract with the animals we eat (as Hugh Fearnley-Whittingstall states eloquently in *Meat*), and it's one that supermarket shoppers in the UK violate hypocritically every day when buying battery chickens and intensively reared pork.

● ● ● ● ●

I sit on the aeroplane wondering what the hell I'm doing. After all my self-righteous justification of dog-eating, I start to think rationally. It's pretty early in my career as a food writer and TV presenter and I've decided to eat the one meal that's guaranteed to upset everybody on the known planet: my wife, my kids and my dog-owning mother, but also everyone who watches food programmes and buys food books ... in other words, anyone who might conceivably be called an audience.

I love dogs. But I also love cats, ducks, pigs, cows, chickens, rabbits, quails, chinchillas, goats (I especially love goats), cats and mice. I don't believe that any of them has any less of a right to avoid being eaten. But that doesn't necessarily mean that they *should* be eaten. Or does it? This is the problem with being a thinking carnivore – you have to spend so much time and effort justifying your actions. Part of the joy of being a vegetarian must be that life is so much easier.

Seoul

We arrive in Seoul. It's one of those super-modern, dystopian fantasy cities lit by neon signs and vast electronics ads. It's corporate, sober and impersonal, in marked contrast to my guide Yoon-Jung, who is gorgeous, funny and friendly, although she betrays her Koreanness in her ferocious work ethic and propensity to turn lightly pink immediately after drinking alcohol. I like her immediately.

Although I'm knackered, I've heard that food here is a real adventure and this fires my gastronautical zeal so I drag Yoon-Jung out to the nearby Itaewon Galbi restaurant for an induction into the strange and wonderful cuisine of Korea. We eat semi-fermented raw crab (which tastes like rotten crab, unsurprisingly, and much as I try to enjoy it … I don't). Our table has a charcoal grill in the middle, and the waitress brings us a variety of ribs, prawns and chicken that we cook ourselves. This is my kind of eating: hands-on stuff, with a sea of extra bowls of kimchi (fermented cabbage with chilli, which tastes great, but doesn't half make you windy), red pepper sauce and various vegetables. Yoon-Jung turns lightly pink, and we all turn in for an early night.

My First Dog Farm

Talk about being thrown in at the deep end: it's my first day and I am on my way to a dog farm. I overslept this morning, so I'm already in a bit of a fluster. 'Dog farm!' Ye gods, it's such an alien concept to me that it sends shivers down my spine, like the idea of a child farm. But I mustn't be a slave to sentiment: fear and ignorance is how prejudice evolves, and just because it's unusual doesn't mean that it's bad.

Look at me! I'm drowning in moral turpitude and I haven't got out of the car yet.

Korean dog farmers are notoriously secretive, and the industry as a whole hates the Western media, which it blames for vilifying a traditional national dish, so Yoon-Jung has scored a major triumph in getting me access to Korea's biggest dog farm. But to achieve this, she's had to talk to some pretty shady people.

I meet Dr Dogmeat in a motorway lay-by. Yup, you heard right: Dr Dogmeat. He's actually Yong-Geun Ann, professor of food nutrition at Chungcheong College, but he's become known as Dr Dogmeat due to his research into the cultural, moral and nutritional significance of eating dog. He clearly likes the nickname, relishing the notoriety it gives him and using it as his byline on the myriad papers and articles he writes.

He has come up with 350 uses for dogmeat in various products, and it's fair to say that Dr Dogmeat represents the pro-dog-eating lobby (all his work is unashamedly, and occasionally hysterically, pro dogmeat). He's not particularly friendly, but he wants to show me how reasonable and decent the dog industry is, and he's taking me to Korea's biggest dog farm to prove his point. We drive in convoy, following his 4x4 into the countryside.

Rural Korea isn't particularly pretty: it's an agricultural wasteland where little love is given to outside space, which I find odd in such an overcrowded country. The countryside seems to have suffered rampant, unregulated development at the hands of economic necessity, and in the middle of rolling fields, you'll often find an incongruous tower block.

On the way, Yoon-Jung gets a call on her mobile. Apparently there will be a Korean TV news crew at the dog farm, and they want to film me as I take a look around. They are already there, so I don't have much choice in the matter.

Yoon-Jung's phone rings again. There are now two separate TV news crews at the farm, both of whom want to film me. This is getting ridiculous. Yoon-Jung thinks that Dr Dogmeat and the owner of the farm have tipped them off.

We finally arrive at the dog farm to find, in addition to the two TV crews, a delegation from the local government office and at least two photographers. It's not entirely clear what they're doing here, but they say they want to ensure fair media coverage of the farm. This is odd, because a) in Korea there are no regulations that apply to the dogmeat industry so there's nothing to be fair about; b) none of them speak English so they wouldn't know what I was saying anyway; and c) if they didn't like something I said or did, what exactly are they expecting to do? Smash our cameras?

The dog farm doesn't look anything special – much like any busy, slightly rundown working cattle farm. The only difference is the sound of a large number of dogs barking. I meet the dog farmer, Mr Yong Bok Chin. He doesn't appear to be the devil incarnate, although he does have a business card with a picture of a cute dog on one side, and a picture of a restaurant on the other. In fact, he's handsome, solid and friendly, if a little nervous of all the attention.

I'm given a bright blue disposable suit to cover my clothes, and some paper shoe covers. I look thoroughly ridiculous, and I'm feeling oddly stiff in front of all the cameras. Mr Chin leads us off to a large iron shed and my journey begins.

As Mr Chin opens the door to the shed, the dogs go crazy. I don't know if it's like this at Crufts, but the sound of 3,500 dogs barking in unison is quite painful. And immediately after the cacophony comes the smell. It's horrendous. Imagine concentrating three months' worth of excrement from 3,500 dogs in a single barn. It's hard not to gag.

So what's a dog farm like?

Extraordinary and unsettling. There are several thousand metal cages, most of them about 2 × 3 × 3 metres. Each cage houses two or three dogs with a fairly small amount of room for them to run around – they aren't free range, but neither are they battery farmed. The cages are raised off the ground so that the excrement falls through the bottom. There are no concessions to comfort, no toys, no beds and no names – they aren't treated as pets in any way, but I still feel a blind, residual affection for them: they wag their tails, try to lick me and run about, barking excitedly.

So is this really bad animal husbandry? Well, call me heartless, but I'm not so sure. It certainly isn't bucolic bliss and the smell isn't nice, but the dogs are very healthy, well fed and, if tail wagging is a good indicator, they seem happy. Many play with their cage-mates. It is a shock to see animals I view as pets being raised this dispassionately, but the psychological assumptions I'd made – that they need treats, love and human affection – are tempered by the fact that these are livestock and have been raised much as cows might be. Although they look like pets, they haven't been treated as man's best friend, haven't run for sticks or won medals for their fine bone structure or well-performed tricks.

The dogs look happy enough, although what I can't see is their behaviour over a long period: perhaps they are frustrated at being locked up, and perhaps they fight each other when humans aren't looking. I realize that, like any livestock, it wouldn't benefit their farmer if they were unhappy or ill, simply because they'd fetch a lower market price.

But the idea of a dog farm is still strange to me, and I start to feel a little sick. We wander up and down the rows of cages, and I try to disguise my shock. Eventually I leave and sit outside to take stock of things.

I talk to Yong Bok Chin and try to understand why he farms dogs, and how he feels about it. He says that farming is as difficult here as anywhere.

'I wasn't making money from traditional farming, so I started rearing dogs for market, and now I make a decent living.'

The government hasn't tried to stop him and he feels happy that his animals are well cared for. We talk about the whole concept of pet ownership, and he claims that people in the West put too much store on pet dogs because the family unit has begun to break down, whereas Koreans have much stronger family ties.

I ask him if he has a pet dog, and he surprises me by saying that he does. I ask him if he'll eat his pet when it dies, and he nearly falls off his chair with laughter.

'Of course not – no – if he dies I'll bury him.'

I suggest that this is odd, considering his profession.

'These dogs are farmed dogs, livestock for meat, and he's not. So he wouldn't be very tasty. The taste is different. I wouldn't eat him,' he explains.

The Korean TV crews keep bugging me for an interview, and I finally give in.

'Why have you come here?' they ask.

'To try to understand the dogmeat industry,' I say.

They become aggressive, accusing me of bias – they've seen another BBC news report, and it was very one-sided and xenophobic – why would I be different?

I'm shocked at the ferocity of their attack – they have no grounds for claiming I'm biased – I've barely said anything yet. I tell them that I'm here to try to understand Korea, and that I will happily eat dog if I think it's a decent industry.

'Well, is it?'

'Give me a chance! I've only been here for half a day – why don't you ask me that again when I've been here for two weeks?'

They take this as an invitation and say that they'll definitely interview me the day before I leave. Damn – I wasn't expecting that.

Dr Dogmeat's Bosintang

I head off for a restaurant that, coincidentally, is owned by Chin, and I get my first glimpse of dog as meat. Chin brings some cuts of dog into the kitchen: an entire hindquarter including a tail, a back and rack of ribs, some intestines and strips of fat. It all looks identifiably canine as he drops it into a vast pressure-cooker full of water. Again, it's disconcerting to see but I'm surprised that I don't feel more of a sense of shock, although it's probably because the fur has been burnt off and the carcass cleaned, so the result looks very much like any meat prepared for eating. Chin puts the pot on to boil, and beckons me into the dining area. Apparently Dr Dogmeat wants me to see something.

He shows me some enormous posters he's had made up to advertise 350 innovative uses of dog he's come up with. Dog oil face cream – I kid you not (helps prevent freckles and pimples, apparently), dog oil hand cream, dried grated dog (for seasoning), and sliced dog penis snacks. In fact, there's a whole poster dedicated to the joys of dog penis – Chinese dishes of prettily fanned penises, and every possible cooking method from pickling, jerking, sautéing, braising, air-drying and grating. It's a veritable orgy of dog chopper. I have to admit that I'm slightly baffled at the evangelical fervour of Dr Dogmeat, and I ask him 'Why the obsession with penises?'

He says, 'Only those who've tried it can tell you what the effect is.'

Which makes it a small and elusive study group, I'd guess. But I'm certainly not going to criticize someone for eating one hunk of protein over another so I stumble, shell-shocked, back to the kitchen.

Dogmeat is very tough and has to be boiled in unseasoned water for a couple of hours before use. I ask Chin if he remembers the actual dog we're cooking, but he says that there are far too many for him to have any personal connections.

Once the meat is boiled, inexplicably, Dr Dogmeat takes over from the women in the kitchen and shows me how to make dogmeat stew. He slices a variety of oriental greens, spring onions, cabbage, leeks and taro and lays these in a wide, flat pan. He takes the belly cut of the dog and pulls the ribs out, and then cuts the remaining meat and fat into long slices. The meat is laid on the vegetables, and red chilli pepper sauce is spread over the top. Over this is poured a litre or so of fatty stock, and the whole lot is placed on a portable gas burner on the table for guests to mix in extra condiments.

So this is bosintang, the infamous Korean dogmeat stew that has caused outrage across the Western world, nearly lost Seoul the Olympics and the football World Cup, and provides something like 60 million meals across Korea every year. It smells good, like a rich pork stew, and I sit cross-legged next to Chin and Dr Dogmeat looking at it in silence whilst three different TV crews film my reactions. I feel quite defensive, and I don't want to give away any emotions. I start having second thoughts about coming here at all – what good can possibly come of this? If I eat the dog, I will upset most people I know, but if I don't eat it I'll be a hypocrite, throwing away all my long-gestated carnivorous principles.

You could cut the atmosphere with the Sword of Damocles that I can just make out hanging from the rafters.

To dissolve a bit of the tension, I ask Dr Dogmeat why he thinks Westerners care so much about the eating of dog.

He responds with a startling viciousness: 'It doesn't matter what you think about it. Just leave us alone. The problem starts when you tell us to change our ways to match yours.'

I'm taken aback because I've been careful not to express any opinions yet – I'm here as a journalist, so all I've done is ask questions. My dislike for Dr Dogmeat deepens instantly, and I now realize that there's only one course of action open to me: I need to wait. I can't make a decision this big on my first day in Korea.

I announce (a little too grandly) that although I think that Chin's animals have been decently raised, when you've got the world's TV cameras pointing at you, the issue of eating dog is about more than just this one meal. 'I can't make my decision until I've found out more, and in fact I won't make my final decision until our last day in Korea, but you're all welcome back to film it.'

There's a sigh of disappointment in the restaurant, disturbed only by Dr Dogmeat, who takes my comments as a signal for him to throw himself with gay abandon on the bosintang, and he proceeds to slurp it down noisily, presumably trying to annoy me.

Noryangjin Fish Market

We visit the vast Noryangjin fish market in central Seoul. I find fish markets mesmerizing, and what's unique about Noryangjin is the mezzanine level of restaurants above the market where they will cook fish that you've bought downstairs, and serve you rice, beer and kimchi (that stinky fermented cabbage) to go with it.

This would be great, except for the fact that here in Korea they have a fishy speciality all of their own, and it's one that gives me the willies. Sea slug. It's the single most revolting thing I can think of eating, and I've always worried about the day that someone puts one in front of me. Well, wouldn't you know it: today's the day.

I don't chase extreme foods on purpose, but I do like food to be an adventure. I believe that in a world that's having tremendous difficulty feeding its population, we can't turn down any foodstuff – who knows what could turn out to be the new potato, the new rice, corn or wheat (this is also one of the many reasons why I think it ought to be OK to eat dog). So I've eaten civet cat in Burma, Yak's knob in China, ant larvae in Mexico and rat in India. But for some reason, sea slug has always been my culinary nemesis.

With a feeling of dread, I choose a plump-looking sea slug from a nice old lady in the fish market. It wriggles around as I hold it, and it's knobbly and slimy and gruesome and yuck and I can't believe this is edible and I gag involuntarily. I hand over some money and take the slug, along with a vicious but tasty-looking king crab as a side order, upstairs to the restaurants.

I hand over my booty and watch the preparation: apparently it's always eaten raw. Well that's just great. But it gets worse: the lady takes my sea slug out of the bag and chops the end off (I don't know if it's the head or the tail, or indeed whether or not a sea slug possesses either), causing it to wriggle frantically. Then she does something grotesque: she squeezes it to push out the intestinal tract, then hands them to me, saying, 'This is the best bit.'

Oh. My. God.

I have just discovered something worse than eating sea slug: eating raw sea slug intestines whilst the eviscerated sea slug looks on. I am surely going to hell.

I put the stringy intestine in my mouth and chew. Every atom in my body is willing me to vomit, but somehow I manage to persevere and eat the thing. It tastes slightly sweet, but the main sensation is the sliminess and stringiness of the texture. It's almost impossible to bite because it slips around your teeth too much. Urgh. Finally, with a few slurps, it's gone. I'm not proud – in fact I'm a little disgusted with myself – but then a sense of victory sweeps over me and I realize I've conquered my culinary demons. After this, what food is there to be afraid of?

My chef chops the still-wriggling slug into slices that look spookily like deep-fried onion rings. They still twitch and glisten whilst as I sit down crossed-legged to eat them. After the intestines, I feel a cloud has parted, and I can eat the slug itself with gay abandon. The slices taste like raw squid – ever so slightly fishy, but clean and fresh. It's all about texture here: they are tremendously tough, a cross between cartilage and car tyre, and when you finally manage to get your teeth into them, they crunch. I get the sense that NASA could develop a new generation of Kevlar from these fellas. By now, though, I'm blooded, and I wolf them down as fast as anyone can wolf down car tyre.

Later, we drive to the town of Taejun to visit Dr Lee, a renowned expert in herbal medicine, who gives me acupuncture and tells me a load of hokum about which herbs and vegetables are good for a set of imaginary ailments that she dreams up for me. She tells me that seaweed cleans the blood, mushrooms are aphrodisiacs and all sorts of other snake-oil nonsense, then announces that I am a cold person, and I need to eat dogmeat to heat me up. I'm probably cold because I'm trying to restrain my deep loathing of complementary medicine and herbal fruit-cakery, but I stay polite to her throughout.

KAPS

I am still on the hunt for dog-eating opinions in Korea so I drop in on the Korean Animal Protection Society (KAPS). If anyone should be against dog-eating, it's these people. And the founder, Soo, wastes no time in introducing me to the exuberantly friendly dogs she's rescued from dealers and showing me photos of abuse. The photos are truly gruesome – dogs that have clearly been beaten and then hanged, dogs being abused and cruelly transported. But the odd thing is that most of these photos look very old. In fact, they look as though they were shot in the 1960s. I've only got hairstyles and clothes to go on (and admittedly this is Korea we're talking about here), but it looks very much as though the worst abuse happened a long time ago.

Then, when I say that I'm trying to work out if it's OK to eat dog, I get a surprise. Instead of an outraged condemnation of the very idea, Soo says, 'It's a personal decision – I can't tell you what to do. However, your behaviour could influence the behaviour of others in a good or bad way. Because it could have a bad influence, I would prefer it if you didn't eat it.'

Soo has stopped a long way short of saying 'no', which is a very Korean thing: much as they hate being embarrassed, they hate embarrassing other people too. Blimey, how do decisions get made around here?

The Dark Side of the
Dogmeat Industry

Dr Dogmeat contacts me again (which surprises me after his outburst last time), and offers to take me to another dog farm that functions as an auction house, farm and slaughterhouse. I eagerly agree and meet him at another secret location. Again, I'm told not to reveal the name of the place.

I arrive at a farm that's very different from Yong Bok Chin's operation. It's scrappy, filthy, chaotic and crumbling. A small auction is in progress when I arrive, and several cages lie around crammed with dogs. Some of the cages aren't big enough for the dogs to sit in, let alone stand up in, so they lie there looking terrified. Much as Chin's dogs expressed joy by wagging tails, jumping and barking, these express fear by curling tails under themselves, trembling and whimpering. Occasionally they snap at each other and fight for space inside the cages.

The buyers walk on and around the cages, squeezing flesh through the wire to check the quality of the meat. The dogs go for around $250 each. When the animals are bought, they are dragged out of the cages and thrown in the back of another cage on a truck. One Alsatian is so terrified at its treatment that it soils itself as it's being shoved upside down into a cage. I tell the owner that it's a cruel way to treat an animal but he says, 'We have no choice – if they're not treated like that, people will get bitten.'

I take a wander around the dog cages that house about 50–60 dogs. This place is hideous, and most of the dogs look ill and disturbed. They sit in piles of their own excrement and their coats are ragged. Most are thin and show signs of stress such as repetitive actions and twitches, and they cower away from me as I walk past. I'm beginning to feel sick with disgust, so I'm almost grateful when I'm taken to see the slaughterhouse.

It gets worse. The owner shows me how they slaughter the dogs: they put them in an iron cage and clip a wire to it that's connected to the positive wire on a plug, then using an iron bar, they complete the circuit to the negative wire. The cage is basically connected directly to the mains electricity, the fuses are overridden and the dog is electrocuted. The owner plugs it in and shows me – it can clearly get messy because the cage and the bar are a bit rusty, so there are lots of sparks, and the connection is a bit tricky to maintain. He claims that the dog takes four or five seconds to die, and altogether it sounds like a dreadful way to go. Oh, and all this is done in full view of the other dogs.

I ask the owner if this place is legal, and he says, 'According to the law, it's neither legal or illegal. They're not telling us to kill dogs, but they're not stopping us either.'

This place is horrific, and I say as much to Dr Dogmeat. I wouldn't eat any meat – dog or chicken – that I knew had been raised in conditions this dreadful. What was he thinking bringing a BBC journalist to a place like this when the issue is so sensitive? His reply is to tell me not to use the footage that's been shot, but it's too late for that.

I leave the farm, and 200 metres down the road I spot a beef farm, so I stop to take a look. Perhaps I've taken things out of context – maybe all livestock in Korea is raised in grim conditions. I poke my head over the barn gate and I am greeted by an extraordinary sight: the cows are listening to Korean ballads played to them on a stereo (I swear I'm not making this up); they are in large, clean, smart barns with ample room, fresh straw and proper ventilation. There are calves and mature cows living in conditions that I can only marvel at. They look healthy, happy and secure. You couldn't engineer a greater contrast if you wanted to.

Moran Market

To find out even more, I need to visit Moran market, a huge food market a little way out of town that's renowned for selling dogmeat and live dogs for slaughter. It's sort of un-legal (rather than illegal) to sell dog, but in the past, the police have raided it and thrown dog traders out to appease the Western press, so they hate anyone filming there and have been known to get extremely aggressive. With this in mind, I am, for the first time in my life, going to wear a hidden camera.

I meet my two slightly dim, uncommunicative security guards and have a safety briefing. Yoon-Jung has a moment of epiphany and decides that she doesn't agree with filming the dog sellers – she's worried about people losing their livelihoods – so I agree to go on my own, but it's a tricky one, this moral relativism thing.

First, I wander around to get a feel for the market. I love these places – they are little microcosms of the societies they serve and are always full of wild, exuberant characters. There's a whole rice-puffing zone with revolving cannons, underneath which is a gas burner. They heat the rice until it explodes with a colossal BOOM, and it blows into a waiting bag.

They make puffed rice, puffed beans and Lord knows what else. But more importantly, these stalls are a gossip arena for garrulous old biddies who crowd around the cannons. Cheeky, naughty and downright rude, these women enjoy the exploding cannons as much as any lily-livered foreigner, and each explosion is greeted with whoops of joy and squeals of fear.

I buy some charcoal-smoked seaweed sheets from a nice guy who spends his entire life wafting sheets over a charcoal stove. Piles and piles of ginseng are sold on an unprecedented scale; the spindly roots are the cheapest. I buy a pile of the medium roots at 20,000 South Korean won (KRW, informally known as kwon) for 300 g, which works out at a bit more than ten quid. Cheap at the price, until I realize that I can't take them through customs anyway.

Having recc-ed the market, I set up the camera and start filming. One area deals in all live animals, including dogs, black goats, chickens, ducks and rabbits. I'd hate to make any wild assumptions, but I'll tell you this: the people on these stalls couldn't give a toss for animal welfare. Dogs aren't treated any worse – every animal suffers. They are all crammed into small cages, sitting in their own excrement.

The dogs are squeezed into cages in front of the stalls, often sharing the cage with the odd goat. The dogs that aren't bored or snarling look terrified, especially when they're pulled out by the neck to be taken away for a customer. I meet a woman who shows me a few grim carcasses, and I have to remind myself not to be appalled at the sight of a dead dog – we should deal with sights like these in return for our carnivorousness.

I wander up and down, getting lots of shots of the dogs and the conditions they live in and when I feel I have enough footage, I drop off the hidden camera and exchange it for the full-sized one that everyone can see. This outing proves to be very different. I go up to every single dog seller in the market to see if I can ask them a couple of questions, but the moment they see the camera they become very aggressive, pushing me away, shouting and threatening to smash the equipment. Of course, no one is obliged to be accommodating to TV crews, but I am surprised at the level of their anger.

I persist with one guy and ask him why he won't let us film. Eventually, off-camera, he explains that after someone had filmed in the past, a critical programme was broadcast and the government had closed them down. I ask him over and over again why he thinks people object to dogmeat, but he refuses to answer me.

Is it right to destroy someone's livelihood for the sake of animal rights? Well, I don't think we should tell Koreans to stop dealing in dogs any more than they should tell Britons to stop dealing in chickens. But just as I don't think chickens should be raised in battery conditions, dogs in Korea should at least be protected by animal welfare regulations that respect their health, life and means of death – it's really not so much to ask.

My thoughts about dogmeat have definitely changed since I arrived. I genuinely thought I'd have no problem with eating it, that I'd relish the adventure, and maybe even enjoy the discomfort I'd cause to all those carnivorous hypocrites watching appalled in front of the telly at home before they tucked into their battery chicken dinners. It would be obtuse of me to ignore emotional reactions to food, but the reality is that there are huge animal welfare issues to bear in mind.

Bloody Sundae

Yoon-Jung takes me to meet some of her younger friends at a blood sundae emporium (pig's blood, not dog's). Sundae is a young person's dish (although no one manages to explain to me why) and doesn't seem to have anything to do with ice cream (which is a shame because I wouldn't mind trying blood ice cream sundae). Instead it's a huge pan of vegetables and Korean black pudding that you either fry or boil at the table and share with your friends: just the sort of food I love best. It's a mess, but it tastes great – like bubble and squeak with lots of vegetables and black pudding.

I ask Yoon-Jung's friends what they think about eating dog. They are a bunch of college kids, and about half of them have tried dog. The girls all wrinkle their noses at the thought of it and the guys all agree that it's really only popular with older men, mainly because it's supposed to be good for your sex life. I ask them if they think it's OK to eat dog, and the reactions are mixed – the girls all hate the idea of it, but they wouldn't dream of telling someone not to eat food that they enjoy. The guys say that it's fine to eat, but they aren't keen on the taste. I ask what they think about the West making such a fuss over dogmeat, and one guy says, 'The UK does some terrible things too, like invading Iraq. Why do people feel that they can come to Korea to criticize our culture?'

When we've finished talking I ask what mayhem young Koreans like them will cause tonight (it's Saturday). The girls say that they're going to a movie and the guys are going to spend the evening at a friend's house playing computer games. I'm astounded – here are the hip kids of Korea blowing their weekends in darkened rooms staring at computer screens. I spent my years at college acting in terrible plays and trying to get off with girls. I guess you could say that I was also wasting my life in darkened rooms, but somehow I'm glad I did it my way rather than theirs.

Cooking with Buddhists

I wind my way through a grim residential area of square metal houses plonked indiscriminately on scrubby yards mixed with shabby light industrial units. Suburban Korea isn't a pretty place. Eventually the sea of grotty houses parts, and I find myself at the base of a pile of huge rock steps leading up to a beautiful, if garish, Buddhist temple. This is the Wonjeoung-ri temple, comprising the Institute of Korean Buddhist Food. I'm taken into the main temple to pay my respects to Buddha, then I'm whisked off to meet Jeuk Moon, the chief priest, for a cookery lesson.

As we talk, Jeuk Moon becomes more relaxed. He says that you can smell a meat-eater, but when I offer him my armpit and ask him to guess what my last meal was, he graciously declines. I ask what his favourite food is and he replies that food is an earthly pleasure and that monks aren't supposed to dwell on it … but if he's drawn on the matter, he'd have to plug for fried bean rice.

I ask if there's anything that he misses from the outside world and he thinks for a while. He says he'd really like to wear a suit. I suggest that if the monk thing doesn't work out, he should give me a call and we could swap jobs for a while. He promises to bear it in mind.

I like Jeuk Moon; he's dignified and humble yet he inspires instant respect. He's calm, smart, spiritually purified and perfectly rotund. Everything you want from your Buddhist priest.

We have a lot of fun cooking – he teases me for anything I get wrong, but stubbornly refuses to accept that my food tastes better than his, which it patently does (OK, spiritually it might be inferior, but try telling that to a set of taste buds). We cook deep-fried thingy, wrapped whatsitcalled and steamed rice with stuff (even Yoon-Jung couldn't decipher the names). The wrapped whatsitcalled is particularly beautiful, the sort of dish a feckless food writer would prepare simply because it would look gorgeous in a photo – raw enoki mushrooms, shreds of water chestnut, ginseng root, juju strips and half a pine nut, all wrapped in a thin strip of ginseng or cucumber. It tastes OK, but not spectacular – a subtle combination of gentle sweet flavours.

The rice is packed in bamboo cups with water and all manner of oriental gubbins: lotus seeds, nuts and roots of this, beans of that. We cover them in paper and tie them up with string. Out in the exterior kitchen, a massive iron cooking pot sits on a log fire, warming up under the watchful gaze of a portrait of Buddha. We pay our respects to him, and Jeuk Moon stokes the fire before leaving for evening prayer. I am to meet him later to eat all the food we've cooked.

I am taken to the temple. At the back sit three chirpy, fat golden Buddhas joyfully contemplating nirvana. Behind these are thousands more tiny ones on shelves that line the entire back and side walls of the temple. It's like being in a religious version of Hamleys. It's so much happier and calmer than our Christian churches and I begin to think that this Buddhist thing is right up my street.

A monk sings a dirgey prayer and I am told to follow his lead with lots of genuflecting, and I enjoy it. I also do lots of prostrating while the monk sings his songs and rings his funny wooden bell. I haven't a clue what's going on, but it's very nice, very calming and somehow makes me feel purified.

Dinner's next. I'm shown into a room with plush cushions on the floor, including a particularly comfy one that clearly isn't reserved for me. Eventually Jeuk Moon arrives and sits himself down on it with great ceremony. I'm a little nervous because all the cheekiness and fun from our cooking lesson has dissipated and he's become stony faced. It's time for me to bring up the main topic for discussion – something that I haven't warned him we will be asking about: eating dog.

The room is almost silent except for the slurping of soup and tinkling of wooden chopsticks and I take the plunge: 'Does the idea of eating dogmeat upset you? Does it disgust you?' I ask clumsily.

Quick as a flash, Jeuk Moon barks at me: 'No talking during dinner.'

Oh, great.

And so we sit there eating in silence. I'm not ashamed to tell you that I *hate* eating in silence. Call me spiritually impoverished if you will, call me worldly and impure, but I can't think of anything worse than four people listening to each other slurping.

After an excruciating 30 minutes of eating, Jeuk Moon finally declares that dinner is over, and he is ready to talk.

So, to the vegetarian issue: 'People can be reincarnated as animals so you could end up eating a person, even a relative.'

'And dogs? Would you get into that crazy situation where by eating a dog you might be eating a relative?'

'Ah,' he says, as if he knew that this bloody dog question was bound to crop up eventually. 'Yes, that's logical from a religious point of view. A good Buddhist wouldn't eat dog because he might be eating a friend or old relative.'

So do you think Koreans should ban the consumption of dogmeat?

No, no, no. 'It's a food tradition that some of our ancestors enjoyed, so it shouldn't be criticized or condemned.'

Eh? Even a man with the weight of religious doctrine behind him won't criticize his fellow Koreans. I'm beginning to feel that Koreans have such an irrational fear of embarrassment that they turn a blind eye to things that upset them: it's just not done to criticize other people here, and I'm not sure if this makes for a particularly healthy society.

In the morning, after being told off for not eating the vast mound of horrid, tasteless rice porridge I've been served, I am invited for a last audience with the chief priest at a traditional tea ceremony. He's in ebullient form and he shows me a picture frame on which is written 'Drink your tea' in Korean. He explains that a famous Buddhist priest he knew always responded to complex theological questions with the phrase 'Drink your tea', meaning that the answer to a direct question was not necessarily a direct answer and knowledge doesn't necessarily come through rationalization. Hmm. Sounds a bit of a cop-out to me.

I have my photo taken with Jeuk in front of his temple, and leave feeling enlightened, though what exactly I'm enlightened about I'm not sure. I was enlightened of 280,000 kwon (around £152) for my stay, plus a few quid for some fetching candles bearing the words 'May all your wishes come true'.

On the way back I drop in to the enormous Olympic Stadium. Given that it was during the build-up to the 1988 Seoul Olympics that the world really started taking a pop at Korea for eating dog, it seems like a symbol for the way the issue has been brushed under the carpet. I challenge my producer Alex to a lap of the track, which I complete in world record time (probably), although he retires hurt after 70 metres.

Petian Castle

I visit Petian Castle, a gloriously kitsch temple to dogs the entrance of which is marked by a 6-metre-high fibreglass bone. Outside is a patch of scrubland for your pooch to crap in, and next to it is a pool for it to swim in (closed September–May). Inside is a mini-mall comprising an extensive dog supermarket, a beauty parlour, a photo studio for pet portraits, a veterinary surgery, meeting rooms, offices and a restaurant. Everything the obsessive pet owner could want. The restaurant offers a selection of meals for humans, and a fine chicken breast dish for their pets. The chef isn't very keen on speaking to us – maybe he feels professionally humiliated at having to cook food for dogs, I don't know.

It's schnauzer day, and there must be 40 of the yapping little terrors here, along with their owners. These people are potty about dogs – one girl says that her dog is a substitute child and that she spends one third of her income on the snappy, yappy little brute, which sports a garish dress with a skirt that sticks up in the air in an oddly indecent fashion. Another dog wears a pink velour track suit that I swear wouldn't look out of place on Vicky Pollard.

Excellent: a chav schnauzer!

You could say that dog owners are just as bad as dog eaters: they incarcerate animals in an alien environment and use them as fashion items, symbols of wealth or emotional props, and have them put down when they are no longer viable pets. Dogs are meant to live in the wild, and breeding them for human comfort is tantamount to torture. It's all in the delivery, see.

I meet 'Hyper', a Korean canine TV superstar who appears in a hit soap opera every week and gets treated as an actor rather than a performing dog. Apparently it's a great privilege for me to meet him. I ask if Hyper finds it easy to get laid with all that fame, and his owner sheepishly says, 'He likes girls'. What a life.

This ought to be a great place to find some dog-loving fanatics virulently opposed to the dogmeat industry but everyone I speak to has the same reaction: 'I'm not a fan of dogmeat myself, but if someone else wants to eat it, that's fine. Who am I to stop them?' I try winding them up into a righteous frenzy, but they're having none of it. When I ask about animal rights, they all have a vague sense that animals should be protected, but they seem more concerned about the government providing better dog-walking parks than protecting the welfare of farm animals. It's as though they haven't really thought about it.

When I take a look around the boarding kennels, I'm shocked to find a stinky block of steel cubicles. If I'd been told it was a dog farm, I'd have found it as disconcerting as Mr Chin's farm. The dogs have nothing in the cages to entertain them, they can't see each other, but can hear each other barking incessantly and they look frustrated and a little disturbed. At least in the farm they could all see and play with other dogs.

My guide to the castle is their glossy dog magazine's editor, and although he reckons that dog owners are often a bit too obsessive, bordering on abusive, in their approach to caring for their dogs, he is not to be drawn on the subject of eating dogmeat.

'Each to his own,' he says. 'Who am I to judge my fellow Koreans on something they've been doing for years?'

'Well, you're a dog expert,' I proffer, to no avail.

'It's up to them.'

Christ alive, why won't anyone in this country express outrage at some level?

I leave Petian Castle without a clear answer – no one seems to care too much what happens to the dogmeat industry and its unhappy dogs. It's as if they see pets as a different *species* compared to animals raised for food, despite the fact that they look exactly the same, wag similar tails and bark like each other.

Facing the Music

It's my last day here so I invite all the stalker Korean TV crews to join me at Chin's restaurant to see if I can bear to eat dog. I arrive at the restaurant at dusk and I can see lots of people and camera kit inside. I'm nervous, not so much because of the attention, but because I find it uncomfortable that such a delicate personal decision has to be played out in front of the world's media.

My problem is this: I've seen the terrible conditions that some dogs are raised in, and that's enough to make me hate the whole idea. But Koreans eat 1–3 million dogs every year. It's a huge industry that, despite some ham-fisted attempts by the government to ignore its existence, isn't going to go away. So surely the only way to improve things is to enforce proper animal welfare standards – standards like those of Mr Yong Bok Chin.

And there's the dilemma: Chin's dogs – the dogs that are on the menu today – were raised in decent conditions, and if I want to encourage anything, it's for people to eat dog that's been raised like these.

Just before entering I call my wife Georgia for moral support, but there's little forthcoming.

'You know what I think. You wouldn't catch me eating a dog.'

Is that all?

'Well, if you want to explain to your daughters that you've been away eating dogs …'

I'm on my own, which is the way it ought to be.

The restaurant is packed with punters who want to watch me eat. One of them reveals the real reason why it's so popular with the guys: 'If you eat it, your energy surges, it gives you a real boost. You really feel the power. If you're low, it gives you energy and helps you to work more enthusiastically and cuddle your wife better. You can go for it twice instead of once!'

His wife bursts into squeals of laughter and enthusiastically agrees, 'He's much better after a plate of dog!'

I'm still confused when I sit cross-legged next to Chin. The cameras line up in front of me and I hope for some lightning bolt that will resolve my conundrum, but none is forthcoming. A bowl of dog stew is laid in front of me, along with a similar bowl of chicken stew.

I stare at the bowls of stew and run over the events of the last fortnight in my head, and the one niggling thing that I can't resolve is the sight of those dogs living in God-awful conditions next to a cattle farm whose animals were so well-cared for.

I unpack my thoughts on camera: 'I think that eating dog is fine in principle. And I think that Mr Chin is a decent farmer who cares for his animals well, and if this was just about his dogs, I'd be happy to eat it. But in front of all these cameras, everything that I do has a wider meaning. If I eat it, I'll be approving an unregulated industry that is free to do what it wants to dogs, and it's got to change. And you can't drive this industry underground. A million and a half dogs are eaten each year in an illegal industry already. So you aren't going to stop it, you're just going to cause more and more suffering for more and more animals. Sorry, mate, but I'm not going to eat it.'

There is an audible gasp from around the room. I promise Chin that if the dogmeat industry does get regulated and conditions improve I'd be happy to return and eat dog with him. He is desperately disappointed, but he seems to understand.

● ● ● ● ●

The next day, as I wait for my plane, I see the story played out on Korean national TV. They use a photo of me with an outsized head, and track my journey around Korea, reducing it to a kind of cartoon – it is all quite jolly and it seems that although they scorn my refusal to eat dog, they are relieved that I hadn't embarrassed anyone. God forbid.

The moral turpitude and false sincerity here has drained me. I feel an enormous sense of relief that I'm heading off to a simpler place next: the Arctic, where subsistence hunting and extreme weather must, admittedly, be physically difficult, but I hope they make the morality and psychology of food infinitely, deliciously simpler.

PS

Before the series was broadcast on the BBC, I appeared on *Richard & Judy* to talk about it. They were very nice and showed lots of clips of the show. The next day I got this email (not from Richard or Judy, I hasten to add):

'I think you are a fucking bastard for going over there and taking part in it. I hope you and whatever family you have die a fucking rotten slow and painful death because you would deserve every second of it.

My sister is 12 years old and that advert [sic] is something she will remember for the rest of her life you cunt-faced shit. Fucking drop dead now, God I'll be wishing and praying for you to drop fucking dead.'

IGLOOLIK, ARCTIC CANADA
Walrus and Pizzas

CANADA

POPULATION: 33 million

PERCENTAGE LIVING ON LESS THAN $2 A DAY: 16%

UNDP HUMAN DEVELOPMENT INDEX: 8/177

CORRUPTION PERCEPTIONS INDEX POSITION: 14/163

GDP (NOMINAL) PER CAPITA: $38,951 (14/179)

FOOD AID RECIPIENTS: n/a

IGLOOLIK

POPULATION: 1,500

GLOBAL INUIT POPULATION: 150,000

UNEMPLOYMENT IN IGLOOLIK: approx 50%

UNEMPLOYMENT IN CANADA: 6.1%

AVERAGE AGE IN NUNAVUT: 22.1 years

It's 4 a.m. I'm sitting, wide awake from jet lag here in Room 1 of the Tujormivik Inn, an isolated, snow-bound hotel in a strange land of desolate beauty. I've just snuck across the freezing cold corridor to the freezing cold bathroom where I found, sitting atop the loo, a paperback copy of *The Shining*. For any of you who were asleep during the 1980s, *The Shining* is a story of gruesome horror, blood-splattering death and spiralling insanity set in … an isolated, snow-bound hotel in a strange land of desolate beauty. As I lie awake, I wonder if this is a sign that our trip will descend into a doom-laden, Stephen King-style nightmare, and it's a long time before I eventually fall into a troubled sleep.

When I wake, I look out of the window. Oh Christ! Two questions: 1. What am I doing here? 2. How soon can I go home? This is Igloolik, an Inuit village in northern Canada, deep inside the frozen tundra of the Arctic Circle. It's very, very bleak: the land is ice-bound for much of the year, it supports almost no vegetation whatsoever and is as flat as a pancake. Temperatures drop to around -65°C in the depths of winter. The houses all look like Portakabins and are inhabited by an ancient people whose way of life is being ripped apart by the modern world. Worst of all, there's no booze. And if you're hoping to hear of a proud indigenous community coping with it all, you'll be disappointed. This is a fractured society that's struggling – and broadly failing – to cope with the pressures of the modern world: crime is high, domestic abuse rife, a 10 p.m. curfew has to be enforced to stop youths running amok, and a local paedophile was only recently locked up, having terrorized the kids of the town for years.

That said, things are looking up: Igloolik has just celebrated its first year with no suicides. This might seem little cheer to a town of only 1,300 people, but with joy in short supply around here, it'll have to do.

And why have I come to this godforsaken place? Simple: these people hunt to eat, following a way of life that has existed for thousands of years. But it's being turned upside down by global warming, the effects of which are five times more devastating here in the Arctic than in the UK. They don't hunt in your posh gents' pheasant-bagging, shooting party way, but as part of a real, dangerous, visceral and vital way of life. None of it is pretty: they hunt ringed seal, walrus, beluga and bowhead whale, caribou and the odd fish, and it's bloody and rampantly carnivorous and it'll upset your kids if they see it (it certainly upset mine). But vitally, the environment in which they hunt is a clear and tragic example of the human consequences of global warming, dramatically changing their way of life year on year. The Inuit who live here are the canaries in the global warming coalmine, and the rapid changes they have to make in their lives every year are a pretty good indication of the changes that will affect all of us sooner or later.

● ● ● ● ●

Here's a basic one-minute guide to the Inuit:

Around 150,000 Inuit live in the Arctic areas of Canada, Alaska, Greenland and Russia. Don't call them Eskimos because they just don't like it, right? They are traditionally highly carnivorous, with meat from marine mammals, fish and caribou making up a large part of their diet in a land of little vegetation. The traditional Inuit belief system is animist – all things have a form of spirit, which may be invoked by the shaman. They are said to have inhabited the Arctic for 4,500 years, living a precarious life as itinerant hunters and fishermen.

The arrival of European whalers and fishermen en masse in the early 1800s brought disease and social disruption and had a disastrous effect, but, in truth, nobody really seemed to care much about the Inuit until the cold war, when the Arctic suddenly became strategically important, and both the USA and USSR eyed it as unclaimed territory and even a possible northern crossing. Canada protested, but they couldn't really claim sovereignty over something that they didn't administer, so they began to take a belated interest in helping the Inuit.

It's easy to be sentimental about the Inuit and their plight but they, like most nations and peoples around the world, have a dark side to their history. Their past is full of bloody, vengeance-based traditional justice systems, raiding their neighbours, vicious inter-clan feuding and hostility to outsiders. It's not surprising, seeing as they survive so precariously, but still. Infanticide used to be relatively common, especially amongst the Copper Inuit, and it was usually female babies who were abandoned, causing a general population problem. The Inuit had to be tough to survive hostile places.

State intervention has been a mixed blessing: modern medical care helped significantly to raise the birth rate, but meant that traditional hunting and fishing could no longer support the increased population. Social security, housing and education brought the Inuit together into structured and static communities, but their culture was based on self-sufficient nomadic hunting and fishing, traditional skills and ancient wisdom. Self-sufficiency has been replaced by reliance on the state, and there is a general frustration that they are now a small, relatively impoverished minority, whose traditional skills, wisdom and values are of little value to the modern world.

The Canadian Inuit suffer extremely high levels of suicide (six times the national average, and concentrated amongst younger men), substance abuse, unemployment and crime.

On a more optimistic note, Inuit arts are becoming very popular around the world and tourism, mining and real estate *might* offer economic potential.

● ● ● ● ●

I take a walk on the beach, and despite the fact that it's well into winter, the sea hasn't started to freeze over. The beach is covered in snow and the ground is frozen hard, but the sea is ice-free – other than the first few metres of slush, which looks like a huge gin and tonic. If only. It shouldn't be like this in October, and the Inuit are eagerly awaiting the long-overdue, proper winter. When it does finally arrive, the sea around Igloolik will freeze over completely and 24-hour darkness will set in. This has limited appeal to my unenlightened, temperate-zone mind, although the fact that lovemaking activity is thought to increase substantially must be nice.

I meet my guides Harry, John, Conrad and Theo, who will be taking me hunting and showing me how modern Inuit live. They are cheery and confident blokes with a dry sense of humour, thick accents (especially John's, which sounds like a badly tuned two-stroke engine) and terrible teeth. Theo is clearly the guv'nor, a small, weathered guy who speaks good English, but looks me up and down like I'm a lily-livered townie who wouldn't last a minute without his help. He may have a point. We make plans to go hunting in a couple of days and return to our hotel.

Back at Tujormivik Inn I taste one of the grimmest meals I've ever had the pleasure to subsequently throw away. It's an insult to a turkey sandwich (which is really saying something) made from yesterday's Thanksgiving turkey leftovers. Chunks of turkey lie cold and glutinous between two vast slabs of the whitest of white breads, and the whole thing is drowning in a slurry of floury and flavourless white sauce. A note tells me to slip it into the microwave. I scrape the meat from the sandwich and throw the rest away. I'll need the protein and I guess that food must be hard to find in the Arctic Circle, so I'm grateful nonetheless. I fantasize about a nice pinot noir to warm my soul, but only manage to upset myself.

Beluga Whale Sashimi

I wake to hear gossip in the hotel kitchen that beluga whales have been spotted near the harbour, so I drag on my huge, duvet-like clothes and hurry down to the beach.

BAD FOOD

When I get there a beluga whale frenzy is going on and there's a sense of excitement in the air. Boats stuffed with entire families arrive back from the hunt, and throw huge hunks of whale into the shallow water, which runs red with blood and whale bits, mostly *muqtuk*, the rubbery skin and outer layer of fatty blubber, which they eat both raw and cooked.

Word has spread around town that there's been a big catch, and a steady flow of friends and family begins to arrive with carrier bags to collect a slab of *muqtuk* to take home. It's a bloody but heart-warming scene as the catch is shared throughout the whole community. The more elderly Igloolikans seem particularly pleased.

Danny, one of the younger hunters, explains how they found an adult and an infant beluga off the town harbour promontory early in the morning. They harpooned them then shot them with rifles. This is the whale-hunting season, the only time of the year when they migrate north past Igloolik and although there's international pressure to ban commercial whale-hunting, the Inuit have always maintained a right to hunt limited numbers for food.

Beluga whales are heartbreakingly beautiful – a little bigger than most dolphins, with bulbous heads, and they are elegantly and disarmingly white. They are born a slate grey but grow whiter as they mature, and it's a beautiful, ghostly, diaphanous white. Danny offers to let me try beluga *muqtuk*. This may be bad news for my career, for my relationship with my little daughters and, of course, for my stomach because, like walrus, beluga can cause a particularly nasty parasitic disease called trichinosis if they're infected with the larvae of the trichina roundworm. I ask my new friend if he's ever suffered food poisoning, but he says no.

OK, then, let's eat whale: Danny shows me how to cut off a piece of skin and cross-hatch it with my knife. When I bite into the skin it's incredibly tough: imagine ripping a piece of car tyre off with your bare teeth. At first it seems to taste of nothing at all, but then I recognize the slight fishiness of very fresh raw squid, but with a tough, rubbery texture. To be honest, I'm not sure if it's nice or not, and my teeth have great difficulty tearing through it – the Inuit must have terrible trouble as many of them have few if any teeth mainly due to their insatiable appetite for sugar. I chew hard but still can't seem to break down the skin. The fatty blubber, however, melts in my hands until they're covered in grease, leaving behind a strong gamy/fishy stench that stays with me for the whole day.

I pick up a whole tail and roll it around in my arms. It's a very graphic piece of meat, with a small, dark red core, white blubber and tough skin. Danny tells me that although they love the fat and skin, they aren't keen on the taste of the meat so they leave it for the dogs.

I thank him and take my leave, picking bits of raw whale from my teeth. I can't help it, but I feel pathetically sentimental about this beautiful creature and slightly guilty that I've eaten its flesh.

On the way back to the hotel, I drop into a small prefab unit that houses the Igloolik Co-op, the oddest supermarket I've ever set foot in. It was founded to help the Inuit profit from the fur trade, but it's now the source of pretty much everything the townspeople need. It has a down-at-heel feel and focuses on selling sweets, crisps, processed cheese, hot dogs (there are dozens of different brands, though the hot dogs themselves look identical) and, ironically, frozen food. Masses of frozen food. The entire left-hand side of the building is a wall of upright freezers packed with all manner of chips, potato shapes, pizzas and frozen burgers.

The manager, John, is a Newfoundlander (known locally as a Newfie) and speaks with a curious mixture of broad Irish brogue and American twang that makes him sound like he's putting on a silly accent. John is conscientious but pragmatic. 'People want fast food rather than fresh food,' he says, as he proudly shows me his shelves of Doritos and biscuits, and he readily admits that his biggest sellers are the chips and hot dogs. But he has more to contend with than your average Co-op: crippling transportation costs.

Everything fresh has to be sent by train to Churchill on the mainland, then flown from there to Igloolik, although there are also a couple of ships every year for long-life canned goods and non-food items. The cost of transporting this stuff is astronomical, and although some is subsidized by the government, everything is horrendously expensive. For example, basic fresh food such as potatoes, flour and apples (which nobody wants anyway), adds an extra £2 per 500 g in freight costs alone.

John admits that food in his shop is expensive, wages around here aren't very high, and in any case, most of his customers are on income support. In fact, unemployment in Igloolik is running at 50 per cent, and most of the jobs here are the result of government projects. John shakes his head at the situation. 'It's difficult, very difficult.' In these circumstances, hunting large sea mammals isn't a cultural throwback – it's a vital way of supplementing the food supply.

Arvirsiurvik

I meet Theo, Harry, Conrad and John the next day to go on a hunting expedition. The boats are stranded halfway up the beach by the tide, which Theo implies is our fault, though I'm not entirely sure how he's worked that out. We all shove and lever the boats inch by inch down into the water.

The town mayor arrives to see us off and tells me more about the effects of global warming: 'It's late October and normally there would be ice forming on the beach, but you don't see that at all. It's very late. People are seeing more and more varieties of animals that we don't usually see up here. Birds that don't normally come up here are starting to show up. The downside is that the ice is too thin in late fall for the hunters to go out and catch the seals that they normally would. People are desperate to go out but they can't.'

Although the pack ice is gathering in the sea off Igloolik, the Inuit are forced to continue using their boats to hunt (by now they should be hunting caribou on top of the ice using skidoos or dog sleds).

Theo does everything he can to make me feel barely tolerated. He eyes my cold-weather gear with disdain and treats me like the yellow-bellied southerner I am, reminding me that he and his ancestors have lived and hunted here for 4,500 years.

'You've never been somewhere as cold as -20 before, have you?' he laughs.

'Well, I did spend a week in Lapland where it was -40.'

He doesn't like hearing this, and walks off to join his cousin Harry who's standing on the gunwale of the boat. Now, the Inuit are a proud and noble people, consummate hunters and boatsmen. They are also occasionally very cack-handed, and at that exact moment Harry slides off the icy deck and plunges head first into the water. A shiver of *schadenfreude* compels me to burst out laughing (if only it had been Theo), but, it's actually pretty scary: the water temperature is below freezing (sea water can be liquid down to -2), and Harry's extremely lucky that he fell into only two feet of water. He jumps out, deeply embarrassed at his mistake in front of me, a southerner. He strips off his outer layer and tries to shrug it off as nothing. Theo scowls.

We are making our expedition in two small boats with very large engines. The one that Marc and I jump into has a tiny cockpit that just fits Harry and John, so Marc and I sit on the back deck, huddled in our voluminous jackets and salopettes.

My real Arctic expedition finally starts as we head south on a couple of open boats to spend three days hunting and camping in the wild. Theo has said we'll find walrus, maybe beluga whale, and probably lots of seal. Once we're moving, the cold numbs my chin so that I sound drunk when I try to talk.

The boats speed out towards the hunting grounds at 40–50 km/h, and every now and then we hit a patch of iceberg mixed with slush. With each bang against solid ice the boat shudders and a shiver of fear goes up my spine. The journey will take us a good three hours, but only two hours into the trip our driveshaft goes and to Theo's increasing embarrassment, we have to be towed the remainder of the way by the other boat.

When we finally arrive at Arvirsiurvik ('place to find bowhead whales'), 100 long km from Igloolik, a blizzard kicks up. This place is isolated, bleak and featureless, and Theo warns me that polar bears often wander the shoreline looking for food. There's a plywood box that serves as a survival hut, and we pitch a tent next to it in the driving snow. John hacks out a berg of sea ice half the size of himself for drinking water – it has been floating for so long that the salt has leached out of it.

In the hut I set up a small stove and make beef stroganoff for our little team from a huge packet of dehydrated survival rations mixed with melted ice. It looks wonderfully similar to vomit, tastes thoroughly disgusting, but in the circumstances it's very welcome.

There's a question I can't get out of my head: why do these people live here? It's brutally cold, the food is grim, its supply is precarious and shop-bought goods are poor quality and expensive. Theo tells me that he gets a real sense of pleasure from following a way of life that the Inuit have always led; he also enjoys the isolation of hunting on his own or with one of his brothers.

Arvirsiurvik might be isolated, but as I sit here in the tiny 2 × 3 m survival hut writing my diary there's precious little peace. My two smelly friends Marc and John are snoring like klaxons next to me; it sounds like two men throwing up every ten seconds, but I smile like a proud parent – at least they're asleep after all that cold. The thing about extreme travel and exploration is that you buy all your fancy kit and expensive flasks, torches, knives and -50°C boots, you hire your satellite phones, your BGAN satellite uplink, and you end up in a shitty little hut surrounded by sweaty gear, snoring friends, junk and damp clothing everywhere – it feels like being back at university.

BAD FOOD

I don't sleep at all during the night. Not because of the freezing cold, quite the opposite: it is sweltering hot. At some point during the night John turned the camping stove to full blast and the hut has transformed into a sweaty, airless sauna. I get out of the sleeping bag and lie on top. It doesn't help. I strip down to my underwear, but I'm still sweating like a pig, and I can't breathe. I endure it for a few hours, tossing and turning, thinking that I'm just having trouble adapting to these ancient Inuit ways. Finally I open the door a crack and let the air flood in. It's like drinking a pint of cold lager on a blazing hot summer's day. I turn the gas down and am just about to fall asleep when everyone else decides it's time to get up.

Seal Hunt

My filthy mood evaporates when I stumble out of the hut – the morning looks clear and dawn is just about to break. I watch as the sun floats free from the horizon and the sky explodes into an apocalyptic spectacle of red and orange set against the pure white snow and dark blue, berg-strewn sea. It's mesmerically beautiful. I sit there marvelling at it in silence, and I feel privileged to witness something this gorgeous. I wonder if this is the reason the Inuit don't want to leave.

Theo and I take a walk to talk about polar bears and chat about hunting. He gives me a lesson in marksmanship (I make mincemeat out of a couple of icebergs) and tells me that he was born just around the corner from this bay in an igloo. His family were traditional nomadic hunters, following migrating animals for food. He learnt to shoot very young and caught his first seal when he was just five – not because hunting was fun, but because it was crucial not to be a burden on the family's food supply and to start contributing to it as soon as possible. Here in the wilderness nothing's easy – you even need a rifle with you when you leave the hut for a pee, although with only a 20-minute rifle-training session from Theo to prepare me, I'm more likely to shoot Marc than I am to shoot a rampaging polar bear.

It's time to go hunting properly so, having eaten a little preserved whale, we get set to tackle the ultimate cute-but-edible sea mammal, the one creature that gets everyone dewy-eyed: seal. To the outrage of animal lovers around the world 300,000 seals a year are culled in Canada. The Canadian government insists that seals are not endangered and that it is necessary to control their number as commercial fish stocks are vanishing. There are 5 million still in the area and the cull will not stop until the number drops well below 4 million. Theo has no truck with the seal lovers and in any case, he's hunting to eat.

We putter around the icebergs for a couple of hours and eventually Theo spots a young seal in shallow waters – I can just see the little dark blob of its nose every now and then as it pops up for a breath of air and to see what we're up to. I keep silently wishing it to go away, but that's not really in the spirit of things. We finally get close enough for Theo and Conrad to take a shot at it but they both miss. We wander around an inlet trying to find it; it occasionally surfaces and we give chase. After five or six attempts Theo hits the seal, but it's still alive and swims away. The search continues and after a couple more shots, it's all over. The seal can't swim, but it still seems to be alive. One whack on the head with a boat pole and it's finally dead.

It isn't a particularly pretty way to go, but at least the seal had lived a free-range life. More importantly for Theo, this one animal will feed four or five families for a couple of days. I try to see it in terms of protein, despite the fact that its huge, sorrowful eyes stare at me, filling me with guilt. We draw up to some nearby pack ice and Conrad drags the seal out. Theo explains that, overall, about 25 per cent of food for Igloolik residents comes from hunting, although for poorer people it can be as high as 50 per cent. Seal is a great source of iron and vitamin B, but the use of blubber for oil and lighting is becoming irrelevant now that most houses in Igloolik have mains electricity.

Theo and his nephews skin and butcher the seal, eating pieces still warm and steaming in the cold as they work. It's a gruesomely bloody spectacle. Theo skins it, although he says that after Paul McCartney became associated with seal-protesting, the price for the pelts nose-dived, destroying a source of income for them, and stripping away another layer of their culture.

The guys all cut away at the carcass and eat hunks of it raw – Harry and Conrad are fond of the liver, while Theo prefers ribs. John hacks out an eyeball and eats it whole. He offers one to me, but I decline, opting instead for a chunk of meat. It's strange to eat still-warm seal, and I can't say that I relish the idea, but it tastes like fine, well-hung beef fillet and not at all fishy.

I don't feel guilty any more, and it would have been a far greater tragedy to let any of the animal go to waste.

Walrus

The following day we head out in search of walrus. Theo says that he had seen hundreds of them a few days ago, so he's hopeful that we'll find something. However, the trip isn't a great success. After hours of searching around, we finally find a dead one floating in the sea. Theo thinks it may have been shot the day before, but escaped its hunter. He decides to take it back to our base to use as bear bait – the idea is that it'll stop the bears from attacking us.

We drag the walrus into shallow water. He's enormous and must weigh nearly a tonne. His tusks are only 30 cm long, unlike those of fully grown males, but he's still a marvellous sight. Most extraordinary are his whiskers, which look like they are made out of thick plastic. Theo says that these used to be sold as opium-pipe cleaners, but the bottom's fallen out of the market.

We drag the walrus onto the beach using pulleys, and then I help to hack it apart. It's strange butchering a vast mammal whose bone structure I don't understand, and it has an immensely strong hide, slightly furry and tough as hell to cut into. Once you get through the hide, there are several centimetres of fat until you get to the meat, which lies in huge, amorphous deposits in places I don't understand. I cut into it to separate it into manageable hunks as Harry sets his sights on its penis bone – a huge 60-cm-long club that sits mainly inside the boar. It has to be stripped of skins and sinews, but when it's done, the penis bone is eye wateringly large. Theo goes for the skull, an even more difficult and gruesome task, but one that will reward him to the tune of $44 per kilo.

After the effort of such large-scale butchery we sit down to snack on some *muqtuk* that the guys have brought with them. There's beluga meat and some raw frozen caribou meat which is utterly delicious, like strong, well-hung beef. I'm definitely beginning to feel a bit queasy – not from the strangeness, but from a lack of fruit and vegetables. I think my breath is beginning to smell a little, and possibly my skin is too.

Back in the hut we roll out our caribou skins and our massive sleeping bags, known as Big Agnes, with an inflatable bottom and -20 insulation. I'm hoping to God that I'll be able to sleep tonight.

Stranded

I sleep briefly, until John's snoring really picks up steam and wakes me up again. I'm starting the day with a pounding headache and a deep sense of resentment, but I hope this will pass.

At first light, we look outside. The good news is that the boats are still there. The bad news is that it's blowing a crushing, lip-shattering gale, with a bit of snow thrown in for good measure. We're not going anywhere. The walrus meat hasn't been touched by the polar bears. I had promised Daisy that I'd see bears and bring one back for her – I hoped that a picture would suffice –but it doesn't look like it is going to happen. With nothing to do and nowhere to go, we all go back to bed, but John's still honking and spluttering so I still can't sleep.

My heart goes out to his poor wife. She must be overjoyed every time he goes out hunting. 'Off you pop, love,' she must say. 'Of course I'll miss you. Yeah, bye. Thank Christ for that, I'm going back to bed.'

We're well and truly stuck here for the day, and the ice seems to be building up around the boats in the bay. Help! I really don't fancy being here until spring.

● ● ● ● ●

Oh shit! We're trapped. It seems no one was listening to my plea last night. When we wake up in the morning and look outside we find that three icebergs weighing around 4 tonnes each have jammed the boats in during the night, and they are now stranded halfway up the shore. Added to that, the winter ice seems to have arrived en masse, piling up in the bay around us, and it's on the verge of cutting us off completely. The only gap is a couple of times the width of the boat, but the ice is shifting and building up all the time. And if that isn't bad enough, there's a terrible fog that would make the journey back to Igloolik treacherous. It all adds up to big trouble. I really don't want to spend the winter here.

We have only one option: we start attacking the icebergs with axes, harpoons and anything else we can lay our hands on. Slowly, slowly, chunk by chunk we break apart the ice, Marc showing a particular aptitude for the task. By lunchtime we've made little headway and in any case the tide is going out so even if we do get through the ice we still have to get the boat to the water. The weather remains a big problem, though, and as a reminder of the danger, just up the hill from our hut there's a monument to a group of seven people who died nearby while trying to get home in the fog.

By early afternoon I'm exhausted, but if we persevere it might just be possible to break through enough ice to make a dash for Igloolik before dark – as long as the floating icebergs in the bay don't block us in.

Finally we clear two of the icebergs, and after some vein-throbbing yanking on a rope and pulley blocks attached to a nearby rock, we inch the boat across the shore into the water. Just as my strength gives out, the boat lurches into the shallows and floats, to cheers from all of us. I'm ready to collapse, but we still have to drag our kit down to the boats. Eventually we're ready to go, and luckily the gap in the ice is just clear enough, so we squeeze through and say goodbye to our little hunting station.

The fog clears to let us out, but as soon as we get into open sea it returns, along with a snowstorm. It's too late now – we can't turn back, so we float through field after field of slush and bergs and it seems as if the sea has completely changed its nature since we left Igloolik; it now feels hostile.

Eventually I can see Igloolik as a dark smudge on the skyline, but there's a problem: the pack ice has made it to Igloolik before us. I'm gutted, after all that; to be stuck out here doesn't bear thinking about. John thinks he might be able to force a way through, so we inch forward, bumping and grinding the boat against ice and rock, shoving them aside with our feet and hands, until finally we make it to a small jetty. I've never been so elated to arrive at a bunch of huts in my life.

Rotten Walrus

By the next day the miserable weather and the ice in the bay clogs the shore and traps all the boats. Wind is blasting across Igloolik, so we have to stay inside watching terrible Canadian TV and snapping at each other. Everybody's in a foul mood. To alleviate the boredom I decide to tag along with the world's most northerly pizza delivery boy.

A few years back the Tujormivik Hotel bought a pizza oven and now the chef, Charlie, makes up to 6,000 pizzas per year. They are expensive at $35 for two, but they are, after all, delivered by snowmobile. You just call Charlie and he'll make you a pepperoni, Hawaiian or Arctic char confection. It's your basic Dominos-style, thick-crust number, laden with cheap cheese and swimming in fat, but the good people of Igloolik love them.

Charlie packs us off with pizzas to deliver, and we hop onto a couple of snowmobiles – one for me and one for Marc. Our destination is apartment 43C, which houses three gorgeous little kids, three sweet ladies and the largest television I have ever seen in my life. Pizza is a once-a-week treat for them, and the kids all say it's their favourite food. Sylvia, their mother, says that although traditional country food (like seal, walrus and caribou) is still important to her and to Inuit culture as a whole, fast food is also an important part of their life.

'It's not really healthy, but it's a real treat and this summer animals seem to be even more scarce, so we've been having more store-bought food then usual.'

Her kids say they don't like igunak, although they are keen on caribou, seal and walrus – and Coca-Cola. Sylvia sighs. 'Back when our parents were trying to survive it was a constant struggle from day to day not knowing if they would have enough food or enough heat, and now it's like, "We live in a house, we're already warm, we've got food on our shelves and everything else. What else is there to worry about?" Nowadays I see kids into computers, or watching TV or playing games; they're not really paying attention to our culture any more. And because of that, trying to keep the traditional skills is getting harder and harder.'

Sylvia works as a nurse at the local clinic, and she's glad for the opportunity and the money, yet healthcare is one of the main reasons the Inuit began to abandon their nomadic lifestyle to gather together in static communities. She voices the confusion I've sensed since I got here: she doesn't want to lose her culture and traditions, yet she and her kids are busy embracing a shabby simulacrum of the modern world in an isolated, remote community where only a small proportion of its benefits are realistically attainable.

The bad weather continues into the next day so hunting is impossible again. Instead, Harry invites me to his house to try some igunak, a unique local delicacy. Harry lives at home with his mum and dad and various younger members of his extended family. The house is similar to all the others in Igloolik – a Terrapin Hut-like construction on stilts.

When I arrive there's no sense of ceremony and they don't get up or say hello. The TV stays on, and there are a couple of squeaking UHF radios – one for emergencies and keeping tabs on their family in boats and another for town gossip. His parents are unilingual – they speak only Inuktitut, the local Inuit language full of clucks and clicks – but they are sweet and friendly.

Harry explains that it's rare to have strangers in your home – the Inuit have enough on their hands dealing with their vast extended families, so who needs the bother of strangers?

He takes me outside to fetch the igunak. I've never been shocked by a slab of meat before, but this is a revelation: out of his shed Harry lugs a vast hunk of mouldly, slurry-covered meat about the size of your average engine block, wrapped in polythene. He unwraps it and instantly a foul and loathsome stench rises up, but before I can vomit over him, Harry starts attacking it with an axe. Call me naive, but it's the first time I've ever seen an axe used to cut a steak. He hacks off the end, pronouncing it fit only for dogs, and simultaneously the smell gets ten times worse. Ah, yes, he says, nose twitching in what looks like olfactory ecstasy. He hacks off a huge 4-kilo section of the middle, and we take it inside. He lays out a piece of mucky cardboard on the kitchen floor and suddenly everyone in the house, plus a bunch of strangers who appear out of nowhere, fall upon it in what I can only describe as a frenzy while I look on in amazement.

Igunak is a speciality of Igloolik and is famous throughout the Arctic region. It's made from huge slabs of raw walrus meat that are rolled up, wrapped in plastic and secured with rope. These are then buried under piles of rocks and left for a year. First they rot during the summer months, then as winter sets in, they freeze. The idea is that they freeze before botulism takes hold – either way, the stuff offers up a fearsome stench, a little like durian fruit, but mainly like … well … imagine what rotting walrus might taste like: you don't really need ever to have smelt it – your imagination will be right on the money. This stuff is vintage 2005, now over a year old, and it is pronounced the bee's knees by Harry's folks.

It's valuable stuff – this batch is worth $500 Canadian, and everyone in town knows about it. They'd heard that some bloke from London had convinced Harry to open a batch, and after a decent delay of about five minutes, they all start arriving and phoning for a chunk.

I kneel on the floor next to Harry and dig in – no one looks up to offer me advice about which bit to eat so I grab the nearest piece. Someone throws me a knife and I slice off a few chunks. It tastes, frankly, disgusting. This might not sound surprising to you, but I have a pretty high tolerance for strange tastes and odd foods, so I was really hoping that I'd enjoy it. I try another piece, but no. Really, really disgusting. I persevere and keep eating more and more of it, hoping that I'll break through my disgust and start enjoying it. No. I try a bit of the intestines. No, that's worse. Harry warns me not to eat too much – first timers often make themselves sick on it.

You don't say.

I wonder if igunak is just an elaborate joke that they play on journalists, but the young kids are tucking in too – it's a kind of igunak madness.

'Why do you like this stuff?' I ask.

'It's an acquired taste,' Theo says. 'We grew up on it, and when the new batch comes out at the start of the winter season, it's a cause for huge celebration.'

After 30 minutes or so, everyone collapses, spent from ingesting this toxic waste, and then more neighbours arrive. Just as when I arrived, there is no ceremony: they just drop their coats and shoes, smile at no one in particular, and hunker down on the floor to eat their fill. One elderly woman calls up on the UHF radio to ask for one of the young lads to bring some over as she can't walk.

● ● ● ● ●

The stormy weather continues , and I'm overcome by the desire to go home. I've tried to like Igloolik, I really have. But the truth is it's a bloody miserable place. Physically, it's a grid of terrapin huts clinging to the side of a small slope. There's no vegetation and no physical features other than snow and ice, the weather is gruesome and there's nothing to do.

Marc and I are thoroughly disconsolate by now, so it's time to crack open the emergency supplies. Igloolik is a dry town and it's illegal for visitors to bring in alcohol. Luckily for us, having been warned that if the weather came in we'd be stuck for days, we'd decided to smuggle in a few litres of hard liquor, which we now drink like naughty teenagers. It transpires that Marc had scarfed all the bourbon himself one particularly depressing evening a little while back, so we mix the gin with 7-Up to make it vaguely palatable. It's a little like drinking lighter fluid (especially at the strength that Marc pours it).

That night we drink rather a lot, and when we wake up, temperatures have plummeted to -25 and it seems as though winter may finally be here.

Although extreme cold sounds like bad news to me, the town is abuzz with excitement. These people are wired differently: they genuinely love the cold and the new hunting opportunities it brings. It's very disturbing that winter is about a month late – I've noticed similar disruption to weather patterns back home, but up here in the Arctic Circle the shift is much more dramatic.

Theo takes us out hunting on snowmobiles, but the trip doesn't go well. We don't find any animals – Harry says they are confused by the shifts in the weather. Theo does his best to keep things interesting by paddling out onto a patch of unfrozen water in a precarious-looking coracle-type kayak, but you can tell that his heart's not in it.

We sit staring out beyond the ice at the ocean, scanning the water in vain for walrus. Quite what Theo would do if he saw one, I don't know. I don't fancy his chances of shooting one from the shore, let alone dragging it in using his tiny boat, but I'm sure he has a plan. In any case, we watch in vain for a couple of freezing hours. My feet are beginning to get that searing cold pain from standing on the ice, but I daren't complain in case it gives these hardened hunters more reason to pity my pathetic southern ways.

To my relief, we finally move off and drive for an hour around the island, looking for a place to hunt. We stop every now and then, but we find nothing. My face is so cold from the wind chill that it feels like it's about to snap off. I try to ignore it, but when I smile, it looks like I'm doing a vampire impersonation and my lips are in danger of disintegrating. I give up trying to communicate and just sit there. Then Theo's machine breaks down, belching clouds of thick smoke and he has to abandon it. Soon afterwards, the skis on Harry's machine collapse and we have to cannibalize parts from another machine to get it going. Eventually it breaks down irreparably, so we tie it to the last working machine and head away from the hunting grounds.

It's fair to say that our snowmobile hunting trip is an unqualified disaster, and we limp back into town. I sense that Theo's getting grumpy, although John and Harry are in good spirits. Marc and I scuttle back into the Tujormivik Hotel and our faces slowly defrost. I am secretly glad that there is only one more day of hunting left before I start the long hike home.

But at our early meeting with Theo the next day it's immediately apparent that he's an angry man. There seem to be two reasons for this: first, that the snowmobile breaking down was our fault, which is an interesting reading of events (we forced them to drive on terrain that was unsuitable, apparently); and second, that one of Theo's friends told him about a news article I'd written. Nothing to do with me writing about the social problems in Igloolik (which I had been worried about), and everything to do with the fact that I said it had taken them seven or eight rifle shots before they killed the seal.

So Theo is humiliated and apparently furious with me, and he's come for his expenses for having helped us. I wander off into town, keen not to cause more trouble. I go on a little tour of the town with one of the two policemen who keep the peace here. He tells me that domestic violence is one of the big problems, but the townspeople are to some extent self-governing. He's about to go south on holiday, and he can't wait for a beer.

I wander down to the bay, which is now packed full of ice. After the ice had blown in, the sky cleared and everything froze over. The hunting season is finished for anyone whose boat is still here in the bay – there's no way of getting boats out now as the ice stretches for hundreds of metres.

The change in the climate is dramatic this far north, and summer sea ice is melting at a rate of 9.6 per cent per decade, which is bad news if you're a polar bear or an ice-dwelling seal. But the most disturbing part of the trip is not the killing and eating of large sea mammals, but quite the opposite: the complete lack of them. Theo, for all his grumpiness, is one of the best hunters around, but although we had modern boats and rifles at our disposal, all we managed to find during two weeks of hunting was one small seal and a dead walrus. It's a huge amount of effort for precious little return, and a hunting-based culture may well be doomed in a place where people's cupboards are full of cans of subsidized food, and a pizza is just a subsidized phone call away.

● ● ● ● ●

To torture myself with contrasts, I'm off somewhere really hot again now. I've been telling my family that this one's going to be really difficult, but deep inside I'll admit that I'm over the moon. How bad can the Caribbean really be? I'm heading for Haiti.

HAITI
Hell's Kitchen

POPULATION: 10 million

PERCENTAGE LIVING ON LESS THAN $2 A DAY: 80%

UNDP HUMAN DEVELOPMENT INDEX: 154/177

CORRUPTION PERCEPTIONS INDEX POSITION: 163/163

GDP (NOMINAL) PER CAPITA: $528 (150/179)

FOOD AID RECIPIENTS: n/a

MALNUTRITION: 47% of the population

It's a hot sticky night on Ocean Drive, the frouffed, bouffed, promenading fleshpot of Miami's South Beach, Florida. From my plate a lobster stares forlornly at the Ferraris, Range Rovers and Hummers that crawl the strip. The lobster seems to have been involved in a strange military torture experiment – it's been turned inside out, but is still attached to its shell. I sincerely hope this didn't happen whilst it was still alive.

To the casual observer, Ocean Drive is the epitome of brash American glamour: beautiful whitewashed art nouveau buildings oozing glitz and cash, facing a glorious wide beach of white sand along which ladies with taut bodies and big hair saunter. Up close, though, the ladies and the buildings alike seem tacky, and the restaurants offer shabby food, dreadful service and spectacularly high prices.

The sloshing of filthy lucre around here verges on the obscene, but in a contrast that would be hilarious if it weren't so tragic, just a couple of hours beyond that white sand and through the sweaty night lies Haiti, one of the poorest places on the planet. I'm hoping to get there tomorrow, and the lobster sitting in front of me is a heavy-handed gesture to help me feel the contrast.

• • • • •

After a series of airport cock-ups (US airport staff are almost as nasty as their odious immigration colleagues), I miss my flight to Port-au-Prince, Haiti's capital, along with about 50 Haitians who all arrived on time but stood in a queue for hours. The airline doesn't seem to give a toss – it's already got our money, so why should it care?

Stepping out of the stale, cool air of the plane into the shit-flavoured sauna that is Haiti, I am almost immediately covered in a slime of sweat that I know is unlikely to dry off for the next two weeks. So it's with gratitude that I hop into a huge white Land Cruiser lent to us by the UN's World Food Programme. Charity workers across the world despise the UN for driving these big expensive cars around poor countries, but I confess to a guilty relief each time I get in them – they can negotiate God-awful roads, they're safe, clean and even mildly air-conditioned. Attached to the bull bars is a vast short-wave radio antenna, lending a slight (possibly false) sense of security. When you're working in difficult places these vehicles make life just a little bit better. I'll be spending a fair amount of my time here with the UN military and the WFP, so I hope I'll get a couple of days' use of these.

A Brief History of Haiti

We don't hear much about Haiti apart from tales of voodoo and the latest military coup, so here's the potted guide: Haiti has been given a rough ride by the world since 1492 when it was discovered by Columbus. The kindly Spanish managed to annihilate all the native Taino Amerindians within 25 years, but kept the place going as a handy staging post. In the 17th century, the French took charge, importing tens of thousands of African slaves to work the forestry and sugar-related industries.

In 1804, after a brutal struggle, Haiti had a brief high point when it became the first black republic to declare independence, having hosted the only successful slave rebellion and defeated Napoleon as well as the English and the Spanish. But it was pretty much downhill from there, when Haiti proved less of a match for the world's businessmen. It was totally isolated by slave-holding countries eager to avoid their own rebellions, and then devastated by the French who refused to recognize independence unless an indemnity of 150 million francs was paid to compensate French plantation owners (they do look after their farmers, the French). The indemnity was paid, but the government was thrown into debt and the economy was crippled, and it's never really recovered. Haiti has been in a state of perpetual poverty and political violence ever since.

The USA has mucked about in Haiti a fair bit: they refused to recognize independence until 1862 and then, in 1915, worried about growing German influence, the USA invaded, occupied and set about improving the country ... to no avail. The 1930 Forbes Commission concluded that 'the social forces that created [the social instability] still remain – poverty, ignorance, and the lack of a tradition or desire for orderly free government'. Roosevelt got fed up and pulled out in 1934, setting off a cycle of vicious, brutal and corrupt leaderships that inevitably ended in coups, including those of Papa Doc (François Duvalier, elected on an official count of 1.32 million votes for, 0 against) and his son Baby Doc (Jean-Claude Duvalier), two of the nastiest and most corrupt leaders to grace the world stage. Jean-Bertrand Aristide briefly came into power before a military junta decided it knew better. After three years of hell, the USA invaded again in 1994 and brought Aristide back. His rule eventually descended into corruption and violence and, would you believe it, another coup in 2004 ... whereupon 1,000 US Marines arrived to help. Again.

Haiti is a social relativist's dream, a benchmark of misery by which we can all judge our lives to be so much better. It is the poorest country in the western hemisphere and aid and donations from abroad make up nearly 25 per cent of GDP. Plus, if you take a quick look at the stats at the beginning of the chapter you will notice that it stands at no. 163 out of 163 countries in the Transparency International Corruption Perceptions Index. Enough said.

When I arrive I get an update on the security situation here: don't drive after dark, don't go out in the city after dark, don't enter Cité Soleil, the sprawling slum that houses the poorest Haitians in Port-au-Prince, and don't eat the food. Great.

Embed with MINUSTAH

Next morning I wake early and head straight for the UN army base. It's my first ever military embed, a strange arrangement whereby journalists live and patrol with soldiers in order to get a realistic impression of what life is like on the front line. Here in Haiti the clumsily named MINUSTAH, the United Nations Stabilization Mission in Haiti, has been struggling to control the armed gangs of the country since it was created in 2004. There are 7,000 troops (mostly Brazilian) stationed here, trying to restore order in a country where the government is too weak, poor and under-resourced to do the job itself. Before the UN arrived there were up to 300 kidnappings here every month, and gun battles regularly raged on the streets of the capital, including an enormous one a few months before my arrival.

I get a cold but polite reception at the MINUSTAH barracks. Unsurprising really as a few months previously a BBC crew had managed to get an interview with their commander on the pretext of asking about the progress of the UN operations, then sprang allegations of child sex offences implicating Brazilian soldiers. As a result the BBC name is synonymous with excrement here at the Brazilian base.

I meet Colonel Pedrosa, who will be running my trip. The Brazilians run an army unlike any I've ever seen before. UK and US troops are obsessed with hierarchy, saluting endlessly as they move around a barracks, and keeping the place in the sort of strict, impersonal order you'd rather hope your army insists upon. Not the Brazilians. They wander around base hugging and waving, joking with and taking the mickey out of their superiors, and there's not a salute to be seen during my entire morning here. They're a little like the nascent Afghan army I met in Kabul, but without the moustaches.

They kit me out with a flak jacket: hot, very heavy and not actually offering much protection. There are two metal plates the height and width of an A4 sheet of paper, and 1 cm thick. There's one at the front and one at the back. The rest of the jacket is just a structure to keep those plates in place. The idea is that they protect the major internal organs which, if shot with a high-velocity rifle, could fail and kill you. You can live without an arm or a leg, but you really don't want a bullet in the guts. It's not that much of a consolation when you're heading into the unknown, I can tell you, and in the feverish heat of Haiti, it's the last thing I fancy wearing.

The ensemble is topped with a thick, heavy, bright blue helmet with UN stencilled on the side in white. It's so heavy that I feel a little like a weeble. They make soldiers look harsh but fair, protectors of the people, but with a killing-machine edge. I, however, look like a pillock.

EATING WITH AMERICA'S NEIGHBOURS

I sit in the back of a pick-up truck next to a soldier who faces backwards, scanning his gun around the streets as we head to a secondary base. Here we get in one of three huge white APCs (Armoured Personnel Carriers). From afar, these look like high-tech fighting machines, but once inside I realize they're just noisy, scorching-hot steel boxes on wheels. I poke my head out of the top and get a great view and an odd feeling of power ... mixed with the uncomfortable knowledge that I stand out like a big white weebly target.

We head off in convoy towards the sprawling slum area at the centre of the city where a quarter of a million people live in squalor and extreme deprivation. Our commanding officer, Captain Ferrarez, shows me the divot that was blown out of his rifle when he led a raid a few months ago. He takes me on a tour of military checkpoints and observation posts and then we enter the notorious Cité Soleil.

Cité Soleil aka Hell on Earth

I must admit that before I arrived I had read lots about Haiti and it was clear that life here was poor and difficult, but at the back of my mind I kept thinking, 'Yeah, but it's a Caribbean island, for crying out loud. How bad can life really be?'

Cité Soleil feels like the nearest I have come to hell. It's dark, crammed, stinking and wretched, and every house, school or water tower is covered in a terrifying acne of bullet-holes. I've never seen anything like it – not even in Afghanistan. In the areas where the major shoot-outs have taken place, there's a concentration of bullet-holes around windows and doors, but it's not just a few holes, it's *thousands*. Rubbish and excrement lies in piles on the streets, children run around naked and all the time the sun beats down. There's little food, no hygiene and scant hope of a way out for people here. There are few jobs on Haiti and no sign of the investment that might provide jobs – mainly because the place is so corrupt and unstable that you'd have to be either insane or in possession of your own militia to feel confident investing money here. There's no running water or sanitation, and with no jobs, these people seem to have barely any possessions at all. They seem to be living a life stripped of human dignity, enduring appalling conditions. Everywhere I go, kids and adults alike hassle me for money, and I don't blame them.

Most places I've visited have had a deep conflict at their heart, whether it's religious, political or cultural. It is often infuriating and brutal – as in Afghanistan and Burma – but there are reasons and structures to the conflict that can be dissected and understood. Here in Cité Soleil the conflict is chaotic: unpredictable gang warfare fed by absolute poverty and desperation in a place where hope has dried up. And although it's deplorable, it's also understandable that people with no hope turn to violence. This is a place where extortion and theft aren't just social problems – they are also an accepted means of employment: a kind of subsistence money-farming.

The Brazilians are different from your usual UN peacekeepers because rather than patrolling and running for cover when things get a little tasty, they have decided to meet the gangsters headon, mounting aggressive raids using a fearsome amount of firepower in the heart of the slums where the Haitian police haven't dared to go in years. This has landed them in hot water at times, especially when, on 6 July 2005, they raided the base of a 'gangster' called Dread Wilme. In the ensuing firefight, during which an astonishing 22,000 bullets were fired, the dreaded Dread was killed, but so were several civilians (estimates ranged from five to 80). MINUSTAH admitted that civilians were killed during the raid but confused the issue by claiming that 'gangs were seen killing civilians following MINUSTAH's operation' and that the UN acted in self-defence. Other operations include a major gun battle in February 2007, and there is often talk of inevitable collateral damage.

I suppose, given that the assaults against the gangsters seem to have been effective, and therefore there will hopefully be less violence and fewer deaths and kidnappings in Cité Soleil, that the ends could justify the means, but that won't pacify the relatives of the innocent dead. And I can't help thinking that gangs don't disappear when you kill the leader, they just go underground with their weapons and hatred. And in any case, with an organization as informal and unregulated as a gang, how do you know who's in and who's not? That said, the Haitian police have just managed to enter Cité Soleli for the first time in years under the protection of MINUSTAH, and the gangs appear to have been largely dismantled for the time being. They may be lurking underground, ready to surface as soon as MINUSTAH goes home, but at least there's a sense of stability that hasn't existed here in decades.

I ask if I can walk and chat to some of the residents, so we get out of the APCs and go for a weird sort of stroll: ahead of us crawls one APC, I walk surrounded by a dozen heavily armed soldiers, and we are followed by the other two APCs. It doesn't make for calm nerves, taking a walk amidst such terrifying firepower, but I get the sense that no one's going to mess with us.

The residents stare at the soldiers, but I can't tell if it's resentment or respect in their eyes. I chat to several women who say, 'We thank God they are here,' and that they have restored order, that they couldn't walk the streets before they arrived. The soldiers punch fists and give high-fives to people as they walk, the kids seem happy to see us and men grin nervously and wave. Mind you, if a group of heavily armed men trooped past my house and waved, I think I'd probably wave back with a nervous grin whether they were gangsters or UN soldiers. The kids pull at my bumbag and pockets trying to make me give them some cash, but the soldiers warn me not to give anyone money or else there'll be a riot, and people might very well die as a result.

I find a woman selling strange clay plates, which turn out to be mud cakes, made from dirt and eaten as a delicacy. I buy a few and they taste very much as you'd imagine clay to taste, but with a strange gloopy, almost chocolatey consistency. It's quite a nice sensation although it does clog up your mouth. Apparently the cakes are full of minerals and are especially good for pregnant women, although people sometimes also make a face cream sludge from them.

We stop for the night in Strongpoint 16, an old market building slap bang in the middle of the worst area of the slums. It has been covered in sandbags and camouflage netting and taken over by the army. There must be 20 of us here, and we each have a small bunk-bed in the open air on the top floor of the building. I feel very vulnerable, both to the mosquitoes of Cité Soleil and the strongmen of the slums who could, if they wanted to, overrun us with ease as there are only a couple of guards on duty through the night.

Dinner is delivered from the main barracks: cold feijoiada, the classic Brazilian meat, beans and gravy, a dish that always creates copious flatulence in my system. It's gratefully received by all of us, but for my hosts' sake, I'm pleased we'll be sleeping in the open air.

And then, just as we're settling down, for some insane reason the commander decides to take us on a night patrol through the slums. Night patrol? Eh? This is the most dangerous slum on the planet, and we're going to cruise around it at night? I know they've got a job to do and all that, but this seems like a terribly bad idea.

Out on the streets, the mood of the people has changed and I can hear the occasional abusive shout from the shadows. This time we don't venture out of the APCs, but drive through the slums pointing searchlights into corners, illuminating people eating, drinking, some just sitting in the dark and, at one point, a man and woman who look distinctly like we've rumbled them having sex. Such is life lived under the concerned searchlights of a UN peacekeeping mission.

We spin around the slum's main streets, making the MINUSTAH presence felt, but the soldiers become a little concerned because there's a bad smell in the APC – possibly engine trouble, but with strong top notes of dog mess. I check my boots with the rest of them, but shake my head innocently, and we decide to return to Strongpoint 16 without delay.

Despite the mosquitoes, the open air and the cacophonous banging and crashing of the slums, I manage to get some sleep and wake only at dawn when the sun peers over the sandbags to burn through my eyelids. The soldiers all wake at the same time and tuck into a breakfast of long-life yoghurt, crackers and honey.

I sit with one of the soldiers for a while, watching the day unfolding from his lookout point. The people on the streets below are in a hurry, starting the day's task of scraping together enough money to buy something to eat. If this sounds over-dramatic, it's not. When you have next to nothing, the task of getting food for yourself and your family becomes the most important thing in the world. But with no opportunities for employment, the chronically poor will do anything they can, often starting with scavenging. One man has salvaged a crumpled hat from somewhere, and he walks along the road trying to sell it to everyone he meets. A great many people walk the streets with a shoe perched on their head, and I wondered if this was some sort of cult of supplication until my guide Mario explains to me that the shoes are for sale.

We go on patrol again and the streets are full of people with something to sell. Wherever I walk, people stop me to try to sell me something: usually cigarettes, clothes or charcoal but a fair few more obscure items too, such as a motorcycle headlamp, an ancient porn mag and at one point an artificial leg. I was quite tempted by the leg, actually. And if you don't want to buy, they'll simply ask you for money, relentlessly harassing, pleading, pulling at your clothes and putting arms on your shoulders. Everyone wants money, just a little something to get by. And if you've got a camera, they will try to step in front of whatever you're filming, and then demand money for having been in your shot. It's irritating and intimidating but completely understandable: if I had nothing, I'd be pounding the streets doing whatever I could to buy my food, and if some English bloke turned up with a camera that was worth more than I was going to earn in my entire lifetime, I'd feel well within my rights to tap him for some cash.

I speak to a young man who tells me that two days ago he and a few friends managed to break down a car for scrap and earned a dollar, but his local gangster found out and when he returned home he was ordered to hand over the cash at gunpoint, and there was nothing he could do. This is how life is in a country where 70 per cent of the workforce is either jobless or under-employed.

The northern section of Cité Soleil spreads along the coast and we wander towards it to get a sense of the scale of the place. From afar, I wonder if this is where slum-dwellers come to breathe in some fresh air, take a break from the pressures of slum life, perhaps even take a swim. As we arrive, however, I realize how ridiculous that would be. There's no beach, no sand, and the seafront is basically a mound of rubbish that hasn't yet been washed away. One of the horrible burdens of the slums is the lack of rubbish collection, so whatever doesn't lie around in heaps on the streets is washed slowly but inexorably towards the sea. The water is a rotting swamp of filth, shit, oil and insects, and Cité Soleil just stops abruptly at the water's edge, excreting and leaking its essence into the Caribbean.

In any case, rather than being drawn to the ocean people here shy away from it, preferring to huddle next to other houses for protection against the typhoons and hurricanes that regularly rip through the area. Mario tells me that no one, not even the fishermen around here, can swim.

Finally, we help out with a 'hearts and minds' mission run by the army to distribute food and hope in the slums. It's a big old cheesy PR exercise, but seems to be very popular: about 100 soldiers take over a building and set up a kitchen to dispense hot-dog rolls filled with mince. Hundreds of people turn up, although the rules are strictly kids first. Over half the children in Haiti are malnourished, so they are understandably eager to join the queue, some of them coming in several times over. I help to hand out the food for a while then chat to some of the kids who've been trying to steal extra food.

I ask them if things have improved since the UN soldiers arrived. A little girl says, 'A load of gang guys were walking around last night with machetes. They slashed some poor people.'

'Do you think most of the kids in Cité Soleil are hungry?

Boy 1: 'Yes, and many of our parents have died.'

Girl: 'My father is dead.'

Boy 2: 'My father is dead.'

Boy 3: 'My father is dead as well.'

I don't know how many, if any, of the kids are telling the truth, but they're only about six years old, so it's a strange world that they are living in to make this stuff up.

As well as handing out food, the soldiers throw a party to get the locals on side. Two very energetic and very irritating clowns bounce around taking the mickey out of all the adults, to the squealing delight of the kids. A DJ sets up his sound system and plays music that gets everyone dancing, there's a fella giving free buzz-cuts, and someone else handing out free bottles of water.

The UN forces aren't aiming to make any long-term structural improvements – they don't have the resources to lay on a spread like this very often, but if it makes the Cité Soleil residents happy and friendly towards them, their work will be a shade easier and less dangerous. And it's no bad PR exercise for them either, especially when they need to counter the bad press over their actions here in the slums.

Finally I'm taken back to the MINUSTAH base and I hand in my helmet and flak jacket with a sense of gratitude mixed with relief.

● ● ● ● ●

Just outside Port-au-Prince is a huge sugar cane farm. During French rule Haiti was the richest colony in the New World and the world's leading sugar cane producer. Half a million slaves were brought here to work the plantations. I join Jacques, a sugar cane cutter who has been working these fields for 20 years, and offer to lend a hand. His friend lends me his machete and Jacques shows me how to hack the thick canes at an angle near to the base. It's extremely difficult, sweaty work, and the vegetation is full of bugs, flies and snakes that don't take very kindly to me destroying their homes.

Jacques makes $5 a day, which for this kind of work seems like a tiny amount of money, but as 78 per cent of the population live on less than $2 a day, he's pleased for the opportunity. After a while we take a break and chew on some cane to refresh ourselves – Jacques says that he eats this stuff all day – but when I get back to hacking the cane, I realize that the sticky, sugary sheen all over me has made me infinitely more attractive to the bugs.

Haiti used to produce 6 million tonnes of sugar cane a year, but the big farms have mostly disappeared due to political turmoil, gangsterism and extortion. The woman who runs this plantation initially agrees to talk to me, but halfway through our interview she gets scared and has a change of heart, pleading with me not to show or name her. Her father-in-law and two of her brothers-in-law have been killed by gangsters and she runs the daily risk of being kidnapped simply because she has a successful business. Her minders arrive and insist that she leaves for her home before it gets dark.

Voodoo

That night we are invited to a voodoo ceremony. Although Haiti is overwhelmingly Catholic, the vast majority of Haitians practise some form of voodoo, assumed to be rooted in the animist practices of the West African slaves brought over by the French. I'm not particularly keen on toying with voodoo, although not as anxious as my wife, who is terrified of my dabbling in this kind of thing and is half-expecting me to return biting the heads off chickens. I've assured her that all those reports of animal sacrifice are just myths.

I meet Max Beauvoir, a Western-educated biochemist turned voodoo priest who runs a temple on the outskirts of Port-au-Prince. He is surrounded by women dressed in white with red headscarves who smile and hug me. I'm already feeling a little intimidated, not least by the sudden and violent downpour that soaks us all in seconds. We retreat to Max's temple and he leads the singing, chanting and clapping, alongside the drinking of hefty spirits and some odd candle ceremonies. Four men drum at a ferocious pace and the women wail and dance, dragging me along to join them in some undisguisedly suggestive dancing. I'm beginning to feel carried away by some indistinct spiritual awakening, although it's probably just a combination of alcohol and trepidation. And the suggestive dancing.

We go back outside, and there's a great deal more dancing, drumming, singing and wailing, with Max standing in the middle talking in a loud, ominous voice and chanting some sort of incantations or prayers. The women drag me into dancing with them and I'm beginning to understand the rhythms they are moving to. It goes on for what seems like hours and starts to blur into one long strange and dark experience. I get hotter and hotter as the dancing gets wilder, and the sweat pours off me as the rain soaks me through. I realize I'm losing control, and my dancing becomes wilder and easier.

Suddenly there's a goat at my feet and I'm told to wash it with some branches of herbs dipped in water. It seems remarkably calm despite the noise. I'm told to walk the goat around the ring twice and feed it the herbs, then I'm wrapped in a sheet and taken away to have my face washed and to drink some herbal liquor. One of the women falls into a trance, dancing and acting like … well … this will sound odd, but she starts moving like a chicken, clucking and screaming, and thrusting her head forward and back as she walks. Max tells me she's channelling Erzulie, the goddess of love but, unlike other spirits, she can't speak, she can only cluck. I'm taken away again to dance, and while I'm gone, I can hear some ominous noises that sound like a goat in extreme pain.

I'm brought to the front and see that the goat has, indeed, been sacrificed. God, I hope it didn't suffer too much. Max forces me to kneel down, and paints my forehead with the goat's blood. I'm not sure what the significance is, but I'm in another world by now, and I couldn't say which way is up or down, let alone right or wrong.

After more dancing and singing, the drummers beat a fearful last thrashing, and the whole ceremony grinds to a halt, the possessed woman collapses and everyone else slumps in exhaustion. Callum, the cameraman, looks ashen. He tells me what happened whilst I'd been taken away: 'They brought the goat out to the front of the temple and cut off its testicles with a knife. I've never seen anything so horrific in my life. The knife wasn't very sharp and it took a heck of a long time. Then they cut its throat, but it wasn't quick. They had to hack away at it as though they were using a saw. It looked at me, and I'll never forget that look as long as I live.'

Oh my God. I know we're here to observe, not to criticize, but that sounds appalling.

I sit down, soaked in sweat, rain and blood, and try to find out from Max what was going on.

'All those songs and the drums combined and also the dances, all that together makes one vibrate,' he explains.

'I was definitely vibrating, yes.'

'Certainly. And what you don't understand probably is that you were vibrating at the speed or the frequency of the world. The world and you became one.'

I have absolutely no idea what this man's talking about.

EATING WITH AMERICA'S NEIGHBOURS

'Why did you have to castrate the goat while it was still alive? That seems a bit unnecessary.'

'We had to remove the goat's arrogance so that he could go to God in humility.'

'What's the significance of a goat being sacrificed; why does that have to be done?'

'Of course everything was symbolically represented. By eating those leaves, he agreed to be part of the world, part of the universe. I'm sure that tomorrow morning you will call me over the phone to tell me, Max, I do feel fantastic.'

That night I sleep deep and long but have horrible, violent dreams with me as the perpetrator.

The next morning I call Max but he doesn't answer the phone. Perhaps that's the way it should be: I'm left to deal with my own feelings of guilt, and I've promised that I'll call my wife in the morning to reassure her that I haven't gone over to the dark side. I'll have to explain all this without Max's help. Needless to say she's unimpressed by my description of last night's antics, but she's relieved that I'm not murmuring incantations to her.

'Poor bloody goat,' she says.

Burying Liberal Guilt ... Again

We hop into another of those WFP 4×4s to visit a poor and vulnerable area called Chauffard where they run a food distribution programme. We arrive just in time for a food handout run by the local priest, Father Estiven. The assembled crowd is almost exclusively female, and each person has arrived holding sacks to pick up rice, flour, beans, oil and salt. I speak to a couple of the women who tell me that they have travelled three, four and even six hours to get here. Their journey back will be even longer, laden with up to 50 kg of food that they carry on their heads. I try to carry one woman's bag, and I'm astonished at how painful it is. The weight puts pressure on my brain, pushes through my neck and down my spine, giving me a headache, neckache and backache in one fell swoop. Perhaps that wasn't such a good idea. She tells me that she has a four-hour journey ahead of her.

I ask Father Estiven if people here think that the rest of the world has a moral responsibility to help the hungry and he replies, 'Instead of giving us food, teach us to grow it, because if we learn how to produce we won't be dependent and our stomachs won't depend on food aid.'

A woman called Estelle asks if we'd like to taste the WFP rations and takes me to her hut for lunch. We are soon joined by a small crowd of her extended family and neighbours who quickly whip themselves into a frenzy of anti-US rhetoric, even as they use a large can of oil with 'USAid' stamped on the side. 'They ruined our rice farming, they ruined our pig farming and our chicken farming.'

Haiti used to have a strong poultry industry, hatching 6 million eggs a year and buying thousands of tonnes of locally produced corn. However, Aristide's deal with the international community to slash tariffs opened the doors to US chicken imports and the market was swiftly taken over by 'dark' chicken parts that Americans are less eager to buy. US companies sell around $17 million a year of poultry here but 10,000 Haitian jobs have been lost.

The WFP driver says that we have to leave – the weather is beginning to turn and if it rains, his vehicle won't be able to make it back along the treacherous roads. I quickly taste the WFP porridge and it's surprisingly good. Estelle has mixed it with condensed milk and sugar so that her 18-month old twins will eat it. I say a hurried thank you and get on my way back to the car, but Father Estiven is waiting there for me and won't let me go without eating lunch with him. Despite my protests, he forces me to eat a meal of meat, vegetables and rice. His flock really need it more than I do, but I persevere because the women have all left for their villages and for Father Estiven it's a point of honour for me to eat with him. As I have discovered so often over the past months, sometimes it's best to bury your liberal guilt and accept someone's hospitality.

The Artibonite Valley

I head to the Artibonite valley, one of Haiti's few fertile, productive regions, to visit some rice farmers. When the slaves rebelled against the French plantation owners in 1791 and founded modern Haiti, many of them turned to rice farming to provide a living, and for quite a while they did pretty well too, producing a nutritious and deeply flavoured rice. Then it all went wrong.

I've had some help making contact with the villagers from a man who owns land in the valley, but allows tenant farmers to grow rice there. Before arriving in the Artibonite, we stop off at his small tumbledown shack of four rooms on the seafront – it's meagre, but a palace compared to most homes around here. Edouard must be somewhere between 70 and 80 years old, a marvellous raconteur whose family have managed to keep hold of their land and resist governments and gangsters alike through popular support from the tenant farmers.

'My mother was the best whore in Haiti,' he tells me. 'She was very good, but also very expensive.' I splutter into my coffee. 'That's nice.' Edouard regales me with tales of the brutality of the dictators he's seen come and go, and his family's struggles to survive, then sends me off to the village with his son and a present for his tenants.

The valley is enormous – a vast plain flanked by hills, full of good soil (it's so flat here that soil erosion is less of a problem) and clearly well irrigated by the Artibonite River that runs through it. There's a lot of rice growing here, so the situation can't be too bad. As I approach the village there's no one to be seen in the fields, so I drive straight into the centre to find a hundred or so people crowded around a few benches, and I wander through to take a look. They are in the middle of a cockfight. Two bloodied birds hack away at each other in a flurry of feathers until the owner of the loser steps in and drags away his bird. I ask him what he'll do with it now and he tells me, 'I'm going to put him in a pot and eat him.'

'Is he no good any more?'

'No, he's finished.'

Edouard's son drops off a vast keg of moonshine as a gift to the village – it must hold around 80 litres, and they are over the moon. I meet Maye, an energetic and opinionated tenant farmer who also seems to be the head of the village. He tells me that the moonshine is for tonight, and I feel an involuntary wince of pain. Am I going to wake up with the mother of all hangovers tomorrow morning? I push it to the back of my mind.

Maye shows me around the fields and tells me that until 20 years ago the Artibonite valley produced almost enough rice to feed the entire country. It had become one of Haiti's few success stories, but back in the '80s the IMF and World Bank demanded that Haiti drop its import tariffs on rice in exchange for loans. 'Why is the imported rice so much cheaper?'

'It's because the import tariff is low. If it were higher, less rice from America would come in.' In 1994 Haiti's tariffs on rice imports fell from 35 per cent to 3 per cent. Maye says 'The problem is that we can't compete with imported rice.'

The trouble is not that US rice (with a glorious ear for irony, the Haitians call it Miami Rice) is better or that American farmers are more efficient, but that they are heavily subsidized by the government. On a rice crop that cost $1.8 billion to grow, they received a subsidy of $1.3 billion, so they can sell their rice very cheaply, much cheaper than the Haitians can grow theirs. In the '80s nearly all the rice consumed in Haiti was grown here, but now rice production has halved and imports, mainly from the USA, have increased 50-fold. The deal is widely seen as a stitch-up perpetrated by Aristide as part of a pay-off to the USA for returning him to power.

American food exporters rightly point out that their imports have helped to lower prices for poor Haitians, but that belies the truth of the situation. By flooding the market with cheap rice a devastating economic cycle has been started: the local farmers will be put out of business because their rice is no longer competitively priced. They will become impoverished and will no longer be able to afford to plant their fields, creating unemployment and a reversion to subsistence farming where the farmers produce only as much as they eat. The lack of work in the countryside creates more poverty, less ability to buy produce and eventually farming will collapse. Cheap rice has made the country poorer than it was with more expensive rice. On the other hand, the 200,000 tonnes of rice imported to Haiti every year make it the USA's fourth-largest market.

The parallels with Mexico are painfully clear: the removal of trade barriers opens up a poorer country's market to the US, and this is swiftly followed by the dumping of cheap, subsidized American food. There's a brief period of joy at the low-priced commodity, followed by a fracturing or even collapse of local farming. The World Bank and IMF have been accused of rampant, insensitive belief in globalization and free markets, and whether or not it's their intention, poorer countries have suffered whilst the USA has gained. It has been pointed out that countries such as the USA, the UK, Japan and South Korea might offer unrestricted trade now, but they achieved industrialization only whilst they were heavily protected markets. Forcing Mexico and Haiti to remove their trade barriers before they are fully developed (in Haiti's case, woefully underdeveloped) can be hugely destructive.

We visit one of Maye's fields and I try my hand at harvesting the rice. It's hot and sticky, and as we race to create the biggest pile of rice, Maye takes the piss out of me for my scythe work. I ask if he thinks his kids will grow up to be rice farmers. He tells me, 'If they have the opportunity, I don't think they'll ever do this job.' He explains that the one small upside of the Haitian domestic market was a subsidy on fertilizer, but that also disappeared in 2004, making a 45-kg bag cost up to $35, double the price a year ago. He now can't afford fertilizer, and his rice harvest is going to plummet.

In the middle of the village we beat the rice grains off the grass, much to the amusement of Maye's neighbours. Half an hour of harvesting has produced about three bowls of rice.

Maye adds another view of the US rice imports that surprises me: 'If our rice is worthless, it feels like our culture is worthless as well and I feel discouraged about working. You get less back than you spend.'

We return to the village and Maye invites me to eat with his family. His wife Sylvie has prepared a meal of dried fish served, unsurprisingly, with rice. But Haitian dinner etiquette means that she does more than just cook the meal. She also feeds it to him. I am astounded. Sylvie tells me, 'He's my husband, that's why I feed him.'

'But can't he do it himself?'

'I work hard all day long, it's only fair that she is working too, by putting the food in my mouth.'

I find this bizarre, intensely intimate and even a little Oedipal for my liking. The absolute subjection makes it a private, almost sexual scene of tenderness, and I feel as if I shouldn't be here.

Sylvie asks if my wife feeds me at home, and I laugh. 'Who's going to feed me seeing as my wife isn't here?' and quick as a flash, Sylvie's sister starts spooning food into my mouth. It's *really* weird. It's such an intimate gesture that if it was my wife doing this, it would feel unbearably erotic. I tell Maye that I'm going to insist that my wife feeds me from now on and he nods sagely.

That evening the village throws a voodoo party in honour of my visit and that fearsome-looking barrel of moonshine is opened. A few guys bring out their drums and the whole village, children and babies alike, crams into a small wooden shelter to celebrate. Everyone sings and dances, always with a couple of villagers leading the singing. Maye warns me, 'He's singing to the spirits using ancient voodoo. Pretty soon, you may become possessed.'

It appears that this won't be a goat-castrating, blood-splashing animist incantation evening, but more of a piss-up, a knees-up and a sing-along. The most vigorous singing of the evening is reserved for a song about the people who live in the next village along – apparently they're a bunch of thieving bastards, and they smell.

Maye insists I look after his bottle of moonshine, telling me that 'Drinking really seems to help contact the spirits.'

'I'll bet it does,' I reply, and almost instantly the moonshine hits me like a train. It tastes like petrol and works like a cerebral turbo-booster. Before I know it, I've got my hands in the air like I just don't care, and I'm dancing my pants off. In fact I've never danced so well in my life and I get a turn around the room dancing with every one of the village's big mammas. Even Callum and Mario get to shake their funky thangs. I have a wild time chatting and dancing with Maye and his wife and I eventually crawl back to the baking hot mud hut that Maye has put us up in at some shocking hour in the morning. Although the moonshine has stripped away most of my brain, I retain enough residual moral fibre to turn down the head drummer's kind offer of his beautiful younger sister to keep me warm.

In the morning, the mud hut is a fug of sweat, still as hot as a sauna and I am covered in a thick crust of perspiration, moonshine and mosquitoes. My hangover puts me at the far extremes of mortal existence; it's like someone has been using a steam pressure washer to pump a mixture of pig excrement and masonry nails through a hole punched in my forehead.

I stumble out of the hut in search of somewhere to go to the toilet and almost fall over Maye, who is slumped outside the hut looking as though someone's been using a steam pressure washer to pump a mixture of pig excrement and masonry nails through a hole punched in his forehead. This makes me feel a whole heap better and we collapse in painful laughter.

Tiny pigs scuttle around the village, and Maye says that they are another symbol of the USA ruining the country's ability to feed itself. In 1982, the USA had become so concerned at the prevalence of African swine fever that it convinced the Haitian government to slaughter all the indigenous Creole pigs in the country, plunging many families into more abject poverty than they were already experiencing. Small farmers claimed that they weren't compensated properly for their pigs and were forced to mortgage their land and, even worse, many people were so desperate that they cut down trees to sell as charcoal, destroying potential future income and intensifying desertification in one fell swoop.

But hold on! A new breed of pigs was imported, although unlike the resilient little Creole pigs, which were well-adapted to Haiti's rugged terrain and sparse vegetation, the new US pigs required clean water (80 per cent of people don't have clean water in Haiti, let alone their animals), imported feed at around $90 per year (when average income was $130) and veterinary costs. The pigs themselves had to be bought for around $50. The programme was an utter failure … except, perhaps for the US pig farmers who exported them. Incidentally, a new variety of pig has now been developed in association with French agronomists, so there is a glimmer of hope on the porcine front.

We eat a little breakfast of rice and small river fish in full view of the entire village who gather round to laugh at my shabby state. Maye and Sylvie chat about children, food and the future and I make a series of bad balloon animals for the village kids. I get fed again by Sylvie's sister, and this time I get into the swing of it, despite the fact that I haven't really done anything to deserve such a privilege. I have become attached to Maye and his family in the short time I've known them, and these few days in the countryside are another reminder that despite the fact that our lives are so wildly different, we are very much alike. In another world, I could see myself wasting away many an evening chatting to Maye over a pint in my local pub. I'm very sad when it's time to say goodbye. I will probably never meet Maye again, and I will miss him.

● ● ● ● ●

I head out of the Artibonite valley and stop off in a nearby town for lunch. The owner of a food shack points at a pot of sludgy green matter and tells me, 'It's got crab, meat and a local leaf.' Her little restaurant is packed, and she says that selling food is one of the few ways of making money in Haiti. 'It's helped me raise three children on my own and send them to school in Port-au-Prince. I bought my house without a husband, I worked and bought some land and the restaurant. But everybody uses Miami Rice now. Before you could get our local varieties, Shayla and Malangusa. They don't have those any more.'

On the way back to Port-au Prince I get a good view of the desperate state of the countryside. Before I arrived I had read that Haiti has suffered 98 per cent deforestation, but I didn't really appreciate it. Not only are there hardly any trees to be seen, but the soil is almost non-existent, eroded by the lack of vegetation to bind it to the hills. Instead of earth, the fields are almost entirely made up of small rocks, with a light scattering of soil in between them. I've heard the term 'soil erosion' used around the world, but it's always been something of an abstract concept, and rarely so visible to the eye. This land is shockingly bad, and I can't see how anyone can scratch a living from it.

I pass a flood-channel that looks like a huge river of stones. When the rain falls around here it rips downhill, unhindered by trees or bushes and strips the fields of any remaining soil and rocks. In some places a few terraces have been attempted, but they look pretty half-hearted, and must take a disproportionate amount of work when the fields are likely to produce so little. The soil heads south towards the sea and the rocks are left as this extraordinary wave, a symbol of ecological folly.

A Glimmer of Hope

I keep thinking that each new place we go to must be a bit better – surely it can't be worse. Inevitably it is. Cap Haitien is like Port-au-Prince but with less infrastructure, although it does have a fair few remnants of beautiful French colonial architecture. It sits on another soupy swamp of water and excrement.

I visit a school on the outskirts of one of Cap Haitien's slums to see the WFP's school feeding programme. It's made up of three small buildings bisected by an open sewer, and is absolutely crammed – a school that in the UK would cater for maybe 80 children has 1,000 kids who attend in two shifts – 500 in the morning, and the other 500 in the afternoon.

In Haiti, as in so many other poor countries, desperate parents prefer kids to work selling and hustling to add to the family income. Many kids therefore don't get to go to school, so they lack the skills to get employment when they grow up, and so the cycle of poverty continues. The WFP has a successful programme of school feeding whereby kids all receive a free meal at school, which eases the burden on their families. It seems to work very well and because the WFP isn't distributing free food into the market, it doesn't disrupt local economies. And the kids get something of an education. I visit a class and the teacher invites me to sing them something in English. I try teaching them to sing 'Think I'll Go and Dig Worms', but they are completely baffled, so I get them to count to ten instead. It's a wild success.

The meal is a porridge of CSB (corn soy blend) and a stew of vegetables. It tastes OK – filling and nutritious if not actually tasty, but the kids are shy about eating it in front of me so I take my leave.

I am invited by one of the kid's mothers to take a look at her house nearby, and follow her to the adjacent slum. Her house is actually just a room, and it's tiny. Seven people live in a space the size of two double beds. All food preparation is done outside, next to another open sewer, and the few bedclothes that they own are covered in a thick patina of grease and dust. I've been inside for only ten minutes before Mario says that he can overhear people getting angry that we are here, and demanding money for us filming. So we leave.

Much of the early blame for Haiti's ecological damage lies with the European invaders, who used the trees for fuel but also cleared huge swathes of the country for sugar plantations. Nowadays the only trees left seem to be mangoes so I drop in at a mango warehouse near the main airport to find out a bit more. The mango industry used to have a huge trade with the USA, but the trade embargoes of 1991–4 pretty much destroyed the industry after the Americans looked to Central America to supply the market. But in contrast to my experiences so far, there is a glimmer of hope here, with mangoes now Haiti's second largest export product after coffee. The tragedy is that after 1991, people started to cut down their mango trees because no one would buy the fruit, so now, production is difficult. It's made even more so by the fact that most farmers have only a handful of trees, and they have to transport their delicate fruit over the island's potholed roads for hours at a time.

Jean Maurice has a network of these small farmers and has managed to create one of Haiti's few sizeable businesses. 'All the export depends on the small farmer. I'm an average farmer too because I own four or five trees. Most of my farmers are the same.'

He takes me out to his field where I climb a tree with one of his employees and, cackhandedly avoiding the wasps' nests, manage to pick half a dozen mangoes. The Madame Francis variety is grown only here in Haiti and around 2.5 million boxes are exported to the USA every year.

It's another baking hot day so we sit under one of the mango trees to try thefruit. Jean insists that I don't peel it, but just bite straight through the skin and into the fruit. It's amazing. As I rip off the skin with my teeth a powerful burst of mango scent floods my nostrils, four times as strong as a mango bought in London and with a deeper, more intense flavour. Jean explains that this is the flavour of a real, tree-ripened, ready-to-eat mango, whereas the ones I've always eaten have ripened off the tree in refrigerated transit, and the flavour just doesn't develop properly.

Nowadays the few remaining mango trees are at great risk. They are resistant to drought and fire, so they're a reliable crop even for farmers who have just a small plot of land. But with production on such a small scale the industry is vulnerable to desperate farmers cutting down their mango trees to make fuel. If someone chopped their tree down, 'they would probably earn the same amount of money selling charcoal [immediately] as it's bringing in to them every year in terms of selling the fresh mangoes. They could have one child that is sick after the mango season and they need to cut the tree so they can save that child. One crisis and that's your livelihood gone'.

The mango industry is still relatively small, but it does show that Haiti is capable of exporting to America, and this rare hint of optimism comes as something of a surprise and a relief.

Fantasy Beach

There's one other glimmer of hope for the Haitian economy. Just 20 minutes away from the slums of Haiti's second city, Cap Haitien, I drive through some heavily armed gates and enter another world.

On a remote beach in the north of the country is a vision of the Haitian Caribbean paradise I hoped existed before I arrived here: beautiful, clean white-sand beaches with deep turquoise sea, palm trees and tikki bars. I haven't seen anything this organized, clean and idyllic in the whole country. But sadly, none of it's real. Labadee is an artificial nirvana built by the Royal Caribbean cruise company, complete with an ersatz Caribbean flea market selling replica voodoo dolls. Even the palm trees have been imported. And ordinary Haitians are distinctly unwelcome on this very private beach.

I arrive early in the morning and I get to the beach just in time to see the *Voyager of the Seas* appear on the horizon and park its gargantuan, expensive butt in Labadee Bay. Twice a week, huge cruise ships drop in to Labadee and around 3,500 tourists, most of them American, are offloaded, along with their own food, first-aiders and jolly cocktail salesmen.

I watch with astonished awe as these 3,500 tourists are ferried to the beach, where they get to paddle around, jet-ski and watch a badly hammed-up cod-voodoo ceremony.

During their five hours on Haiti the passengers won't leave the beach (they aren't allowed to). They won't taste any local food either – their supplies are all brought over from the ship. Some of them don't even *know* they're in Haiti. I manage to speak to an old lady fresh off the boat. She explains, 'I'm just resting right now, we've been busy on the cruise ship.'

'It's been hard work on your cruise ship?'

'Yep.'

'Do you know anything about Haiti at all?'

'No.'

'Do you know what lies on the other side here?' I point beyond the beach.

'I don't know what's on the rest of the island.'

It's easy to sneer when you're confronted by a phalanx of shiny American tourists, but it's dawning on me that these brash visitors provide exactly what Haiti needs: employment.

David Southby is an Englishman who runs the beach for the cruise line, and he's realistic about Haiti's prospects as a tourist destination: 'We do confine the guests to the site because there really isn't that much on offer outside of the site at this stage. It would be very difficult to bring in any amount of tourists, which is probably what will bring Haiti up and into the future. It's a beautiful place, there are some amazingly beautiful beaches, there is a lot of potential. The infrastructure just isn't here to support us yet.'

He goes on to explain, 'We have 200 full-time staff, plus the additional staff for call days, the musicians and so on, so we've got up to 500 people on site. That's 500 people with a regular income, which is not something that you'll find anywhere else, definitely not to that scale.'

For the tourists, the highlight of the day is an all-American barbecue, but the buffet is an astounding collection of homogeneous comfort foods: chicken wings, frankfurters, unripe tomatoes, burgers and pork ribs. I'll guiltily admit that the ribs are actually quite nice, but the rest is an abomination.

Just across the bay is Labadee village, and a handful of the local workers on the beach come from there. I hitch a ride over, and it's what I'd imagined Haiti would be – a simple but not impoverished laid-back Caribbean village. It's obviously benefiting from tourist income through jobs, but for the families of the workers, the cruise ship passengers might as well be on another planet (although I should add that no one would talk to me without being paid $5, so whether or not what they said was true, I have no idea.

A woman I talk to says that she's never in her life met one of the half million cruise ship guests who come every year. 'We just see them in the distance on their jet-skis. Sometimes they come in very close, but they don't land.'

We return to the beach but it's all over. In the hour we'd been gone the guests all disappeared back to the ship and a short while later the *Voyager of the Seas* was steaming off towards Miami. They had been here for three hours, never leaving the compound, and that was their entire experience of Haiti. In a funny kind of way, they never left America.

Royal Caribbean Cruises pays the Haitian government $6 per person to use Labadee and that's income the country desperately needs. If I was being pessimistic, I'd suggest that at 163 on the corruption scale, it would be surprising if any of that money went back into the community, but Haiti needs some optimism, so just forget I said that.

It's easy to sneer, and these large steel containers packed with nice wealthy Americans seem wildly out of place here in the poorest country in the western hemisphere, but they could be Haiti's great hope for prosperity. Americans don't seem enormously keen to encourage mutually beneficial ties with their neighbours, but they won't turn their noses up at a slice of affordable luxury. The trouble is that the USA seems to have a habit of causing at least as many problems as it solves.

I've never experienced such depths of human despair as I found in Haiti, especially in the slums. It is an image that still regularly haunts me, and I can't help despairing for Maye, Jacques and the people of Cité Soleil who endure so much. I hope the world, and especially the USA, doesn't screw Haiti over again.

Next, I'm heading for Mexico, so close to the USA that you can throw stones over the border. Perhaps they treat these neighbours a little better.

MEXICO
The Tortilla Crisis

POPULATION: 106 million

PERCENTAGE LIVING ON LESS THAN $2 A DAY: 20%

UNDP HUMAN DEVELOPMENT INDEX: 53/177

CORRUPTION PERCEPTIONS INDEX POSITION: 70/163

GDP (NOMINAL) PER CAPITA: $8,006 (54/179)

FOOD AID RECIPIENTS: n/a

MALNUTRITION: 5% of the population

I have come to Mexico to investigate one of the country's biggest problems: the Tortilla Crisis. Don't laugh. You might think of Mexican food as a novelty Friday-night beer-sponge, but tortillas provide around 50 per cent of all calories that Mexicans eat, and the corn that they're made from is the main crop for 3 million impoverished rural farmers. In 1994 Mexico signed a free trade agreement with the USA that caused massive upheavals for corn farmers and sparked an extraordinary revolution led by the Zapatistas, a group of anti-globalization rebels fighting for the rights of indigenous people in the southwest of the country.

The Zapatistas are a well-funded, well-organized, armed group that only ever appears in public in balaclavas and ski masks, and have a habit of issuing rambling proclamations denouncing the USA and threatening the Mexican government. So far, so Marxist revolutionary. But the difference is that the Zapatistas are a group that admits its mistakes, that develops its policies and devolves power. It's led by an enigmatic, eloquent intellectual called Marcos whose true identity remains a secret, and who manipulates TV journalists like us with remarkable dexterity. I'm going to try to speak to the Zapatistas and find out if the Tortilla Crisis, together with the influence of the USA, have torn apart rural Mexico.

Eco Alberto

A few hours' drive out of Mexico City is Eco Alberto, the world's most extraordinary theme park, and I'm on my way there to experience the unique sensation of being an illegal immigrant crossing the border from Mexico into the USA. I can't work out whether it's a huge bad-taste cash-in, a simple exercise in left-wing activism or a training ground for would be fence-jumpers. Either way, I'm joining in.

I meet 'Poncho', the head of the operation who wears a thick woollen balaclava (although no poncho), despite the fact that he's sweating profusely underneath it. He's taking a roll-call of extras from the village who are here to help me get an authentic illegal immigrant's experience.

Along with 25 giggling blokes and a couple of crippled-with-embarrassment *muchachas*, I jump onto one of four pick-up trucks and set off. Ten minutes later I'm dropped off in the middle of nowhere and join these extras stumbling around muddy fields in the pitch black whilst three 'border patrol' vehicles with flashing blue lights, sirens and floodlights chase us around. I can't see a thing, so I run about in a panic, falling over every five minutes, and occasionally hide in bushes.

I wonder what it's meant to achieve. At various points along the way, Poncho stops to offer his semi-poetic, semi-revolutionary, wholly confusing thoughts about truth, brotherhood and struggle: 'This night is in honour of all migrants who have left with the illusion, the dream of finding a better quality of life. Ninety per cent of our community have migrated, leaving behind our land, our culture and our customs.'

I can't really work out if this is a condemnation of desertion or a celebration of escape. Is it about a struggle for wealth and respect in the USA, or is he saying that Mexicans should stay on the land and make the best of it? In any case, there's frequent singing of the national anthem and group assertion that they have pride, respect and certainty in their hearts.

What is clear is that this community has had a terrible time: there are so few opportunities here and Poncho says that the collapse in the market price of corn, the most important local crop, has forced 90 per cent of Alberta's population to jump the border into the USA, leaving behind a social vacuum and a hobbled, decimated community. They've set up this illegal immigration theme park to publicize their plight and to bring a bit of cash and pride into their lives.

At one point I get arrested by the mock border police who fire blank ammunition at me and abuse me in cod-aggressive immigration insults: 'We gats too many of you Mexicans 'ere. We don' like you so go back 'ome.'

They have the acting ability of porn stars, but they clearly love their roles, their faces curled up in mock grimaces. Nonetheless they release me and I continue to run around cornfields and through irrigation pipes as the border police capture my co-migrants.

After another three exhausting hours of this madness Poncho puts a blindfold on me and leads me somewhere he claims is very special. He talks for another 20 minutes about pride, believing in ourselves and giving our souls for our family, friends and Mexico. I'm still confused as to what exactly we are all proud of; the message is confused by his constant reversion to tawdry, sexist knob jokes and extravagant claims about how much sex he has, but this is important stuff for Poncho.

Finally my blindfold is removed and the sight is, indeed, spectacular. We are in a dramatic valley, and thousands of lanterns have been lit all the way up the rock face on either side. The sight sends a shiver down my spine and fills me with non-specific awe. The show is over and I am given a welcome bowl of chicken giblet soup.

This whole mad scheme might seem funny to people on the outside looking in, but my translator, Luisa, has heard that the lanterns were intended to represent the estimated 500 people who die crossing the border each year. These people are suffering huge turmoil, but the question is, why? What has happened to make 90 per cent of a community disappear, considering the dangers involved and the fact that they have to abandon their loved ones to an uncertain future?

Well, the answer seems to lie in a treaty signed in 1994 between the USA, Canada and Mexico. Bear with me here because the following should explain why I'm running around fields in rural Mexico. Plus, think how knowledgeable you'll seem next time you drop into Nando's.

● ● ● ● ●

In 1994 Mexico signed up to a free trade agreement with the USA and Canada known as NAFTA, which dismantled many import and export duties. It's been controversial in all three countries and it has helped in some areas and caused difficulties in others. In Mexico it's been great for the trading middle classes, and it's also created a huge number of unskilled jobs at new assembly plants. But there's been catastrophic fall-out in rural areas. The agreement meant that Mexico removed import taxes on US corn – corn that's sold way below the cost of production thanks to the huge subsidies that the USA pays to farmers – and imported corn suddenly became much cheaper. However, millions of Mexicans, especially in rural areas, are poor corn farmers who survive on what they can grow, selling any surplus to keep themselves afloat, and the NAFTA price crash was devastating for many of them, causing widespread misery to people who were already desperately poor.

When your food security is already compromised and you're living on the edge of hunger, a small shift in your ability to sell your corn has disastrous consequences. And this, in roundabout ways, is what NAFTA did. The result has been extreme poverty, chronic malnutrition and a social vacuum created where communities simply became unviable. In poor, rural areas many people are now either living in miserable conditions, or have left for the USA in a desperate attempt to find work.

As part of the trade agreement, the Mexican government started a programme of land reform to reverse the system of collective ownership (my, how the USA hates collective ownership!) that was common in the countryside, and this has added to rural chaos and resentment. There's an added complication too: the price of tortillas (made from corn flour) recently *rose* fourfold due to higher prices in the USA, presumably due to US farmland being turned over to ethanol production (which uses a different kind of corn). But for various reasons, this seems to have benefited the big transnational corn dough suppliers and not small-scale rural corn farmers.

In 1994, on the day that NAFTA was implemented, the Zapatistas exploded onto the scene, based in southern rural areas where food security is worst affected. Although they are armed with guns, they've rarely been used, but despite this they've been pretty successful. Trouble is, they like to control their image very tightly and recently they've been refusing all interviews. I've got just two weeks to make them change their minds.

Don Chon

It's 5.30 a.m. and I am sitting in a knackered saloon car outside the chapel of Santa Malverde, the saint of prostitutes and burglars, in the most dangerous part of Mexico City. My driver has locked me in and forbidden me to leave the car, and he fidgets nervously as we wait for the legendary restaurateur Don Chon to emerge from his apartment. Chon is renowned for his love of ancient pre-Hispanic foods from Aztec and Mayan times, and it's a great privilege that he's agreed to meet me. The trouble is that I'm feeling decidedly queasy and I haven't slept a wink all night. Gastronomic adventure usually gets me excited, but right now it's the last thing I need.

Chon finally waddles around the corner. He looks short and rotund and very grumpy. We drive to La Merced ('Mercy'), his favourite market, which he warns me is both vast and dangerous. People here don't like being filmed, but Chon has apparently convinced people to speak to me. There are stalls piled high with mounds of cactus buds, all manner of chillies and spices, bushes of leafy vegetables and flowers. Despite my wonderment, however, I feel very unwelcome as stallholders wave me away when I ask to speak to them, and I'm only allowed to chat to the specific people Chon's negotiated with. One guy sweats profusely whilst I talk to him, but he's passionate about the traditional foods he sells – poached duck tripe (very tasty – a little musky, but with a soft, liverish texture), tiny crayfish dyed red, fish wrapped in corn husks and baked. He says it's a shame that modern junk food has taken over the country.

I convince a spice stallholder to give me a masterclass on chillies, and foolishly ask to try the hottest that the guy sells. At first, there's a little heat, but not the face-expanding slow explosion I was expecting, so I try a little more. Bad idea. These are quite dry chillies, so the first taste goes nowhere, and it's only when my saliva starts to break down the heat-packing capsaicin that my head is rapidly set alight. None of this is helping my stomach.

I visit the fly egg man: I'm surprised that anyone has the patience to harvest them because they are minute, the size of fat grains of sand, and greyish-brown. I dip a finger into the pile and taste them: they are entirely devoid of flavour, and the only sensation is the tingle in my cortex at the thought of eating flies, and a crunch on my tongue, like I'm chewing grit. The whole flies are even weirder, like eating shards of straw. Again, they taste of absolutely nothing, and even though they are an historically important delicacy, I find it amazing that people will pay $80 per kilo for them. The stallholder admits that foods like this are in decline.

I try to chat with Don Chon but he's getting grumpier and grumpier as we walk around the market, and I don't understand why – most chefs are happiest in places like this. He takes me to a food stall and orders chicken soup plus a side order of gestating hen with a string of half-formed eggs inside it. Neither tastes of much but it looks fun and the texture of the eggs is wonderful – a cross between hard-boiled yolk and hard-boiled white. He also offers me some chicken blood tortilla. Ah, I finally realize what's going on: he's trying to shock me, and his lousy temper only gets worse when I don't recoil from these strange foods. Oh dear, he's chosen the wrong person to try to shock – this is comfort food compared to half-fermented rotten walrus – and my interested reactions have been making him more and more irritable.

We finally head off to his meat market to pick up *escamoles* (ant eggs), off-white and creamy on the tongue, and *jumiles* (large fleas), which have an extraordinary crunchiness and a flavour that's a cross between fennel and menthol. They'd almost be pleasant if they didn't leave my mouth full of irritating shards of flea legs. Don Chon takes me to his restaurant to start cooking.

He serves me fly eggs fried with chicken egg, cactus and coriander; ant eggs cooked with green tomatoes, garlic and chilli; and whole flies cooked with red tomatoes, garlic, chilli and chicken eggs.

Hmm. It's all quite interesting, but when prepared, the flies and fly eggs taste like a sandy omelette and the ant larvae tastes like salsa omelette. I don't want to sound mean, and I'm all in favour of resurrecting ancient foods and breathing life into lost cultures, but I only really enjoyed his food for the novelty and surprise rather than the taste. I was hoping for a gastronomic epiphany so that I could come back to Britain with a renewed zeal to spread the word about eating insects. But even his deep-fried grasshoppers just taste of old cooking oil.

Chon drops a few hints that he'd rather I buggered off, thanks all the same. He needs to get on, preparing braised snake and (allegedly) some armadillo.

I get up early to visit a *tortilleria* and try to find out more about the tortilla wars. Funnily enough, no one is willing to take the blame for the recent fourfold price increase that sparked riots in Mexico City and brought 75,000 people onto the streets to protest. Mexicans eat 300 billion tortillas each year – that's 3,000 per person.

The tortilla trail starts with the corn growers (usually the massive transnational corporations, such as Cargill and ADM), then leads

EATING WITH AMERICA'S NEIGHBOURS

through a web of distributors and wholesalers, processors and dough-makers until it arrives as a ready-to-bake dough at high-street *tortillerias*. These are where most people buy them, freshly baked on machines that churn them out at around 120 a minute. And it's here that the good people of Mexico pay through the nose, and where the government recently imposed price restrictions to try to keep them affordable. Trouble is, none of the people running *tortillerias* could care less about price restrictions and instead they charge as much as they can.

The owner of the *tortilleria*, Emilia, is sweet and helpful and even lets me touch her cacophonously clanking and yelping tortilla baking machine. She explains that over 50 per cent of calories consumed by Mexicans come from tortillas: 'They are the basic food in Mexico because we hardly eat any bread.'

We chat and make thousands of tortillas, and all is going well until I ask her about the riots and the price restrictions, at which point she becomes evasive and grumpy, and breaks away to argue with someone about Lord knows what on the telephone. Meanwhile, my driver is being harassed for money by some of the local hard men, who want a tax for filming on their patch. I give in and call it a day.

Acteal

I fly to Chiapas in the far southwest of Mexico where the air is clean and clear. Arriving at the airport, I breathe deeply, relieved to have left the filth and cacophony of Mexico City.

Chiapas is one of the poorest places in the country and the birthplace of the Zapatista movement, with a high proportion of indigenous people who often don't see themselves as Mexicans, and resent central government exerting power over them.

I drive to San Cristobal de las Casas, an incongruously wealthy Spanish colonial city of dappled courtyards in an otherwise deprived state. The well-to-do residents were rather surprised on New Year's Day 1994, when the Zapatista rebels chose San Cristobal to launch a Marxist revolution, capturing and ransacking government buildings for a few days before the Mexican army drove them out. Their dismay turned to joy, however, when they realized they'd been put on the left-wing activist tourist map, and world travellers now come in search of righteous indignation, cheap indigenous crafts and decent coffee.

Acteal, however, is a different story altogether. The town was the scene of a horrific massacre in 1997 when 45 people, mostly women and children, were brutally slaughtered by government-allied paramilitaries because the village sided with the Zapatistas in a dispute over land. It now lives in a state of perpetual mourning.

I meet Miguel, the current village leader (leadership is constantly rotated to avoid corruption), who blames the USA for forcing Mexico to give up on co-operative land-holding and allow private ownership as part of the free trade agreement, and hence for the massacre itself. He explains that during the 1960s and '70s the Acteal peasants were given parcels of land as part of a widespread land redistribution. Soon after this, wealthier landowners started to bully the peasants away, or simply reoccupied the peasants' land (a common consequence of agrarian reform), but the Zapatistas encouraged people, including those in Acteal, to assert their rights and to occupy more land, and this put them in active conflict with the local landowners who ran a militia called Peace and Justice which, Miguel says, carried out the massacre.

Miguel takes me to the church where the victims were first attacked, and then to the place where most of them died, starting with the village leader. We visit the tomb where the bodies now lie, and I shiver when I see the pictures of the dead: women, boys and girls, a few men, and most awful of all, a five-month-old baby. How could anyone do this?

I ask if the village still supports the Zapatistas and Miguel says they agree with their aims, but not with their methods. After this vicious attack destroyed so many families in the village, they now want peace more than anything. I notice they still talk in a Zapatista-esque language of struggle, though. 'Our struggle to retain our land will never be over,' Miguel says. 'It is our destiny. The government is too strong to be beaten, but we are too committed to lose.'

We go to the village cornfields, and Miguel tells me that corn is their life. 'According to our Mayan tradition, we were created from corn, yellow, white and black.' He goes on to say that the conflict began because of the free trade agreement. 'They wanted to take away our lands so that we would become their slaves.'

After exploring the cornfields, we return to the village and eat bean soup with tortillas and chilli with Miguel and the men of the village council. For every meal there's always a pile of tortillas to hand, wrapped in a cloth to keep them fresh.

I leave Acteal, shocked at the scale and viciousness of the massacre.

It's absurdly early when I get up to visit Petrona, a beautiful elderly woman who's renowned for her cooking. She's agreed to show me how to cook a classic Mexican food called tamales: steamed parcels of corn dough filled with bean paste. They're a Mexican classic but are only made for special occasions. Mention them to Mexicans living away from home and they will turn misty-eyed and start missing their mothers.

Following Petrona's instructions I spread out a thin layer of corn dough onto a damp teacloth, enough to cover the whole thing in a large rectangle. I do it slowly and carefully using the palm of my hand whilst trying to ignore the wailing laughter of the five elderly Mexican women looking on. They find it bizarre that a gringo is daring to cook in a Mexican *madre*'s kitchen. Petrona cackles at my cack-handed doughwork (which isn't actually that bad, thanks very much).

Once I have survived the initial humiliation and made a passable base for my tamales, I spread an equally thin layer of cooked and mashed beans on top of the dough. Then I roll it up like a jam rolypoly, wrap it in corn sheaths, and steam for an hour or so over a wood fire. When I'm done Petrona charitably praises my work. We leave the tamales to steam and Petrona shows me how to make a drink from corn, water and sugar. My God, this corn thing is getting out of hand. We make a huge vat of corn drink, which tastes surprisingly good – although it's sickly sweet it also has a great citric kick – like Tokaji wine, but white and silky.

Our tamales are finally ready, and they're extremely filling and soothing, although they don't taste of much except wet corn and wet beans. Luckily there's also an enormous smoked beef stew, so I fill my boots with that.

On the Trail of the Zapatistas

Making tamales is fun but I'm keen to tackle the big story: the Zapatistas. I head out to the remote countryside, leaving Mexican-administered territory and entering rebel-controlled land, though there's no border and it's hard to tell where the front line is. This, along with the fact that who's in charge in any one place is vague and shifting, makes rebel conflicts rather dangerous.

As I drive further from San Cristobal, the countryside becomes more mountainous and eroded and the people are visibly poorer, living in wooden shacks. The bright, colourful Mexico I've got used to turns monochrome, sullen and ragged. People stare warily at us from their front doors and the plots of land get smaller and more crowded. The countryside around here is mainly steep hills and valleys, often too difficult and fragmented to farm, and fields of corn are small and scrappy. Despite this, there's a surprising density of housing and it's teeming with people, which puts enormous pressure on the land. Each family must have barely enough land to feed itself, which is partly why land ownership here has become a matter of life and death.

I make my way to a village called Oventica, a Zapatista command centre, and it's here that I'm going to try to get access to the rebels. The Zapatistas are notoriously wary of mainstream media, and they like to exert tight control of their message. Since the movement began they have used the Internet and a network of international sympathizers to publicize their struggle, and their manipulation of the media has ensured their survival so far, despite the fact that they haven't had to fire their guns for several years.

It also means that any attack on the Zapatistas by the Mexican authorities can be instantly broadcast to the world via the Web, ensuring worldwide condemnation.

The rebels, and especially their leader, have become famous for their struggle and the way they devolve power and avoid the usual descent into internecine power struggles and corruption that other bedevil other rebel groups.

I'm beginning to think that the Zapatistas might be one of the few Marxist groups it's cool to like – the old student poster boys such as Mao, Che and Castro have all been a bit compromised by their irritating habits of presiding over genocide and summary executions, stamping on rights, or simply by being dictatorial bastards. Marcos, though? Well, he's anonymous (balaclava), humble-ish (calls himself a *subcommandante* rather than leader), he's sexy (bullet belt), and cool (pipe). Oh, and of course he's dedicated his life to the struggle for rights for the oppressed.

A team of scary-looking guys in balaclavas guards the Oventica Zapatista camp, and when I ask to enter, I'm told to wait outside. After an interminable, nervous wait, I'm led in to sit like a naughty schoolboy outside the hut of the main camp committee until I'm finally ordered in for an audience. The walls of the hut are covered in pictures of rebel groups, people in balaclavas and idealist paintings of rainbows and happy children. It reminds me of my childhood in the Woodcraft Folk.

Seven men and women sit on the bench opposite, silently watching us from inside their black balaclavas. I can't help thinking that they must be terribly hot under there. They ask my name, grill me briefly on what I'm doing here, and then give a little speech about how pleased they are that I've come. I get up and leave. Well, that was easy, I think, until I realize that all they've done is grant me an audience with the communications committee next door who will consider my case. In the next-door hut two more hoodies interrogate me. They take some notes and then tell me to leave while they consider my case.

I sit in the camp café for two hours before I get an answer and it's a simple one: 'No. We don't speak to any journalists.' Did it take them two hours to decide that? I have come a long way to talk to the Zapatistas, and I'll have wasted thousands of pounds unless I get to speak to one. I humbly tell them that I'm interested in the NAFTA disputes and it would be a tragedy if they aren't able to put their case. I hope it doesn't sound too much like a threat.

That's lovely, they say. No thanks.

I'm distraught. I ask if I can think about what they've said and then come back to see them later.

'Sure.'

I return to the café, tearing my hair out. Perhaps if we just sit here, something will happen. An hour later I spot one of the committee poking his head out of the door. Apparently they will reconsider their decision if I write down the exact questions I want to ask. I come up with a set of subjects that don't sound too threatening (I'll change them to specifics later), and they send me away again. This is becoming boring.

I have lunch in the café and browse the camp shop, which sells all sorts of glorious Zapatista kitsch: tea towels, tortilla cloths, CDs, stuffed wool figurines of a pipe-smoking Marcos, Marcos on a horse, portraits of the Madonna wearing a balaclava (I kid you not), Zapatista snail purses, and all manner of lapel pins. It's extraordinary: this movement has become a brand. I buy one of everything in the hope that this will stand me in good stead for an interview.

Four long hours later I'm still waiting. Finally Luisa the translator wanders down to see if she can poke her head around the committee-hut door. As she gets there, the committee are all leaving to play a game of football, and they tell her to come back tomorrow. They are clearly playing a power game. They know we need them to be in our film, and they don't care how much they annoy me. I leave downhearted, having wasted a whole day.

While I'm waiting for the Zapatistas to give me an answer, I go to the San Cristobal market to find out about the local food. The market is jammed with people and I taste a few strange insects and try to talk to stallholders. I stop at a juice stall for a pineapple and banana drink and get talking to the owner, Maria, who points to the spice stall opposite. 'That's my husband, Fernandez,' she says.

They are garrulous and friendly and when I tell them I'm investigating food and politics they open up. They give me their recipe for mole (a thick sauce flavoured with sweet chillies, chocolate and endless other ingredients) and tell me about the fights they sometimes have across the market stalls, which have occasionally involved flying oranges and cinnamon sticks. Maria makes me her favourite drink: the deep crimson Vampire, which contains beetroot, carrot and sugar. It's good stuff.

Eventually I hear from the Zapatistas. The committee might let me visit another camp in a couple of days if I go with José, a guy I met when I first arrived in Chiapas.

Perhaps I'll get an interview after all.

● ● ● ● ●

To pass the time, I head off to a town called San Juan Chamula to meet a white witch (also called Maria), who carries out a cleansing ritual on me. I've never been spiritually cleansed before so I'm not sure what to expect, and I ask her not to turn me into a chair or anything weird like that. She doesn't think this is funny.

Maria takes me to her shrine room, which has a huge figurine of the Virgin Mary, plus crosses and corn symbols, and all manner of junk, where she unleashes pungent clouds of incense over me and then proceeds to whack me with leaves, and, most bizarrely, roll eggs over my body, all the while chanting and praying in a strange, indigenous language that sounds spookily similar to the Inuktituk that the Inuit speak.

It's all very calming and uplifting, and I'm grateful for the sensation. I'm not a particularly mystical kind of bloke, but it's impossible to ignore the sense of being cleansed and enlightened. It might just be all the stroking, but I resolve not to give in to my mystic cynicism, and thank her profusely. She hugs me like I'm a long-lost son, and invites me to watch her daughters cook tortillas.

In her smoke-filled cooking hut, three women sit spreading corn dough into thin circles and toasting them on a flat metal plate. When I kneel down and ask if I can try making tortillas myself, they laugh in disbelief, saying, 'Women are creatures of fire, so they belong in the kitchen.' I persevere and spread out my lump of dough, slapping and twisting it. I make a passable tortilla shape, but the girls take great delight in taunting me. I place my dough on the griddle, burning it in several places before it's finally cooked. It tastes awful, and I humbly take my leave. Maria hands me her CV. I've never read a witch's CV before (it's very much like an ordinary mortal's, but heavier on the miracles).

Still on the Trail of the Zapatistas

I drive for hours away from the cool air and smart courtyards of San Cristobal and down into the baking hot, dirt-poor plains of Chiapas. The land is parched and windblown – more like the Mexico I'd imagined. Crooked fences guard vast tracts of worthless, wasted earth, and the sun burns like the breath of a massive, moustachioed dragon.

In this land crops are failing, yet the price of corn has been pushed so low by subsidized US imports that it's no longer worth planting. People are leaving this place in droves for the USA, prepared to take their chances as illegal aliens. I stop in a raggedy town square and chat to a few elderly gents about how difficult it is to make a living here, and they despair at so many people leaving.

I stumble across Jesus and Aramore, two impoverished farmers, and offer to buy them breakfast. They blame the free trade agreement for rural poverty, and America for treating Mexicans worse than dogs, despite the fact that 'the USA needs Mexican labour and Mexican oil'. They sympathize with the Zapatistas rebellion – how else can people succeed against a government that has abandoned them?

I ask if either of them has had any experience of the emigration tragedy, and Jesus breaks down in tears. His daughter escaped to the USA years ago and he doesn't think he'll ever see her again. I think how devastated I'd be if one my own daughters left, and Mexico's simmering national sadness suddenly becomes clear. Rural poverty tears communities apart leaving behind fragmented families and social catastrophe. I feel sick at the thought of a countryside that can no longer sustain its people.

I call José, my Zapatista contact, and ask him to make a last-ditch attempt to get us a meeting with the Zapatistas. I have to leave tomorrow for Tijuana, and I'm getting desperate. José is hopeful, and makes a provisional arrangement to meet me tomorrow.

That night I meet a group of men who were kicked off their land by the Zapatistas in 1994. They were wealthy landowners (and look as though they still are), but they haven't been able to set foot in their old homes. They are calm and structured in their responses, but when I ask if they understand why the Zapatistas have invaded their lands, they claim ignorance. I push the point – surely they are doing this as a way of correcting historic injustices – but the landowners aren't willing to let their guard down. They say that the indigenous people are being manipulated by the Zapatistas for political gain.

I feel cautious sympathy for them – landowners are not historically renowned for their fair treatment of indigenous people, but these guys have clearly been forced off land that they owned. They say that they were only small landowners, not the wealthy oligarchs the Zapatistas claim they are. However, one of them gives us a lift back to our hotel in town, and during the journey he mentions that he's now doing pretty well in the cosmetics business and that the Zapatistas took only a small proportion of his land – he still owns a lot more.

I'm getting desperate about my lack of success with the rebels now, and I'm not feeling optimistic as I head towards the camp where I'm hoping José has wangled us an interview. I am supposed to meet him at a road junction, but after an hour, I hear that he's driven straight past me and entered the camp – he didn't see us waiting. Sod it. I hope we haven't blown our last chance.

I dump the car, hike to the top of a dramatic valley and finally come across the Zapatista camp. It's pretty grim: in a scrappy clearing 20 or 30 listless men and women sit or lie around a large wooden-frame shelter covered in torn black plastic sheeting. A few of them get up when they see me, but it's clear that we pose no threat. I carry a box of fruit that I've brought as a peace offering.

A short-wave radio fizzes and quacks every now and then, and smoke drifts from a couple of fires. Outside a separate cooking shack a young couple stop snogging for a second to look at us without interest, then go back to snogging. So this is what a land invasion looks like. The people here are occupying land that they've invaded mainly to make sure that no one comes to take it back. There's little to do, and there are no crops growing. All they can do is sit and wait.

I find José and run to greet him, but he's furious with me. 'Where were you?' Apparently I shouldn't have entered this place on my own – I've made him look untrustworthy for leading me here. It looks as though the whole interview is in jeopardy, but after talking to him for a while, and offering the box of food to the rebels, he calms down and agrees to make an introduction for me.

Miraculously the rebels agree to an interview. They single out a young boy who will act as their mouthpiece. I'm slightly crestfallen – I don't want to speak to a mouthpiece. The boy sits me down next to a roaring fire and begins to talk. In fact he doesn't stop talking for 15 minutes straight, and that's just him introducing himself and his comrades. The rest of the rebels stand around in the background, listening in and posing for the camera. I ask a few questions about Zapatista aims and feelings, but the boy just wants to drum out the manifesto. I ask about the free trade agreement, and what the Zapatistas feel about Mexico's relationship with the USA. He starts to stumble a bit here, and one of the adult rebels gets frustrated and takes over. The free trade agreement was the catalyst, he says, and both capitalism and the USA are to blame for the Zapatista revolution. Ultimately, this revolution is all about food, hunger and land.

It's weird interviewing someone in a balaclava, much more so than interviewing a woman in a burka. It could be the fact that 20 blokes are staring at me whilst I talk, and without knowing their expressions, I can't tell if they're happy, angry or just bored. But as we continue to talk, other men butt in to take over the discussion and express their frustration and anger. 'We are all landless peasants, indigenous people whose rights have been trampled on by the government. In the 1960s, land was redistributed to many poor people, but soon afterwards the big landowners just bought it up again when they shouldn't have been allowed to. We are angry, and for years the Mexican government has ignored us.'

I tell them that I met a group of landowners whose land had been invaded, and wondered how they could justify forcing people off their farms.

'They say the land is theirs but they are illegal lands, they belong to the peasant. We always say we are the guardians, we are the ones who look after the land like a mother.'

I ask why the Zapatistas have an issue with the USA. He says that they blame the Americans for forcing NAFTA onto them: 'We indigenous people don't accept the free trade agreement because it will destroy our livelihoods. We are already seeing many indigenous people head across the border where they are killed like little birds. That's the end result of the poverty we have here.'

After talking over a blazing fire in baking sunshine for a couple of hours, I am stressed, hot and sticky, but elated that I've finally got to speak to the Zapatistas. I feel comfortable enough to ask the question that every journalist wants to ask, but never dares: 'We've been sitting in the blazing hot sun for two hours now, and I can't help feeling that you're wearing inappropriate headgear for a climate like Mexico's. Aren't you hot underneath all that wool?' My belligerent interviewee lets out a chuckle, and it spreads gently around the camp.

I race back to San Cristobal to meet Maria Urvina, a woman in her 60s whose land was invaded by the Zapatistas four years ago. She wears glasses that are held together by glue and hope, and she has a sad but kindly face. She flusters around her kitchen when I turn up, tidying and shooing children out into the courtyard.

Maria is, it's fair to say, emotionally crippled by the experience. She frequently bursts into tears when talking about the life she used to lead, and she's lost hope of ever getting her farm or her life back. She spends all her time working in a beer shop and looking after her sick brother who has gigantism. 'I'm too old,' she says, 'my life is over now.'

Whilst making me guacamole, she shows me the letter she received from the rebels back in March 2003. It makes terrifying reading: in three terse paragraphs she is ordered off her farm, and the Municipio Autonomo en Rebeldia claims it on behalf of the indigenous people: 'The earth has no owner, it cannot be bought or sold. It does not belong to whoever claims to be its owner, or to the government. This land will be worked collectively for the good of everyone.'

After the letter arrived, she had to leave her farm, never to return. She passionately hates the Zapatistas, and the indigenous people who invaded her land in particular. 'They are lazy, unlike other indigenous people from San Cristobal, and they haven't done anything with the land' – just left it to decline so much that it would take years of work to make it productive again. I ask why the government didn't help or protect her, but she dismisses them out of hand. 'The government doesn't help any of us.' Certainly, the government seems to be too weak to resist the Zapatistas here in Chiapas. Had she bought her land illegally, I ask? 'My grandfather bought the land,' she says, 'but it wasn't illegal.' And now she has nothing, and the Zapatistas occupy land that has apparently been rendered useless.

Crossing the Border

I leave Chiapas and fly to Tijuana, adjacent to the USA. It's not just near the border – it *is* the border. When you exit the airport, the border wall is 50 metres away. It must be overwhelmingly tempting for poor Mexicans when just over that line of concrete and plexiglass lies wealth beyond their dreams. Around 800,000 people cross the border illegally each year, many of them from rural areas like Chiapas. I'm planning to make the crossing (legally) late tomorrow, but first of all I'm going on a whirlwind tour of Tijuana.

There are now an estimated 11 million illegal immigrants living inside the USA. It seems ironic that whilst the USA exports corn, Mexico exports illegal immigrants. Of course, this hasn't been going down at all well with conservative Americans.

My guide on the tour is Lupe, quite possibly the worst driver in Mexico, if not the entire world, and his car is the most flea-ridden, cracked-of-windscreen, shabby and unsafe jalopy I've ever clapped eyes on. A deep funky smell rises up from it, and the smell evolves and worsens the hotter the day becomes. Only the passenger door opens, so I clamber over the passenger seat to get in the back. He's been employed because he's in touch with illegal emigrants and the 'coyotes' who extract exorbitant sums to take them across the border and supply them with fake passports.

Lupe is an ex-addict. He's kind and gushing in his affections, but full of nervous energy and wild twitches.

'What were you addicted to?' I ask.

'*Toto*,' he screams. 'Everything! Crack, marijuana, heroin, coke, crystal meth, glue, speed. You name it. Oh yeah, man, I was a baad person, but I'm clean now, been clean for ten years.'

We narrowly miss colliding head-on with an old VW Beetle taxi-van filled to the brim with a fat family. There's no time for recriminations or horn-honking – I just spot the startled expressions on their faces as they whiz by. 'Oops,' Lupe says.

He takes me at breakneck speed to a Casa del Migrantes – a night shelter for migrants who are on their way from rural areas to the USA. These men (only men) have often travelled days or weeks from their home towns, and they stop here to rest, gather themselves together and work out their means of crossing the border. If you jump the wall in or near Tijuana it's quicker to get to civilization as the US towns lie just over the border, and family or friends can easily pick you up. But there's a higher risk of capture. If you head off into the desert before crossing there's a lower chance of being caught but a much higher chance of dying from exposure in the desert sands. Either way it's dangerous – the wall by the airport is decorated with hundreds of crosses to mark all the lives lost by would-be emigrants.

In the Casa del Migrantes, we meet another man José, who tells me that he's planning to jump the border in three or four days, as soon as he's ready. He's been over a few times before, but spent time in prison for drug offences when he was younger, so he's very unwelcome.

There's no food, no work and no life worth living here in Mexico, he wants to go back over and join his mother. But America doesn't want or like him, he says. 'They need our labour, and they need the money we pay them for corn, but they hate us. Why can't they open the borders? No one in the USA wants to do the tough, filthy jobs the Mexicans are prepared to do, but they need someone to pick their tomatoes, so we are forced to work illegally.'

He's desperate to go, but he's not willing to pay the coyote rate of $3,000 – he'll take his chances in the desert. I wish him luck.

● ● ● ● ●

It's our last night in Mexico so we go out for a drink. Tijuana is a gruesome place, full of strip bars and shockingly young prostitutes in unfeasibly short skirts. We go to a horrible, empty bar built for American frat boys to get tanked in. A deafening mixture of rap and R&B pumps out of the speakers, and we order a bucket of beer. We make use of the bar's novelty sombreros for a team photo, and then make a break for our hotel – we've got an early start tomorrow.

The next day I try to meet some of Lupe's coyote contacts, but when we arrive, everyone in the room is shooting up heroin, and no one's in any fit state to talk. Come back later, they say. I give up, and Lupe takes me to a part of the wall that he's jumped in the past. From a bank at the top of a flood-channel that's straight out of the movie *Grease*, we can see across to the US. There's a McDonalds, a vast Nike store and a gleaming shopping centre just over the wall – it could have been built specifically to taunt the Mexicans. It's clean, ordered, spacious and dull, in wild contrast to the relatively lawless Mexican side, which is a mess of filthy buildings crammed together in a kaleidoscope of vibrant colour.

Lupe looks longingly over the wall. 'I was deported from the USA for selling drugs. I spent three years in a US state prison then I spent a year in a federal prison in Texas.'

I finally take my leave of Lupe and head for the border crossing point. It takes ten minutes with my UK passport and I'm in the USA. The difference is apparent from the moment I emerge from the border crossing: it's clean, wealthy, high-functioning, smart and civilized. It's also boring, faceless, generic and corporate, but that's hardly the point. It's easy to romanticize rural Mexico with its beauty and simplicity of life, but I know which lifestyle the emigrants prefer.

I visit groups of migrant workers standing by the roadside at a large intersection, next to a fast food joint. They come here every morning to wait for work, and stay until 1 p.m. before giving up to go home. Often they'll get a couple of days' work in a week, three if they're lucky. Few of these people are willing to talk to us, worried that they'll just attract more attention from the police and from a semi-vigilante group called the Minutemen. These are people who try to highlight illegal immigration, and have recently been accused of attacking and harassing migrant workers.

I find a group of luckier workers who've been given work for the day. They are exhausted from working on a tomato farm, and they are slumped by the roadside eating cheap pseudo-tortillas from a food van. None will say if they are working legally or illegally, but those who will talk all say the same thing: 'America hates us, but needs us.' Do they sympathize with the Zapatistas and their aims? 'Of course. No one else is prepared to stick up for us against the Americans.'

The truth is that the Zapatistas are a long, long way from here, busy occupying land in a place that these men have abandoned.

They get up and trudge back to the tomato farm to continue living their dream.

I hope that all this border crossing has prepared me for my next trip, which looks like being the most dangerous one of my life. Burma.

BURMA
Cooking with Rebels

POPULATION: 49 million

PERCENTAGE LIVING BELOW THE POVERTY LINE: 25%

UNDP HUMAN DEVELOPMENT INDEX: 130/177

CORRUPTION PERCEPTIONS INDEX POSITION: 160/163

GDP (NOMINAL) PER CAPITA: $230 (173/179)

FOOD AID RECIPIENTS: n/a

MALNUTRITION: 5% of the population

I'd make a crap spy: I get excited way too easily. And right now my shabby attempts at nonchalance could have catastrophic consequences. It's 4 a.m., and I'm about to spend the most dangerous night of my life trying to cross the border illegally from Thailand into Burma with Marc, my producer and good friend. We're standing in a pitch-black hotel car park in Thantend somewhere near the border surrounded by several conspicuous-looking bags of kit. We've just been dropped off by C___, the BBC's International Man of Mystery and Risk Assessment, and our high-risk consultant for visits to dodgy places, with instructions to wait until our contacts arrive and not to draw attention to ourselves.

We could get caught by the Thai army and be deported, or we could get caught by the Burmese army, in which case heaven knows what might happen. Hopefully, though, we'll slip through unnoticed and spend the next two weeks living with the Karen rebels and refugees, trying to find out how they survive whilst the Burmese government uses food as a weapon against them.

I've been lucky over the last few months of bullet- and dystentery-dodging not to have had any major accidents, not to have got shot or kidnapped or brought home a vicious bout of the runs to share with the kids. I hope to God that this isn't the trip where I screw up.

A pick-up truck rolls into the car park and a group of gnarled, baseball-capped guys jumps out. No one says anything. After a tense stand-off, I can't bear it any longer and I say, 'Hi. I'm Stefan.' One of the guys comes forward. 'I'm Black Tom.' You couldn't make this stuff up.

We throw our kit into the back of the pick-up and jump in. Black Tom grins at me, and it's a real smile. Thank God for that.

● ● ● ● ●

Before I carry on, let me tell you a little about Burma and the Karen rebels.

Alongside North Korea, Burma is one of the most repressive, corrupt, brutal and undemocratic regimes in the world, which, until very recently, has had little significant censure from the international community. They've been having a whale of a time repressing all manner of Burmese people and pissing all over democracy, but they've reserved some of their most vicious treatment for the Karen people.

The Karen rebels have been fighting the Burmese regime for 60 years, making this the world's longest-running civil war, and for the most part, the Karen have been losing. The Burmese army has invented some fantastic ways of screwing up life for the Karen, and most of them involve the use of food as a weapon.

The military is trying to starve the Karen out of existence by laying landmines in their fields, cutting off access to farmland and confiscating crops. These guys really know how to repress. As a consequence, the Karen people (who don't really need the junta's help in making their lives miserable as they are already desperately poor) are often forced off their land through hunger, and become refugees in their own country (some have escaped over the border to camps in Thailand, but this is currently illegal). They are liable to die of starvation, and even if they survive, they and their children are at risk from malnutrition, mineral and vitamin deficiency, dysentery and high infant mortality.

Sadly, as the situation gets more and more desperate, the political leadership of the KNU (Karen National Union) appears to be suffering from an internecine power struggle, and the rebel troops are sometimes refusing to accept their orders. The future of the Karen looks bleak indeed, and over the last few months there's been a huge escalation in fighting, and the current offensive is the strongest in ten years. It's widely seen as an attempt to crush Karen opposition once and for all. I'm expecting to have a traumatic couple of weeks.

● ● ● ● ●

Back in the pick-up we chat with our hosts: they are friendly, wiry Burmese refugees who work the border smuggling supplies and information and, tonight, a couple of journalists from Britain. We are driving towards a weaker section of the Thai-Burmese border, and Black Tom warns us that we've got a long and tiring night ahead of us.

Several hours later, the pick-up stops halfway up a jungle road, and we all dive into the trees, following our leader, Tu La Wa, an old soldier of 50 or so who's small and absurdly fit, despite the fact that he smokes endless stinking cheroots. Our rucksacks containing all our kit are left in the pick-up, to be smuggled over the border posing as humanitarian aid (still illegal but less sensitive). I wonder if we will ever see them again.

We begin an interminable trek through the jungle, and it's bloody hard work. The jungle is extremely humid, we are sweating profusely and the mountainous terrain makes walking extremely difficult. Our legs strain at the ridiculous gradients, and we stumble continually on the loose rocks under our feet. To add to the discomfort, after a couple of hours, despite the fact that I wore them for two weeks solid before we left the UK, my new jungle boots have raised a small army of blisters on my feet. Who'd have thought that the mountains in Thailand could be so different from Sainsbury's in Islington?

Marc holds a small infrared camera so he can film the border crossing, but it makes life very difficult for him – the camera screen he stares at is so bright his eyes can't adjust to see where he's going in the murk, and he keeps tripping over. It's all rather exciting in a cowboys and Indians kind of way until Marc loses his footing at the top of a hill. Black Tom and I grab him just in case he falls and, looking to our left, we see a terrifyingly precipitous drop. It looks like we just saved his life so Marc and I start to take things a little more seriously after that.

Marc isn't very fit. He can hold a cripplingly heavy TV camera for hours on end and endure the burden of my constant teasing, but he simply isn't built for jungle mountain trekking. He has to ask everyone to stop for a break every 15–20 minutes or so. This has both good and bad aspects – it's

FOOD AS A WEAPON

not great that we are constantly losing time, but at least I get lots of opportunity to tease him. He gets very grumpy and, in his best scoutmaster voice, tells Black Tom, 'You should only go as fast as the slowest person in the group,' as though it's not him. I, on the other hand, am built for endurance rather than speed. I'm useless at sprinting or Herculean feats of strength, but I can swim, cycle or hike for hours on end.

It's now pitch black, and the atmosphere becomes tense. We have headlamps, but Tu La Wa tells us that we shouldn't use them in case the army spots us. Suddenly there's a big crash and I can't find Marc. I begin to panic and take the risk of turning on my headlamp, to see a huge hole in the path in front of me about 10 metres deep, at the bottom of which lies Marc, on his back with his arm stretched ominously to the heavens. It looks like a trap hole straight out of *Tarzan*. I scramble down to him and discover that the camera sits in his hand.

'Is the camera OK?' he croaks heroically.

Thank God. He's shaken, bruised and scratched, but generally unhurt. I suppress the urge to give him a big hug. He sits for a few minutes to gather himself whilst I scour the jungle floor for bits of camera. We put it back together and even though it looks slightly less camera-like than when we left, miraculously, it still works.

Finally we stop by a small track and collapse, exhausted. Black Tom takes this opportunity to reveal that this is only the start of the night's journey. Great.

We wait for an hour or so, until another pick-up comes along. To my delight, this one is carrying our bags. We jump in and speed off. I am way beyond tired now and the exhaustion, together with the impending fear, makes me extremely tense. My mood is not improved when Black Tom tells us that we still aren't anywhere near the border – we're taking a long circuitous route around army bases and checkpoints just to get to the crossing point.

Suddenly the pick-up skids to a halt, and once again we all jump out and run off into the undergrowth where eight ragged men, who have agreed to help carry our kit, wait for us. We share the stuff out between us and race off, with Marc bringing up the rear and protesting at the pace.

It's another crippling, hot, sticky, mosquito-ravaged walk, and after a couple of hours my legs are beginning to feel dangerously wobbly. There's also a grating sound coming from my knee (too much cross-country running as a teenager). My blisters have begun to grow blisters and Marc has lost any remaining sense of humour he might have had.

Tu La Wa tells us not to talk, which is just fine as it helps us preserve energy and contain our irritation with each other. I've long since given up teasing Marc for being unfit – we're both at the limit of our endurance, but needless to say our uncomplaining Burmese helpers are skipping along like mountain gazelles on heat.

Four-and-a-half miserable hours later, we wait whilst a spotter goes ahead: we are nearing the border crossing point. When he returns we are urged to move on in silence and eventually we come to a large, filthy house raised about 5 metres off the jungle floor on thick bamboo poles. This is a safe house, owned by a Karen sympathizer, and we sit in his open-air, bamboo-floored room and gratefully drink his water and eat some small, sweet bananas.

We're late, Tu La Wa tells us, and we've missed the boat that was going to smuggle us across the border, so we'll have to wait until just before dawn for it to return. We sit down for a moment and fall asleep immediately.

The border between Thailand and Burma is a wide river, and to get across Marc and I will hide in the bottom of a boat. Thai fishing boats are allowed on this section of river, but either side can stop and search them. Tu La Wa says that there's a strange light scanning the river from the Burmese side that they've never seen before, and everyone is nervous. My hostile environments training taught me that the greatest dangers are presented by situations where you are tired and disorientated, and when carefully laid plans are changed at the last minute, but what can we do? We are in the hands of our hosts and they have 60 years of experience dealing with the Burmese army, so we have to follow their advice.

When Black Tom wakes us for our journey, we stumble out of the door and in his exhausted state, Marc falls down the stairs of the hut, twisting his ankle. It's still pitch black as we stagger off down the hill, shouting our thanks to the owner of the house. Tu La Wa tells us to keep quiet from now on, and warns us about a large riverbank that we'll have to climb over as quickly as we can when we reach Burma. This is when we'll be most vulnerable.

The night is absolutely black, and I'm blindly following Black Tom's footsteps. When I eventually hear the river it sounds scarily fast. Too fast for the long, thin, rather wobbly boat that is to be our transport. As soon as we're on our way I spot the light. It's small but very bright, and it's scanning the river from the far side. It looks like a laser, but I can't really tell. We duck our heads down, trying to look like cargo, and the boatman pushes on. The light seems to scan across us a couple of times and flickers green and red, but nothing happens. My heart beats like the clappers and I try not to think about what will happen if the Burmese army catches us.

We motor slowly up the river for half an hour just as dawn breaks, revealing a spooky, misty scene straight out of *Apocalypse Now*. We make it up the river without a problem and as we pull up at the water's edge, I can see a jetty and the infamous riverbank. The engine is cut, and we climb out of the boat in the terrifying silence. We scramble up the sand in a panic and jump over the edge of it to find a small bamboo hut. We're in Burma. We walk past more huts and pathways and stumble into the Ei Tu Ta refugee camp, sick from tiredness and nervous exhaustion. We're shown to a large open-sided hut where we're offered a cup of coffee. We sit there like zombies, and when someone mentions that this is the hut we are to sleep in, we drag out our sleeping bags and collapse.

Ei Tu Ta

I wake blinking into sunlight with a brilliant, sharp headache piercing my skull. I acknowledge the fact that I am alive, not visibly in custody, and uninjured, and fall back into a deep sleep.

Many hours later, I wake up to feel a throbbing, searing ache where my legs used to be. We'd slept the night on a big bamboo frame with just a roof of leaves and a floor raised a couple of metres off the ground away from snakes and bugs. It's home to a ragbag collection of charity workers, camp officials and a French would-be journalist called Roman who's cut loose from his job as a cocoa trader to explore the world.

Ei Tu Ta refugee camp is deep enough into the jungle and far enough away from Burmese interests for the army not to bother attacking it, but not far enough for its refugees to feel totally secure. These people, like the people in northern Uganda, have become Internally Displaced Persons (IDPs). The Thai army across the border is primarily there to ensure that the IDPs don't cross into Thailand: no one wants the burden of refugees, but the Thais are keen on peace with Burma and want to avoid militarizing the area. The most that the Thais are prepared to do is to turn a blind eye to aid that's shipped into the camp from Thailand, but it's difficult to imagine the Burmese allowing any UN agencies or charities to help the Karen on any significant scale. So the 3,000 residents of Ei Tu Ta are trapped, most of them having been forced to leave their homes by the brutality of the Burmese army, they are unable to return, yet unable to escape into Thailand to start a new life.

We sit down for a cup of tea with Peter, the head of the camp. He explains that although the Burmese junta hates the Karen people, they love Karen refugee camps because they know exactly where the Karen people are, and that they are safely disenfranchised, hungry and powerless.

Peter invites me to join him in the camp leader's hut, and I eat a plate of rice mixed with rotten fermented fish sauce (a bit like Thai fish sauce, but complete with fish-heads, bones and tails) and searing-hot vegetable curry. He shows me the food store, where a small supply of rice, fish paste and chillies is handed out to the refugees. Outside it I meet Ing Ling Wa, a nervous young mother who has recently arrived, having spent 17 days trekking with her family with no food other than foraged vegetation. I ask what forced her to make such a dangerous journey, and she explains that the Burmese army had taken control of her village and imposed forced labour.

'The army told the villagers to put a fence around the village, and if you were seen outside the village in the jungle you would be shot.'

This meant that she couldn't visit her fields so her crops were all ruined. I ask what threat she poses to the junta and what the army hope to achieve by doing this, but she just laughs: 'I don't know. I don't understand why they did it.'

Burma's military leaders have a deliberate policy of starving the Karen villagers, but I find it bizarre that they bother oppressing these people when nature has been doing a fine job of oppressing them for centuries. The Karen rebels are under-equipped and relatively small in number, and the Karen people are generally poor subsistence farmers living in an area of mountainous jungle, little of which can realistically be cultivated.

The answer might lie in the nature of the Burmese army, which, although it's big, is also under-equipped and poorly-trained. Armies are a great way of handing out patronage, maintaining corruption and keeping a network of paid lackeys to oppress the rest of the country, so it's in the junta's interest to keep them busy. In addition, the army has now been ordered to become self-sufficient, so it has to steal and confiscate from the locals to survive.

● ● ● ● ●

Just as in Uganda, I find Ei Tu Ta camp strangely beautiful – like a Hollywood re-creation of a simple Burmese village, complete with beautiful kids, smoke gently rising from houses made entirely out of bamboo, bare-breasted women washing in streams, young girls giggling flirtatiously, and men sitting around on their haunches chewing betel nut. There are chickens running around everywhere and puppies scampering at our feet (no, really there were). There's even a rudimentary football pitch.

Peter explains that the camps offer people a better life than their own villages: there's free (if basic) education, healthcare and some food rations, and many people own their own small plot of land to grow vegetables.

I meet the Tu Pa Lai family who arrived three months earlier. There's a tired, submissive sadness to them, and they tell me that their youngest son died from diarrhoea soon after they arrived. They explain that life is better here than in their old village where they were used as forced labour by the army. Despite the fact that here in the camp they have no prospects, no work, no land, no independence and no long-term future, at least they are free from the persecution they suffered at the hands of the army.

They are cooking lunch: rice with fish paste and a few greens they've grown beside their rickety shack. It is a decent meal in sheer calorific terms, but woefully lacking in nutritional basics – vitamins and minerals. They make enough for me too, and I'm very grateful. Marc, however, refuses to touch it for fear of losing control of his bowels. I've eaten so many dodgy meals by this stage that I have nothing left to lose, but Marc eats a bag of Boots nuts and raisins and looks bashful.

As always, it feels strange talking to people about their misery and then walking off to find someone else to interview. This is the journalist's conundrum, I suppose: you dip into people's misery and move on, trying not to feel too grubby.

The sun sinks like a stone at around 7 p.m. and I head back to the camp hut for supper, which is exactly the same as breakfast but bigger. Marc opts to sup from our survival rations again.

I want to call Georgia; I always miss her like crazy when I'm in the more remote and difficult places. We have two satellite phones and a couple of spare batteries, which we have to use sparingly because there is no way of charging them whilst we're here. I call her anyway, I need to let her know I got over the border safely. She's relieved, but still stressed that we're here – she knows that the real danger has barely started.

In places like this there's nothing to do after dark – most people can't afford food, let alone candles, so they just go to sleep after the sun sets. I stay up and chat with Peter and Black Tom, and then call it a night.

Although I'm still exhausted from the journey, I find it impossible to sleep. Our hut-mates all snore like dragsters and I'm essentially lying on a pile of logs with legions of busy little insects living busy little lives, swarming and chewing.

The camp rises before dawn with the sound of banging and shouting. I lie listening to the cacophony until 7 a.m. and then drag myself out of bed for a wash in some freezing cold stream water. Wow, that wakes me up.

Peter takes me on a tour of the camp. It's enormous and growing every week with new arrivals. As soon as a new family arrives, they are given a plot of land on which they start to build their bamboo house, which takes a couple of weeks. Everyone seems to have the basic skills to build a house – bamboo has a limited lifespan of around five years, so everyone has to know how to build and rebuild them on a regular basis. A couple of streams run through the camp, and we wander among allotments and houses of varying ages.

The Nao Gu Putu family are just about to eat breakfast and they wave me over. They arrived in the camp four months ago but weren't able to bring any possessions with them. La Puo, a woman of about 40, explains why.

'In October the army sent four battalions of soldiers into our area. Fighting broke out between them and the Karen soldiers and mortar shells landed on our village. When the army withdrew, we thought we'd return to harvest our crops, but they put landmines around the village so we dare not live there any more.'

They escaped their village and hid in the jungle, but hunger forced them to venture back. 'When my father-in-law returned to the village to find food he moored his boat and the Burmese army found it. They waited for him to return and shot him, cut off his head and took it back to the military camp. Later, they forced his cousin to kiss the head.'

La Puo tells this story without emotion, and I find it difficult to understand if she's angry, grieving, combative or simply relieved that her ordeal is over. The Karen aren't loquacious people, and they seem happiest answering direct questions. This makes interviews extremely difficult as I have to ask some uncomfortably probing questions: unless I ask if any of their family have died, they don't think to mention it. On top of the tragedy of La Puo's father-in-law it turns out that their two youngest children died of diarrhoea.

The Karen are friendly but unused to talking about emotions and opinions – in fact, Black Tom tells us that expressing emotions is a sign of weakness, and God forbid anyone should be seen crying. Crying in

FOOD AS A WEAPON

someone else's house is a big taboo because this curses the house, and you then have to pay the owner to make up for the impending bad luck. A therapist would have a field day here. It is horribly ironic that a people with such a negative attitude to emotion have experienced such misery. Maybe denial is the only way of surviving when life is so full of pain.

They aren't consumed by their pain, though: the entire family howl with laughter when, at their urging, I try the local bird's-eye chillies. A word of advice: don't eat these at home, unless you want to know how it feels to be punched in the mouth.

Jungle Trekking

We leave Ei Tu Ta in search of the Karen rebels. We're going to spend a week living rough in the jungle, monitoring Burmese army movements and checking on the remaining Karen villages.

After half an hour's walking we stop at a clearing and it takes me a few moments to realize that there are 20 or so heavily armed men lurking under trees and in the undergrowth. Tu La Wa introduces me to Major Ki La Wa, the platoon commander, who says that he will be responsible for our safety.

We walk out of the camp along a riverbed, wading through the water. Our jungle boots aren't waterproof – in fact they are exactly the opposite: they're designed to let water in, but more crucially, to let it out again. Jungle trekking involves stomping through endless rivers and streams in the fetid heat, so walking through the rivers isn't as unpleasant as it sounds – it's a great way to cool down.

The Karen National Liberation Army (KNLA) has around 5,000 soldiers, all volunteers who spend much of their time fighting in the jungle. They are a ragged army of flip-flops and rocket-propelled grenades, and they're vastly outnumbered and outgunned by the half-a-million-strong Burmese army. But the Karen soldiers have the benefits of guerrilla warfare, the support of the villagers and 60 years' experience of living and fighting in the jungle. Our platoon travels light, each man taking with them little more than their weapons and ammunition, a small bag of rice, oil, a sleeping blanket, lightweight hammock and a machete.

Marc and I, on the other hand, have BBC health and safety rules to contend with, so we come complete with trauma packs (for major injuries), emergency food rations for eight days, insect repellent, cameras and microphones, batteries, sleeping bags and a set of clean clothing.

We hike off into the hills at a fair lick, stopping frequently to check for Burmese army patrols. Almost instantly I am bathed in sweat from the damp heat, and I start to feel tense and irritable. My mood isn't helped by the fact that the walk seems to go on forever, and I begin to despise the jungle with a passion.

Ei Tu Ti Village

After five hours of walking up and down steep valleys I am exhausted, but we have finally reached our stopping point near the Karen village of Ei Tu Ti just in time for nightfall. A few of the soldiers go to check if the village is free of the Burmese army whilst we set about preparing for our first night sleeping rough in the jungle. Ki La Wa helps us find a couple of trees from which to string our lightweight hammocks, then teaches us to clear the ground underneath to make sure that snakes and rodents don't hide there. If you're bitten by a snake it's a long, long way back to the camp, and they probably won't have the antidote anyway.

I set up my hammock, spray the end ropes with insect repellent to avoid the tree's legion of creepy bitey crawlies joining me in bed later, and attempt to get in. I'm swiftly and humiliatingly ejected from the other side. After an ungainly struggle, I finally manage to get in and stay there. The discomfort is a surprise – the hammock is tiny, precarious and wobbly, and it clamps you into a bowed posture designed specifically to bugger your back.

The major tells us that the village has an animist ceremony later and the villagers have invited us to join them, so we leave our new jungle home and pick our way up the hill as soon as night falls.

The village is a collection of 20 or so bamboo huts in the same style as those in the refugee camp. We're led into one of them where a dozen or so men, women and children are having a feast. The head of the house greets me with a huge smile, then ties red strings around my wrists as good luck charms whilst mumbling words of blessing. 'All your good spirits will come back to you,' he says. That would be nice.

'*Ta blu,*' I say [thank you].

The villagers are fascinated – they've never seen Westerners before, and it's all they can do to stop themselves from poking us with their fingers. They are kind and welcoming, and they've been waiting for us to arrive before starting their dinner, which makes me feel very guilty. The major, Black Tom and I are given a meal of boiled pork – a huge privilege in a place where there is so little food, but after the offence I caused Sabra in Afghanistan, I have learnt that turning down food is a great insult, so I swallow my guilt. The pork is still covered in pig bristles, but it's the first meat I've had in ages, so I wolf it down.

The major explains the Burmese army's Four Cuts, a deliberate policy of starving the Karen. 'When they arrive at a village they loot it, taking all the food. Then they ask the villagers where the rebel soldiers are, and beat them if they won't say. And where they suspect there are landmines they make the villagers walk on the fields.' The army hope that if the villagers are starved out, the rebels will lose supplies.

The Ei Tu Ti village head relies on the KNLA for protection and says 'If they weren't here we wouldn't be here either.' But right now he doesn't want to talk about problems in case it brings bad luck on the village – he wants to sing and drink to bless the coming harvest. He passes me a small bowl of rough and potent rice wine; it warms me instantly. The cup is passed around over and over again, and the villagers all start smoking gruesome cheroots. They begin to throat-sing, a dirgey, moaning noise that no one could translate. After drinking enough hooch to ensure a swift departure into dreamland, I thank everyone profusely, wish them luck and stagger back across the soggy valley to our camp, from where I can still hear the throat-singing loud and clear.

The ominous drone of the singing, together with the discomfort of the hammock, the freezing cold and the constant rustle and scratching of Lord-knows what on the jungle floor below keeps me wide awake until about 4 a.m.

I awake at 6 a.m. with a throbbing headache and the sensation of having wet myself. I feel my sodden sleeping bag, and realize that it has been raining whilst I've been asleep. I'm soaked through. It has also been building up on the leaves above me, and then dripping down on my forehead, adding to the hangover. I look around to see that the soldiers had built themselves fires next to their hammocks, which they stoked every few hours throughout the night. Why didn't I think of that?

We pack up camp soon after dawn and head off to our next camp. I'm already exhausted and sleepy, and I hike in a daze. After four hours of zombiefied walking we stop in dense jungle next to a stream and make a more substantial camp. Two of the soldiers start hacking down bamboo to make utensils for a meal. They've brought a couple of pans with them, but use bamboo to make everything else: ladles, spoons, pans, cups. They pack rice into a piece of bamboo around 5 cm in diameter, top it up with water, put a stopper into it, and then lean it against the fire. The rice steams, and just before the young bamboo starts to burn, it's cooked. They also make a bamboo saucepan using the same principle – it sits on the fire and because it's green and tough, water inside it will boil before the pan burns. You can use each pan twice before throwing it away. This is how the rebels survive carrying so little – they make utensils every time they stop to camp, but leave them behind when they move on.

The soldiers pick some wild banana flowers, thinly chop them and their stalks and boil them in stream water. They also find bo na – a kind of tropical root that tastes of ginger and aniseed – and the major shows me how to strip and cook it into a stew. He tells me that he's been a soldier for 30 years, and he's never even thought about doing anything else. He spends most of his life living in the jungle: 'I miss my family, but I have a responsibility. What can I do?'

I ask some of the younger soldiers what they would do if the war ended, but they haven't got a clue. They have no understanding of life without the war, and in truth they don't believe it'll end in their lifetime.

The food is good and we eat it gratefully. Marc says he isn't hungry, but soon after, I spot him wolfing down a batch of Boots flapjacks.

The major decides we should stay here by the stream tonight and arranges guards to surround the camp. I wander off with the satellite phone, trying to locate a satellite through the jungle cover. I haven't spoken to my girls for four days, so I'm elated when I get through. Poppy goes nuts, screaming, 'Yello Daddy.'

Marc and I make a much better camp this time, building a fire in between our hammocks and making a little bench to keep our kit off the ground. I even set up a strip of plastic as a rain cover in case it rains again tonight. We make some coffee and strip off to wash in the chilly stream, after which I feel almost normal again.

We go to bed early, and I lie awake wondering what it must feel like for these people to welcome journalists from rich countries into their lives. The Karen are stuck here, possibly forever, whereas we have the luxury of coming and going with our high-tech kit to keep our expensively insured bodies as comfortable as possible. And we are being paid for it. Black Tom says that he's just glad we're here, making a film about them – it shows that the world cares, and that if nothing else, at least their suffering isn't going unnoticed. But I can't help thinking that if I were in his position, I'd resent these two wimpy blokes from the BBC with all their expensive stuff.

Bushmeat

In the morning I notice that next to the major's hammock is a vast cow pat. Quite what (or how) a cow was doing here in the middle of the jungle is anyone's guess. I point at the huge turd and ask the major if last night's supper hadn't agreed with him. He doesn't get the joke, and I hope I haven't offended him.

During the night the guards had shot a type of cat and a monkey-like creature called a ki chi, which I've never seen before. Black Tom doesn't know what their English names are. The cat looks oddly like my own faithful cat Tom, so I pay close attention to the cooking process and store the recipe in my memory for when he gets old and grouchy.

I find out much later when we're back in London that the cat is a civet cat, renowned for spreading SARS, and the monkey-like creature is a loris, an endangered primate, though possibly not as endangered as the Karen. The soldiers impale the animals on sticks then burn off their fur over the fire. It smells foul, but it's better than skinning them as we need to eat the skin too – it would be a waste of precious protein to throw it away. We gut and butcher the cat and loris in the stream, and only the lower intestine and gall bladder are thrown away – everything else goes into a pot to be stewed. The civet cat is briefly simmered in water, but the loris needs to be cooked for two to three hours. We make the bamboo rice again to accompany the meat.

When it's finally ready, the major invites me to eat – he gets the first bash at any food, so it pays to stay matey with him. The civet cat is delicious – sweet and strongly gamy, with lots of small, fiddly bones to suck on. I eat a hunk of cat's liver, which is a first for me. The whole thing tastes quite heady and intestinal – they haven't thrown much away, and the innards of the cat have all been cooked up with the flesh. The loris isn't as nice as the cat – a murky, strong and musty flavour, although this could be because of the intestinal overload. Either way, I'm grateful for the meal, and relieved that I don't have to join Marc eating the emergency rations. He complains of gag reflexes, but I manage to bully him into tasting a morsel of the cat. He turns green almost immediately and I feel a little guilty. I look at his rehydrated lunch: pasta with some filthy excuse for a meat sauce. It smells like cat food.

Then there's more walking: hours and hours, miles and miles. The KNLA keep this up for years on end, but I am exhausted after a few days of it. The villages are spread out – the Karen enjoy living in isolation, and the terrain is so difficult to cultivate that it takes large amounts of land to support a relatively small concentration of people.

It's dangerous patrolling the jungle regions because there are no front lines in this war – the area is so vast that occupying it permanently would be impossible for the army, so it has a series of barracks and it tends not to venture far unless absolutely necessary. We drop in on one village close to one of the barracks, which is regularly raided by the army. I ask them if the army treats them badly, but they can't answer – they have no frame of reference.

'Every time the army comes, we all run away and the soldiers loot our food,' they say. But there's no sense of surprise or outrage: they just accept that this is the natural order of things, and there's nothing they can do about it.

That night we stop on a high mountain ridge to camp. It's an unsettling place: we're on the site of a Karen graveyard strewn with pots and pans and clothing for the departed soul to take into the next life. We're also near a Burmese army camp so everyone's on high alert, and night-time guards are doubled. There are five bases and 400 Burmese soldiers in this area, and they are far too strong for our KNLA platoon of 20 men to engage them in a battle.

Determined to keep my mind occupied I borrow a machete from one of the soldiers and hack down bamboo to make a bench. I'm hopeless at it to begin with, and the soldiers try to help me. It's all about getting the angle right, apparently.

Marc and I build a huge fire – we're determined not to get too cold on this mountain. We sit on our bench winding each other up talking about gin and tonics and ice-cold glasses of wine, then put a vast log on the fire and turn in. Soon the fire has grown out of control and I have to get up to try to calm it down. I finally go to bed and sleep fitfully, too hot.

I wake in a pool of cold sweat. I'm really not built for this jungle thing.

We visit another village and are ushered in as honoured guests along with the major. The village head offers us a wonderful treat of big white wriggling butterfly larvae – they are especially rare at this time of year. Tu La Wa dry-fries them in a pan over a fire. They are extraordinarily delicious and taste exactly the same as Jerusalem artichokes: sweet and crunchy, with a soft centre. I even get Marc to eat one.

FOOD AS A WEAPON

This village is almost comically isolated – there are no services of any description, and the people are often on the verge of starvation. They grow a little rice and a fair crop of tobacco, and if they can make it as far as the next village without disaster, they can exchange the tobacco for other foods. There's no healthcare, no education and no protection from the Burmese army, except occasional patrols like this.

I spot a little boy with a testicle the size of a small melon – a tumour or cyst, perhaps. His mother says that every three or four days he feels acute pain and can't breastfeed; she's distraught. I leave some money with Tu La Wa, asking him to make sure the child gets to Ei Tu Ta camp to visit the clinic. Journalists aren't supposed to give money to people because it has a tendency to warp the truth: people will make up tragic stories in the hope that journalists will pay them to talk. But I reason that this boy's condition is serious and specific, and my cash could help. On the way out, Black Tom worries that we've ensured the boy never gets to see a doctor – his parents now have more money than they've ever had before, and it's in their interests to keep him like this in case another Westerner with a charitable bent comes their way.

On the way back to the refugee camp we meet a couple of nervous women who have been scouring a stream for food. It's taken them four hours to catch three minute frogs and a tiny fish about the size of my little finger.

After four hours' trekking (it doesn't feel so bad this time – perhaps we're getting fit) we finally arrive at the clearing on the outer reaches of Ei Tu Ta camp and say goodbye to the soldiers. They've looked after us well, and I'm grateful to have got back unscathed. The major gives us both a gift of a bamboo saucepan and I wish him all the luck in the world.

It feels like we're returning to a luxury hotel: we have a floor! A roof! Food! As we arrive at our shack, a huge crowd has gathered and I smile and thank them for coming to welcome us back. I shake a few hands, but the people look confused. I realize that they haven't come to welcome us back at all. In the middle of the throng stands a rotund, balding, goateed man who looks like a drummer from a death metal band.

Pastor Joe is something of a legend around these parts. A brash Noo Yoiker with a big gob, a desire to do good, and the personal approval of the Lord. He is in town to distribute boxes of toys and clothes donated by the people of Australia, along with the word of God. He's bursting with energy and faith. He tells me that Sylvester Stallone is going to make a film of his life – he spends his life smuggling aid across the Thai border and spreading the good word. It's a tough way to live, but Pastor Joe relishes the challenge.

I want to talk to him some more, but right now just looking at him makes me even more exhausted so I go and collapse in the hut.

Ei Tu Ta vs The Rest of the World

We are invited to try betel nut by some of the camp women. All across Burma, Thailand and India people chew betel nut in much the same way that Westerners smoke cigarettes – it's a habit-forming, mildly euphoric stimulant and it's cancerous. It dyes the teeth red and causes the chewer to salivate profusely and spit bright spurts of red saliva all over the place. Burma is covered in red flob in the same way that London streets are covered in chewing gum.

Betel nut is the seed of the betel palm. It's the size of a nutmeg and it has high levels of psychoactive alkaloids. The giggling women show me how to grate the betel nut using a tool that's a cross between a nutcracker and a pair of pliers. One of the women, Li Do, takes me under her wing and shows me how to lay the gratings on a bitter betel leaf, wipe some lime paste (the ingredient in concrete rather than the fruit) on top, add some tobacco and wrap it up.

The women all proudly show their red teeth – they look like vampires – and tell me that the Burmese find red teeth very sexy. Li Do warns me not to chew, but rather to just hold it at the back of my jaw, otherwise it'll sting and make me feel dizzy.

I put the package into my mouth and try not to chew. Saliva starts to run like a river from my mouth, and I'm overcome by a sensation of intense pain. There's nothing about this experience that's pleasant. I tell Li as much and ask when the good bit starts, but she just laughs at me and teases me that my face has turned red. She says that it should taste sweet and delicious, but I'm overcome by a heavy sweat, a burning mouth and general panic. I'm chewing involuntarily and persevering, but I just don't get it. The girls find my discomfort hilarious.

I start to splutter, and thick red saliva spews forth. I go for as long as I can, but after 15 minutes or so, I can't take it any longer and spit the whole lot out. I'm feeling dizzy and sick and the women are splitting their sides at the sight of whitey making a tit of himself.

Pastor Joe wakes me early – he wants to play a game of football against the camp. Ei Tu Ta vs The Rest of the World. I am a little

FOOD AS A WEAPON

hesitant – I'm leaving tonight on an exhausting eight-hour hike back over the border into Thailand, and a twisted ankle is the last thing I need. Before I go, I also need to see a woman whose baby is in the camp clinic with severe malnutrition. But Pastor Joe hasn't got where he is today by giving in to secular reluctance. He practically drags me, along with his chirpy acolyte Joshua and our French friend Roman, to the camp football pitch.

We stand there in the early dawn light, but no one else has turned up. This doesn't bother Pastor Joe who says we should have faith and warm up. After half an hour of booting a football around, a trickle of people starts to arrive. The trickle turns to a flood, and eventually about a thousand people gather to watch the crazy foreigners make fools of themselves. We borrow a few of the camp administrators to make our side up to a decent number, and the best Karen footballers gather to take us on. I'm sure they are better players than us, but I sense that this one could be close: we have the crucial advantage of shoes.

Oh, how wrong I am. The football pitch is about as flat as the Somme after heavy shelling, and the ball bounces unpredictably and wildly, as though it were a rugby ball. We totter around the crevassed pitch trying not to break our ankles, whilst the Karen glide around as if it is as smooth as the Stamford Bridge turf. They wallop the ball hard with their bare feet and our only saving grace is, of course, Pastor Joe, who is a fearless and bulky goalkeeper. This is fortunate because he is kept very busy. At one point, Joshua scores a goal for us, and the refugees roar enthusiastically.

The balls continue to fly past Pastor Joe, until suddenly I get a lucky break: the ball actually goes in the direction I kick it, I dribble like a pro, dummy past two defenders leaving them flat on their backs, wrong-foot the goalie and ready myself for the *coup de grâce*, then just in front of their empty goalmouth a muddy chasm opens up in front of me and my foot disappears. I pirouette, arms flailing, and fall on my face like a drunkard. A thousand refugees laugh their pants off. We finally call it a day at 6–1, and gather for a team photo with half the spectators. The school bell rings (the teachers have kindly waited until the match is over), and the kids run off.

I return to my shack to tend my wounds, but there's bad news from the clinic: the baby girl that was suffering from malnutrition has just died. I'm devastated. Perhaps I've become biased from spending too much time here, but it feels as though the Burmese junta has just murdered another Karen child.

Just before we leave, Pastor Joe gathers us for a blessing. It's not really my thing, but in the circumstances, Marc and I need all the help we can get.

Night falls and we're ready to move off. As we leave camp, people wave and say 'Ta-ta'. They know that we're going home to a place where there's wealth, opportunity and respected human rights. They also know that we'll be making a film about their lives and they hope that this will help in some way. But there's little real optimism here: the Karen are a broken people fighting a war they can never win, against a regime that persecutes them with impunity. I hope with all my heart that the world begins to care a little more and puts pressure on the junta.

We climb into a wobbly boat and cross the river. We're taking a different route this time in case soldiers discovered the path we took on the way over and are waiting for us on the way back. I could tell you about the return journey in detail, but it's just more of the same: hour upon hour of utter, body-aching exhaustion, sweat-drenched nervousness and vaulting fear. The only difference is that I will, for the rest of my life, feel an impotent rage at what I've seen here.

Burma's brutal totalitarian government seems propagated by greed. A military junta that's unburdened by the expense and restrictions of democracy and can do fantastic business deals when it's using forced labour, when it can take land and resources from its natural owners at will, and when it cares little for the social or environmental consequences. If you are thinking about going to Burma on holiday, bear in mind that whatever the deal, you can be sure that, in one way or another, the regime and its friends are pocketing a fair amount of the cash from it. Russia and China are happy to do deals with a repressive regime, which seems to say a lot about their own politics. India is happy to ignore human consequences in order to fuel its economic boom. And the world doesn't mind what's going on in Burma as long as it stays quiet. The only hope for democracy in Burma is if the small rumblings amongst the international community become a roar.

NOTE: *The facts in this piece have been checked as far as reasonably possible; much of what is stated about the country is common consensus from journalists, politicians, NGOs and protest groups. Many of these groups have an agenda, so I have usually gone with the less hysterical views and tried to tread a middle path through them, and to let people speak for themselves.*

FOOD AS A WEAPON

INDIA
The Rat Eaters

- -

POPULATION: 1,169 million

PERCENTAGE LIVING ON LESS THAN $2 A DAY: 80%

UNDP HUMAN DEVELOPMENT INDEX: 126/177

CORRUPTION PERCEPTIONS INDEX POSITION: =70/163

GDP (NOMINAL) PER CAPITA: $797 (133/179)

FOOD AID RECIPIENTS: 190,000 to 2007

MALNUTRITION: 20% of the population

- -

Everyone falls in love with India eventually. It's partly to do with the swirling, chaotic human soup, the sensual assault and the intricate, bewildering beauty. But there's a guilty secret to our fascination: much of India's beauty is found not so much in its fabulous riches, but in its gruesome poverty, in our wonder at the sheer scale of deprivation. The poorest Indians endure conditions so awful that they seem unreal, like an epic movie of human suffering rather than reality. And the Western visitor wanders around the country in a state of semi-disbelief, mesmerized by the vast gap between the wealthy and the impoverished, fascinated by the lives of its rural poor, the beautiful kids running about in shreds of clothing, the people surviving amidst filth and squalor, the sheer pressure of so many people in such a small space.

India has the fourth largest economy in the world, but despite that, over half of the world's hungry people live here. It's odd because food is India's most successful cultural export (and of course curry has become the UK's national dish). But what's even more shocking is the fact that this hunger isn't just due to the natural growing pains of an emerging capitalist democracy: in some parts of India the poor are systematically kept hungry by the wealthy, and it's all justified by the caste system.

India is home to one-eighth of the world's population (1.1 billion people), and one-eighth of the population of India (that's 165 million people) are dalits – the untouchables. These people are seen as outcasts – below caste – outside the Hindu social order. Many of these people live in grinding poverty, disenfranchised from Indian politics and society, and with little hope of escape.

Caste discrimination is now, strictly speaking, illegal, but it's still going strong in the countryside, where the poor are routinely exploited and abused. Many rural dalits are desperately poor, perpetually living on the verge of hunger, and because they are so powerless they are highly susceptible to abuse by the wealthy, especially through food and land. There are widespread accusations that the Indian police systematically collude with the discrimination and support the Brahmin: the highest caste who usually wield the real power in India.

In the Hindu belief system you live an ongoing cycle of reincarnation until you reach *moksha*, or liberation, and in each cycle your caste is assigned to you depending on how good you were in the last life. It's a more or less fatalistic approach to earthly existence (and maybe it has positive uses) but it's also been used for centuries by the higher castes to keep the poor in their place, and to ensure the continuity of their own power and wealth – you've been born a dalit, ergo, you must have been bad in a former life. Ergo, tough shit.

I've come here to discover how untouchability has kept so many people hungry in a country whose economy is set to rival the USA within 30 years.

The Rat Eaters

I'm in Patna, the state capital of Bihar, in the northeast of India. It's a filthy, crumbling mess of a city, with tens of thousands living rough on the streets; it is renowned for corruption, bad government and a high level of discrimination against the dalit. I'm planning to head out to the countryside where, rumour has it, there's a sub-caste of the dalit, the very lowest of the low, called the Musahars – literally, the rat-eating people. My Indian guide and translator, Anoj, is extremely sceptical that anyone gets so hungry that they'd eat vermin: 'It may have happened in the past, but not any more,' he says.

In this area several armed groups, including the Naxalites (pro-dalit Maoist rebels), have emerged to assert the rights of the dalit, fight the wealthy landowners and claim land for the peasants, but in return the landowners have funded their own armies, such as the Ranvir Senato, to resist their claims, and my most difficult mission is to make contact and meet with these paramilitaries before heading out to the countryside. It's dangerous to meet them in town where there are informers and policemen everywhere, so they are very wary of us, with good reason as it turns out, because straight away there's a catastrophe. Somehow Anoj manages to screw up the meetings so that the Naxalite rebel contact is sitting waiting whilst I chat to their arch rivals, the notorious Ranvir Sena army. How the hell has this happened?

After trying to negotiate my way through a tricky few hours with a barrel-load of lies, it seems that neither group of rebels is keen to chat – in fact they're furious. I try telling them that I'm from the BBC, I have to remain neutral and I'm interested in both sides of the story, but it doesn't seem to wash.

It's a really bad start to the trip so I decide to find some authentic Biharian curry, plus a pint or two of Kingfisher to ease the tension. I drop into various curry joints, but either they don't serve beer, or they are too filthy to bear. Finally I stumble across a temple to 1980s' chic full of chintzy sofas. They sell beer. It'll do fine.

Refreshed and slightly more optimistic, I visit Patna's central food market the following day. But it's very difficult to talk to anyone. White people are pretty rare in Patna and the locals stare at me with a lobotomized gaze and a crowd of men follow me around in a bizarre human wave. I explore the chaotic, stinking market, trying to get a feel for food in Patna, but every time I stop people push forward until I am squashed in the middle. I take refuge in some grimy food stalls, but it's hard work.

I persevere, though, and spend some time wandering around the street stalls looking at vast mountains of sweets, buns, pancakes and all manner of breads. I stop at one breathtakingly filthy stall where the chef lets me make fresh golden yellow jalebi sweets. I squeeze flower shapes (well, that's what they're supposed to be) out of dough from a scrofulous cloth straight into hot ghee (clarified butter). They puff up and fry hard, at which point they are dropped into a sugar solution to soak, and then piled into mounds (on which the flies feast) for sale. It's hard to imagine a more calorie-laden opportunity for botulism spores to grow.

I'm useless at it to begin with, but my technique improves as I persevere. By the time I'm done the crowd has grown enormous, and they clap and cheer my efforts, which is sweet but undeserved, and I buy a few kilos of the sweets to say thank you.

The crowds continue to follow me until it becomes too difficult to work so I find a small sit-down curry joint and pay the owner a few rupees to close his murky restaurant to customers for an hour so that I can eat and talk to him. He glows with pride when I tell him that his food would stand up well in any Indian restaurant in London, but he warns me that in rural areas people are desperate for food and hunger is widespread.

Paraiya

I get up early the next day and set off on a four-hour journey to a rural village called Paraiya. In geographical terms it's not very far, but the roads are so potholed that our driver can go only at walking pace. It's tiring sitting in the car being thrown around as if you're on a tiny boat in a violent storm, and I become desperate for a break. Eventually I can take it no more and shout 'Stop!'

We stop at a roadside shack and eat kachori – fried dumplings stuffed with various pastes made from vegetables. They don't taste of much, but they're served with a slurp of very hot spicy pulses and sauce – it's a decent breakfast. It always surprises me how people eat curry for breakfast – it's quite a jolt to start the day with food that takes your breath away with its ferocity. I take a look at the filthy, fly-blown kitchen and wonder if I'm taking undue risks with my stomach again, but I figure that I've built up so much immunity from eating in squalid places over the past year that nothing much can hurt me now.

Four enormous breakfasts (sullen driver included), plus ten cups of sticky, sweet chai cost 80p. The tea is served in tiny clay cups that are thrown away after a single use. This seems a waste in such a poor country, but it's best not to argue with the system. The clay gives the tea a dry taste similar to … well … clay, but it's nice. The only problem with the place is that it's swarming with flies.

As we pass through the countryside I look out at the never-ending network of rice fields. Every patch of spare land is being used to grow food, which isn't surprising for a country with this kind of density of population. What I do find surprising is that there are people *everywhere* in the fields – all of them busy tending, tidying, or guarding.

That afternoon I stop at the offices of an NGO called Nav Bharat Jagriti Lendra and drink some chai with Ramswaroop, a kindly balding man who fights for the rights of the dalit and reminds me of Gandhi. He has a habit of farting long and loud in public without a hint of embarrassment, a skill of which I am enormously jealous (I'm not sure if Gandhi did the same).

We wander around the village. All the buildings are covered in cakes of mud and straw, and I wonder if it's something symbolic to do with dalit fatalism. Ramswaroop tells me they are dung cakes, used as fuel for cooking. A little girl called Indu shows me how to make them: take a bucket of cow dung and another of water. I get my hands in deep (best to remove your watch first) and squidge it about with my fingers to make sure it's fully mixed in, ignoring the rising feeling of disgust at being up to your elbows in shit. Then we make balls of dung the size of a large fist, and roll that in straw or rice husks, and set them aside. Once they are all rolled and ready, Indu takes one and taps it gently against a tree to flatten it, then, when it's cake-shaped, she slaps it against the tree with a large 'splat'. I try my hand at it, and make a big shitty mess of the tree and myself. Eventually I get the hang of it, and I finish off the rest of the cakes until the whole tree is covered in dung. The cakes are left to dry for a week or so, then used like wood for fires.

I ask why people bother going to the effort of making dung cakes rather than just throwing some wood on the fire and Ramswaroop explains that it's not easy getting hold of wood, especially in a country as densely populated as India, where deforestation has devastated rural areas. There's just no wood left near most villages, and it's one of the reasons why cow ownership is so important despite the fact that Hindus don't eat beef: the cow can be used for milking, but also for processing organic matter into cooking fuel. People who own no livestock often have to spend huge amounts of time and effort walking miles out of the villages just to gather enough fuel to cook.

Soon after dawn, we strike off across the shallow riverbed, heading for the next door village, with Ramswaroop farting merrily as we talk. This is the desperately poor village of Paraiya, medieval in its filth and poverty, but within a matter of seconds we are surrounded by a sea of tiny, ragged, heartbreakingly beautiful children, squealing with laughter and getting under our feet.

I'm struck, once again, by the poverty paradox: in the morning light the village – with its simple mud huts, children playing in the dirt, women washing in rivers, smoke drifting up from tiny stoves, baby goats and enormous cows fighting for space between people, and a patchwork of paddy fields – looks idyllic, and it's tempting to think that life here has an innocence and simplicity that we in the West long for.

Anshuman, one of the village elders, invites me to share his breakfast in front of his crumbling mud hut. He serves rice with a thick white sauce and I ask what it is. 'It's the water from the boiled rice. We use it instead of curry. We have it for breakfast, lunch and dinner.'

His entire family live on rice with rice sauce, and it's diets like these that cause half of India's children to be malnourished. You can't get the minerals and vitamins you need by eating only rice.

Some TV presenters and gushing food writers will have you believe that dirt cheap peasant food from across the globe is good, wholesome and delicious. But with the truly poor, that's simply not true. Most of the food they eat is bland and depressing such as CSB (corn soy blend) flour mixed with water. In Uganda it's flavourless ugali, in India it's plain, low-quality rice, and the locals make no show of enjoying it. 'Look at what we have to eat,' says Anshuman. 'It's terrible.'

In many of the poor countries I've visited it's very difficult to talk to women – they are not expected to speak on behalf of the men, and their concerns are routinely dismissed. I try talking to Anshuman's wife Mina, asking questions like, 'Do the landowners treat the dalit badly around here?' but she just can't seem to answer. It's as if she's stuck for words, and after persevering for half an hour or so I give up. It seems that the less educated people are, the shyer they are. It appears to be part of the cycle of deprivation – the poor, and especially the female poor, are less assertive because they feel less able to express themselves and hence their problems don't get attention. They are surprised to the point of terror that anyone, especially a foreigner, should want to know their opinion about anything.

Anshuman, however, is confident and voluble: 'The landowners do everything in their power to keep us in our place,' he asserts. I ask if he supports the Naxalites, but he dismisses both them and the Ranvir Sena (the landowners' paramilitary group) as irrelevant. 'How can they help us with politics when all we need is food?'

I pay Anshuman for the food I've eaten and he takes me out to the rice fields to show what he does all day. Rice provides the main income and employment for more than 50 million Indians like him, and right now it's one of the year's several harvest times (these fields usually provide three harvests every year), so Anshuman and his entire family work from eight until six every day in a local landowner's fields. The children never go to school because they're needed in the fields too. The entire family lives in a shocking state of feudal serfdom, in thrall to the landowners. 'They pay us just enough rice to keep us alive so we can work their fields, but not enough so we can sell it to make any money or own any land ourselves.'

I try my hand at harvesting. It's backbreaking work. I cut one row of rice about 2 metres wide and as I do a large crowd gathers, shocked and amused to see a white guy in the fields. I ask Anshuman if the landowner would know if he stole a bit of rice?

'Yes, the villagers would tell him that I had stolen the rice.'

'Why on earth would they do that?'

'They want to keep us in our place.'

The strength of caste fatalism means that the poor would even inform on each other to make sure no one breaks out of the system. I find it terrifying. I say, 'If it was me, I'd just be tempted to come out at night and nick loads of rice. But that's just my feckless Western attitude I suppose.' Anshuman shrugs.

Word gets out to the surrounding villages, and people start arriving on bikes to take in the scene. I feel a little embarrassed – I want to know how hard their work is, but it's ended up feeling like a celebrity visit to Africa. When I get to the end of the row, the embarrassment is compounded by everyone breaking into applause and someone offering a bucket of water to cool me down.

I can't tell whether Anshuman resents this pandering or if he's enjoying the attention that he's getting. I give Mina her knife back, and worry that I've trivialized her life with this grandstanding. Oddly enough, the undeserved applause and water make me feel more angry about the way the dalit are forced to live.

Back in the village I find a woman called Dreya threshing rice and I ask her if I can try – I've only ever seen raw rice in books. It grows very much like grass, and at the ends of the stalks grow little beads of rice. The whole stalk is cut in the field and left there to dry, then the grains are beaten against a rock to separate them from the grass. It's bloody hard work.

Dreya is an angry woman, one of the first women I've met here who isn't afraid of expressing her frustration. She tells me her daily routine: 'I have no land of my own so I work in someone else's fields from 8 a.m. till 6 p.m. in return for some rice.'

She gets this food only for a few months each year, during harvest time. The rest of the year she often goes hungry, although occasionally she and her husband might get a small job and can buy some more food. 'We don't get money. We just get rice. We farm and they give us rice, not money. They feed themselves. They let us starve ...'

'What do you do between harvest times?'

'When we earn we eat; when we don't earn we don't eat.'

She's angry and unhappy, and suddenly she's none too pleased to be surrounded by a journalist and 100 of her neighbours, all of them watching her work. She talks about her anger at both the government and the Naxalites. She reckons that neither have done any good for her. She says that people are often forced to vote under threat of violence.

Suddenly there's a commotion. Rats! Someone has spotted a rat, and everyone rushes back to the fields, us included. Maybe the rat-eating isn't a myth after all. We arrive just as a group of men have trapped two of them. The first tried to scarper after the lair was discovered with a shovel, but it didn't get far. There's much excitement, shouting and pointing, and the men are clearly full of adrenalin. They dig up the lair and pull out a second rat by the tail.

Despite all the wild-eyed excitement the rats are pretty tiny – more like mice, if you ask me – but this is a place where protein is an extremely rare treat, and these guys have been very lucky.

The rats, on the other hand, are very unlucky. The men pull the tails one way and the heads the other until their necks break with a light 'snap'. There's a fair amount of twitching afterwards. In many ways, this is as good as the feudal deal gets for the dalit: in return for saving the landowner's rice from pests, they are allowed to keep any rats they catch. I had thought that Hindus were vegetarians, but it's probably best to keep this to myself – other than rice, these people get very little to eat, so who's complaining?

When the three men kindly invite me to try their catch, I accept. They cook the rats over a makeshift fire of straw and twigs. First they are rolled on the fire to burn off the fur, then when the skins have been thinned by the flames, the men pick open the stomachs to eviscerate them, saving the liver. They are then roasted over the fire for another ten minutes or so, and when they're blackened from the flames, they are ready to eat.

It's an odd feeling putting a rat in your mouth. These seminal experiences should really be private affairs, but I've got a pushing, shoving audience of 100 people. I wonder if this is the point when my stomach finally says 'enough is enough' and delivers me a crippling bout of salmonella. But if I bottle out from the scary bits, all our interest in the Musahars is just poverty tourism – like looking at the poor from the comfort of a tour bus. I have to get involved.

So I sink my teeth into the hind quarters of a charred, grilled rat, and it tastes pretty good, if a little burnt. A little like baby chicken. Whenever I've visited a new conflict zone and tasted something unusual, my friends always say 'I bet it tastes like chicken', and it hardly ever does. But rats really do taste like baby chicken. It's sweet and flavoursome from the crispy skin, yet surprisingly fatty, and disconcertingly rare inside. I reason that it's been so burnt in the fire that it must be OK to eat. I chew the meat off one of the legs, then hand it back, conscious not to take too much food from them. When I hand it back to the rat-catcher, he upstages me by putting the whole thing in his mouth, chewing it and then swallowing it whole: bones, skin, skull, the works. Then he beams at me.

I visit Dreya again to ask about how the dalit live. I wonder if she feels that it's a difficult life – perhaps it just looks difficult and unhappy to me as a Westerner? She's sarcastic about the question. 'Of course I'm unhappy,' she says. 'Look at my life.' That puts me in my place.

That night we eat with Ramswaroop and he explains how the dalit are treated by the wealthy. The higher castes see them as unclean, and refuse to eat from the same plates, eat food that the dalit have touched, or even to walk on the same paths (the dalit are expected to cross the road when someone of a higher caste passes). The dalit must use different wells, live apart from the rest of the community, and any ownership of land or animals is seen as an affront to the higher castes.

We spend another day in the village, chatting with the Musahar then we're taken for lunch. It's the most gruesome and uncomfortable spectacle: Ramswaroop takes us to one of the larger village houses and sits us down with the elders. A group of 150 or so people gather to stare at us (they don't do anything, they just stare) and we proceed to eat a meal that he's paid for. The food isn't particularly special or good, but when 150 rat-eaters are staring, it's hard to swallow a pakora.

I tell Ramswaroop how uncomfortable this is, but he's dismissive. They aren't resentful, he says, just interested. It feels too weird for me, though, and puts me off my food, so I thank him and go to play with the kids instead. I've got a handful of modelling balloons in my pockets, and

I make some balloon dogs, giraffes and elephants. There's practically a riot when I hand them out.

It's finally time to leave so I thank everyone, shaking hands and dishing out hugs where they're likely to be accepted. I've got mixed feelings about leaving: it'll be a relief to be back in less difficult surroundings, though – I've rarely seen poverty on this scale, and certainly never seen it so systematically enforced.

I'm still trying to negotiate meetings with the rebel groups, but neither the Naxalites nor the Ranvir Sena are minded to chat. I wonder if we should give up, but it feels important to get the other side of the story, so I decide to head for the centre of Bihar so that we'll be ready to drive to meet them if they suddenly agree.

On the way, I bump into another dalit subcaste beside a murky pond: the snake eaters, a nomadic people who catch snakes in the fields for food. A young man is at home in a shack of tarpaulin and twigs, and he shows me a highly poisonous cobra he has caught. Vicious-looking thing it is, too. It seems like a precarious way to get a meal.

The Ranvir Sena

I leave for the town of Bodh Gaya on the next stage of our long, increasingly fraught, roundabout journey in search of the Ranvir Sena – up until now I've heard so much from the dalit that in order to get a balanced view I need to speak to the wealthy landowners. I get the feeling that I'm running out of time. My attempts to set up a meeting with the Maoist Naxalites seem to have failed – they refuse to be tied down to a meeting point, nervous about putting their security at risk.

I decide instead to concentrate on finding the Ranvir Sena so drive for hours to Jahanabad to pick up a contact who says he might be able to introduce us to them. We need to drive on to a village in the south, and he reckons it'll take us two hours. We squeeze into the car and after *five hours* of slow and painful driving we arrive in R___a, a tiny medieval-looking hamlet of cow dung and rubble. It's already dark. I've had to promise not to reveal the name of the village or the people in return for a meeting, but there's still no certainty that they'll turn up. I sit and hope.

After much toing and froing between the rebel contact and the villagers, I am led out to the pitch-black fields; the BBC security team would take a dim view of this. I power up the satellite phone and call the office in White City to give my GPS co-ordinates to my researcher James, telling him to panic if we don't call again in a couple of hours. Quite what he can achieve from west London, I'm not entirely sure, but it's all I can do. The villagers seem suspicious of my phone – perhaps I'm a government agent trying to bust the rebels. But would a government agent really be so stupid as to put himself in this kind of danger? Only a journalist could be this reckless.

I wander around the fields in the dark looking for the paramilitaries. After an age, I stumble across the rebel army of the Ranvir Sena in the pitch black (how they manage to find their way around I don't know, but they don't use torches). There are a dozen or so fighters, all carrying rifles of varying age and effectiveness. Their faces are covered in scarves, and they are all silent except for the leader, who calls himself 'Dinka'.

My relief at finally finding the rebels is tempered by my unease at sitting down with a visibly angry armed group who could easily kidnap me if they wanted to. I don't want to make these people any angrier than they already are, but at the same time I have to ask some provocative questions.

Dinka talks with righteous indignation and heavy gesticulation about his need to protect his land, his caste and his family. He immediately pitches his army as the protector of poor, downtrodden landowners, accusing the Naxalites of stealing land and massacring landowners for no apparent reason. I suggest that they do have a reason: to fight the wealthy, even if he doesn't agree with it; they are poor and desperate, and motivated by centuries of persecution. He's not interested. I ask what he'd do if he was in their situation with no possibility of escape and with his family starving.

'I'd abide by the law – I wouldn't fight,' he says. 'Exploitation happens to all classes, not just the poor.'

I say that I'm not sure if I'd resist the temptation if my family was starving by force.

He says that the Ranvir Sena have been portrayed as the villains of the piece, when in fact all they're doing is protecting their land. 'Sure, I hit my labourers every now and then, but how else can I assert my authority? We've been involved in many attacks against left-wing groups. If someone destroys my farm, can I not hit him, abuse him out of rage? They graze their cattle on our land and steal our grain, then we abuse and beat them.' Christ alive.

To begin with, he denies that he has ever been part of an attack – he was merely part of the administration of the Sena. Later, though, when he's got his fellow army members together for a show of strength, and to display their guns, he is more forthcoming – he's been part of a battle against the Naxalites during which they had killed three Maoists. It made him very happy, he says.

Funnily enough, I don't really take to Dinka, nor his ridiculous claim that he's fighting to create an egalitarian society. How does he work that out? I sense that he's just a bully. All this conflict over food and land could only happen in a place that's desperately hungry.

I say goodbye and call the office to say that we haven't been kidnapped. 'Oh, good,' says James.

We set out in the dark (another bad idea – this area is renowned for banditry) and drive to a safe house 3 km away. It takes about 45 minutes to get there, on the worst roads I have ever bounced along, and I arrive to discover that there's no electricity, water or food. We share rooms and sleep on the hardest beds known to man – they are actually low tables – all they offer is a slight levitation from the floor and the bugs and snakes that live there.

Tomorrow I am hoping to meet the Naxalites, but unfortunately they are even harder to pin down than the Ranvir Sena. Fingers crossed.

After another sleepless night on a hard, sweaty bed, I get up and drink chai, which seems to have appeared from nowhere, then wander around the village – another beautiful medieval scene straight out of a movie – an art director's dream. The houses have no walls so the inhabitants effectively live in the open air in utter poverty.

I'm baffled at how this cycle of poverty can be maintained, so I visit the Hindu priest at the village temple. He claims to welcome the dalit to his temple, although Anoj, my translator, doesn't believe a word of it. I ask if he thinks the dalit deserve their fate, and he says yes, the dalit, the poor, the lepers and disabled all earn their state after being bad in a former life.

This fatalism is really dangerous: not only are the dalit expected to remain poor and dispossessed in a system sanctioned by their religion, but this destitution is supposed to feed down through the generations. The children of a dalit will be dalit, as will their children and their grandchildren, and they are all expected to be poor and destitute too – there isn't supposed to be an escape from the cycle.

And this is where the situation in India feels so gruesome and unfair. In the war-ravaged wastelands of central Africa, the one thing people have is hope and optimism fed by religion. Sometimes it's blind hope and sometimes people's dreams don't happen, but when you have

FOOD AS A WEAPON

nothing, it seems obscene that something as basic and unthreatening as hope can be denied to you. But to the landowners and the powerful, hope is the most dangerous thing, and the caste system is what they've used to eradicate it.

I find the priest thoroughly depressing, and he also seems to be a bit of a bully. Village priests come from the highest Brahmin caste and wield enormous power. When a new child is born, parents ask their temple priest to give it a name, and dalit children are routinely given names like 'dirt' and 'filth'. The parent has to use the given name in order not to offend God, and hence the child is forever singled out for persecution.

I hate to criticize an ancient culture, but something really bugs me about India, and that's the way that people treat each other. In everyday life I keep seeing the enforcement of hierarchies at every level: anyone who sees themselves as more powerful, rich or higher caste treats other people – staff, servants, passers by and even colleagues – with a shocking arrogance and rudeness. Perhaps it's a remnant of the caste system, perhaps it's a function of a society where there is such a disparity of wealth. Perhaps we do it in Britain, but it's just less visible.

Across India by Train

As I leave Patna, I wonder if there's a solution to the horror of untouchability. It might sound surprising to say this, but it's possible that money could offer a way out. Many rural dalit take the view that money has no morality and knows no religion, so it should be possible for people to escape their village, move to the city where no one knows their caste, and life instead becomes about money. There's still poverty in the cities, but at least its egalitarian poverty! If the rich get richer, then *perhaps* the wealth might filter down, and capitalism is, after all, supposed to filter wealth down through society.

I want to see if there's any truth in this theory, so I'm off to Mumbai, India's 'City of Dreams'. I had booked some flights, but then I found out that there was a train. I've always had a romantic (OK, neo-colonial) dream about travelling across India by train. I imagine a dining carriage with crisp napery and be-capped staff. I imagine a slow, colourful and dreamy journey, with me reading books about the proud, noble dalit, and sitting in white linen trousers with the wind ruffling my hair, Michael Palin style. I am convinced it will be a life-changing experience.

The reality is very different.

The Indian railways are the country's biggest employer, and the company seems to be working hard to find jobs for all those people with layers of bureaucracy and quadruple bookkeeping. It takes two hours just to get my bags booked onto the train. The train itself is a clanking, wheezing, spluttering hunk of battered iron on wheels. I find my carriage in second class and my disappointment begins to grow. The seats are all plastic, the windows are tiny and mud-caked, the place stinks and there's no privacy. There's no crisp white napery, no be-capped staff and we are told by our fellow travellers that the journey will be 27 hours of slow, trundling agony. Or at least, it's supposed to be 27 hours.

People are fascinated that there are Westerners on their train, and they come up to me and stare. Sometimes they will ask questions, such as 'Where are you from?', but it's mainly just staring. A surprising upside is the food. Stewards constantly pass along the train offering plastic trays of pakoras, samosas, curries and chai. I avail myself of their wares at every opportunity throughout the journey, eating some sphincter-searing chillies and making up for the last week of deprivation.

I hate sitting on my bunk, barely able to see out of the window, so I wander to the end of the carriage and jam open one of the carriage doors with my leg, and settle down to read *Untouchables* by Narendra Jadhav, who broke the caste mould and escaped from his cycle of poverty and persecution to become an eminent banker, and to watch India pass by.

It's not exactly Palin-esque, but I love watching India unfold as the train trundles painfully slowly through the countryside. Every travel writer on the planet waxes lyrical about the chaotic beauty of India, but amidst the beauty is the ever-present grinding poverty. And from my vantage point I see it all: mile upon mile of rice fields, millions of ramshackle huts full of people, filthy kids playing in the dust, the pressure of 1,000 million souls scraping a living from a country the size of the USA (population a mere 300 million). The land is overworked, ruined and wasted for miles and miles, but the fields are full of people working, the stations are full of people selling food and drink, and at every level crossing there are hundreds of people standing with their bicycles, pressed shirts and beautiful saris on their way to do something. Indians always seem to be busy, always striving, always going somewhere.

What strikes me most about India, though, as we travel through the countryside, is the incredible mix of smells. Rural India smells strongly of sewage and human excrement, but oddly enough it's not a bad smell.

FOOD AS A WEAPON

It shifts and evolves as I travel across the country, and it gets combined with the smells from animals, people, cooking, agriculture and even wine. We go through a district of vineyards that seems to go on for miles. They aren't planted in the anal-retentive style of European vineyard, but they look pretty good.

As night falls, I return to my carriage and the seats are pulled down into bunks. Suddenly I am hijacked by a group of engineers, one of whom has heard that I'm making a film about food and insists that I try some of his mother's home-made bhajis and brinjal (aubergine) curry. 'She's a terrible cook,' he says, but they taste great to me. The men are all tremendously friendly, and we chat for hours, even though we're all desperate for some sleep.

Finally they leave and I crawl into my plastic bunk. This is going to be a sweaty night. I fall asleep pretty quickly, but in the middle of the night I'm woken up by some people who get on the train and claim they were originally allocated these bunks. My bribe to the train steward clearly didn't do any good. I bribe another one and apologize profusely to the new passengers, and they wander off to a different carriage, a little disgruntled.

When I wake I take a tour along the train. I've been in air-conditioned second class (there doesn't appear to be a first class carriage), but a few carriages down is 'second class, no air con', and people are crammed in a little tighter at three bunks high as opposed to our two. I meet Muralie, a polio victim from a lower caste who survives by sweeping the train for tips. He tells me that his life has been ripped apart by caste conflict.

'My father was a daily wage labourer but we were given a plot of land by the government because of my disability. The villagers killed my father because of the plot – they belonged to the upper castes, the Brahmins and the Thakurs. They smashed in his head, put out his eyes, and his limbs were twisted and broken; finally he was hung upside down.'

Stories like this are common across rural India and atrocities against lower castes have risen dramatically in the last year, allegedly instigated by upper castes with the prime motive of grabbing land.

When I finish interviewing Muralie, he becomes aggressive, asking what I am going to give him in return for the interview. I explain that I am making a film about the caste system and food, and that perhaps it will help to have his story told, but he wants me to give him money. I explain that the BBC doesn't pay people for interviews. He's disgusted with me. What can you do for me? He keeps repeating. I wonder if I'm abusing these people in some way. I'm not here to change the world, but to tell its stories and perhaps somehow that will help to force change. But it's true that none of this will help Muralie eat tonight.

I continue down the train and find third class. There are bunks here but there's such a desperate crush of people that at least a quarter of the passengers have had to stand for the last 20 hours. The few that have a seat are perched on top of each other, and it takes me an age to get anywhere. I stop and talk to some of them. Many are dalits from rural Bihar who've managed to scrape together enough cash to escape, and are hoping to leave their caste behind to start a new life in Mumbai. They are lucky, they say. Most people aren't able to leave – they can't find enough food to eat, let alone save money for a train ticket. Many of these people have family living there who will give them somewhere to stay, but it's going to be difficult.

Back in second class I speak to another dalit, Rajesh, who says, 'I am going to Mumbai for the first time. I have my people there. There are so many friends. Some of them drive auto-rickshaw, some drive trucks, some sell vegetables. If I have some talent, I would like to use it.'

Half a million people migrate from rural India to Mumbai *every year*, often to escape the dalit hunger-poverty trap. Rajesh says that hunger is used as a way of suppressing his family: 'In villages this is a big tragedy. People suppress the working class; they make sure that the working-class people remain uneducated. They make an effort to stop them from going to school. They want the labour class to remain in the dark.'

City of Dreams

I finally make it to Mumbai, Lord knows how many hours late. I'm exhausted from lack of sleep, but excited to be here at last. My enthusiasm wanes a little when my luggage is held to ransom by a succession of people who demand bribes for its return in the form of 'import tax'. This appears to be a fluid amount, there are no receipts available, and no justification, despite the fact that the man demanding it clearly works in a local government office. Indian bureaucracy is so mesmerizingly complex that people use it as a tool for all sorts of extortion. When I finally buy my luggage back, someone else comes up with another tax that I need to pay. Four different people need to be paid off before I am reunited with my pants. Suddenly Mumbai doesn't seem so welcoming.

My anger and frustration evaporates, however, when I discover that all the hotels in town have been booked up for the arrival of the Chinese president, and the only rooms available are at the ultra-luxurious Taj Mahal hotel. The BBC has managed to find me a more customarily drab hotel for the following night, but for one night only I will sink into the incongruous luxury of fine linen and fine dining offered by the Taj. Sadly, by the time I arrive it's too late to enjoy anything the hotel has to offer, such as the pool, and I've got such an early start in the morning that I won't really get to enjoy it, but hey.

Do I feel guilty that we've left rural poverty and landed in the lap of luxury? To be honest, I'm too tired to let it worry me, and I collapse for a good night's sleep and let it slip from my mind.

Mumbai is as fabulously wealthy as it is destitute. It has a rapidly expanding middle class, shops full of fancy clothes, cars and assorted bling, as well as the largest, most miserable slum in Asia. The contrast is odd, and I find it hard not to feel anti-wealth. I have to remind myself that just because there are impoverished people in India, it shouldn't mean that others can't earn good money. The gap is admittedly vast, but who am I to tell people that they don't deserve to enjoy their wealth – in India or in Britain? It's all too easy to resent the wealthy for their money, but I do have this residual hope that although some inequity is inevitable, wealth ought to filter down through society eventually. Certainly, the contrast here in India is hard to bear.

We visit Indigo, the most exclusive restaurant in Mumbai. It's full of the rich, the powerful and the beautiful, plus a fair smattering of braying American bankers. The owner, Ravi Anchan, has an army of staff working in his kitchens and a lot of them are dalits benefiting from the money that the rich spend. What the poor of Mumbai need are jobs, and caste is irrelevant to him. 'The only real class divide, as in any cosmopolitan city, is money. Caste implies a certain amount of fatalism, whereas money doesn't. Everyone has the chance to go after that great pot in the sky, especially in Mumbai.'

He gives me a free dinner, and I sit on the open-air terrace. It's spectacular, and I could be in a fancy Indian restaurant in the middle of London or New York. When I leave, however, our taxi has to take evasive action to avoid running over a woman sitting in the middle of the road howling and crying, holding her hand out for money.

Dharavi

Dharavi is the biggest slum in Asia, and home to more than 600,000 people. Over half of them are dalits who have migrated from rural India in search of a better life, but most of them live on less than £1 a day. When they get to the city of dreams, this is where most of them end up. There's no running water, healthcare, rubbish collection or proper housing. It's a sea of tiny shacks, with people crammed on top of each other in a shocking concentration of humanity, and all of them living amongst raw flowing sewage. The place smells horrific and in many ways rural life in Paraiya seems idyllic in comparison: at least in the country there is ample space, beautiful rivers to wash in, places for kids to run around and play.

But the difference is that in Dharavi there is hope. It might sound sentimental, I know, but it makes a world of difference here, where, for all its faults, the anonymity of the city makes it a meritocracy and systematic caste discrimination is replaced by the slightly less rigid discrimination of poverty.

One of the most horrific things about Dharavi, though, is the relentlessness of it. There's no escape from the poverty, filth and discomfort for the residents; they can't take a break from all this hell and sit in a park, or go for a walk. The people who live here have to endure it constantly. There's nothing in Dharavi except more Dharavi, and it goes on for miles.

I meet a few people, and they show us the extraordinarily small spaces they live in. This is an affront to human existence. One woman shows me her tiny room, about the size of a small bathroom. She tells me that seven people live in it. I can't actually see how seven people could lie down here at the same time.

There's a set of steps at the back. 'Where do they go?' I ask, wondering if she has another room.

'They're for the family that lives upstairs,' she says, pointing to a platform that sits precariously above her room.

Other rooms have no light whatsoever, but one woman proudly shows me her TV and shrine inside her dingy black hole of a room. Some others have stereos and bicycles, although they are rare exceptions. But they have managed to move here and get jobs, they hold their heads high and they are relatively optimistic amidst the squalor.

I meet a young man called Ramprakash who arrived a year ago and survives by selling children's shoes that squeak with each step. His tiny shack is clean but extremely difficult to live in. I buy a pair of his shoes for my daughter Poppy, and have to practically fight him to accept the money. It comes as a shock to me that he rents his shack. Even in slums, you can't just build a house from wood and plastic sheeting – every scrap of land is owned by someone, and they will want to be paid for it. Ramprakash rents his shack from a dalit who has managed to escape the slums.

But amongst all this, I finally discover a real story of hope. Twelve million people in Bombay live in its various slums, trying to escape the cycle of poverty. One way of getting out is to become a dabbawallah. These men (always men) are tiffin-carriers – porters who take people's tins of packed lunch to work for them. Most middle-class Mumbaians want to eat homemade food in their office, but don't want to carry it on the crowded trains. It seems to be a snobbery thing – it's just not done to be seen to carry your own tiffin, and if you can afford to get someone else to do it, why not? If it sounds ridiculous, it is, but it's another way that wealth feeds down to the poor. For a small fee, they do the carrying for you, picking up the tiffin box from your wife after you've left home, and delivering it to your desk. They also pick up the old tin from yesterday's meal and it gets delivered back to your wife again before you get home. Most dabbawallahs never meet the person they deliver the food to.

I went on the rounds with a dalit dabbawallah called Ballaral. He told me that despite the wild complexity of the system, he never delivers a tiffin box to the wrong place. Over 200,000 lunches are delivered every day by around 5,000 dabbawallahs, and *Forbes* magazine recently claimed that there's only one error in every 6 million deliveries.

It's particularly ironic that Ballaral does this work, when in the countryside he wouldn't be allowed to touch the food of a higher caste member for fear of contaminating it. Higher caste children regularly abused Ballaral when he was growing up in rural India but here he has shaken off the stigma. It's been replaced by a simpler poverty prejudice. 'Some people don't let us into their home when we go to get the tiffin. Sometimes people even refuse to give us water.'

But at least it's better than systematic caste discrimination, and now that he has a proper job he can support his two children and his parents, as well as his brother, and his brother's wife and son. He earns £60 every week, which is a princely sum in Mumbai.

He says, 'I have a ten-year-old son and an eight-year-old daughter and by the time they grow up the caste system may be over. But I might not live long enough to see that.'

A week after we left, dalits rioted across the country demanding an end to discrimination.

• • • • •

India is touted as an emerging economic superpower, and it has one of the largest economies in the world. But the media tends to ignore the fact that it damn well ought to have one of the biggest economies, seeing as it has such a vast population. Over half of the world's hungry live here, for crying out loud, and 25 per cent of all Indians live below the poverty line. And all the hype about the modernity and dynamism of the country is lost on anyone who's really explored India. The place is a *mess*: its infrastructure is dire; it's desperately poor; and its turgid, bloated bureaucracy and endemic corruption is hampering progress.

I wish the best of luck to the middle classes, and the new technology companies and industry of India, but those 25 per cent who are desperately poor expose the grubby underbelly of all that progress. And with corruption, patronage and caste discrimination all alive and well, the wealth of those middle classes might never filter down.

The best memory I have of my time in India (and please excuse me if this sounds sentimental) was a moment as I left the Dharavi slum. On the side of a football-pitch-sized sea of raw effluent and rubbish was a large wooden box on legs. I peered into it and got the shock of my life. Inside were four beautiful little girls, all around six or seven years old. I asked what they were doing. 'Homework,' they said in Hindi. Then 'Hello, mister,' in English. And I sat with them for a while, giggling and pointing at the book they shared. And that's the image I took away from India: four beautiful little flowers of hope, sitting literally raised above the slurry, studying for a better life and wearing smiles as brilliant as rays of sunshine.

CHINA
Cooking with Communists

POPULATION: 1,321 million

PERCENTAGE LIVING ON LESS THAN $2 A DAY: 46%

UNDP HUMAN DEVELOPMENT INDEX: 81/177

CORRUPTION PERCEPTIONS INDEX POSITION: =70/163

GDP (NOMINAL) PER CAPITA: $2001 (107/179)

FOOD AID RECIPIENTS: n/a

MALNUTRITION: 12% of the population

I'm hurtling towards a love affair at around 865 km/h. If all goes to plan I will land in Beijing in another four hours or so, and shortly afterwards, I expect to fall head over heels in love with the place. I should admit right now that despite all the cultural and historical importance, as well as the sheer size and power of the place, I've never really *understood* China. I've never felt affinity or empathy, even though my first-ever girlfriend was born there (OK, we were four and we only ever held hands, but still). I do have several things in common with the Chinese, however: like me, the Chinese are obsessed with food; they have a natural love of weird and wonderful ingredients; and they aren't shy of adding a bit of drama and spectacle to mealtimes. So I'm hoping that food is the perfect way to get under the skin of the Chinese, to understand a country that's changing at a bewildering pace and to try to understand what makes the world's next global superpower tick.

Is that too much to ask?

You're probably thinking, 'This place is a modern marvel, host to the 2008 Olympic Games and the world's second largest economy. Where's the danger zone here?' Well, despite all the international fawning over China (let's face it, it pays to be mates with the world's next superpower), it's still an authoritarian, highly militarized totalitarian regime; there's little freedom of speech, no political party except for the Communist party and there's widespread corruption. More importantly for me, China's relentless drive for economic growth has devastated agriculture, created a huge gap between the urban rich and the rural poor and caused comprehensive social damage. In spite of all this, I'm sure I'll find that China is a spectacularly successful country full of rich and complex characters – all I need is to find them.

It's taken me three months to get clearance simply to visit China to make a film about food, and I've been warned by the BBC to expect all manner of official intrusion. In order to get a permit I must agree to have a minder at all times, and to pay $100 a day for the privilege. And we're under strict instructions from our bosses not to mess them around and film things we shouldn't, otherwise the authorities could ban the BBC altogether.

Welcome to the Kung Fu Restaurant

I arrive at Beijing Airport to a murky soup of a day. The dust blows into Beijing off the Gobi desert, blotting out the sun and creating a shroud of general misery.

I meet my guide Yan Yan and the China TV (disconcertingly called CCTV) minder Penny, who couldn't look less like the miserable communist cadre I'd been expecting if she tried. She's a tiny, sweet and disarmingly pretty media student who says that she plans to make herself useful carrying bags and keeping an eye on the van. And another eye on us, presumably. I get the sense that there's going to be conflict between Yan Yan, whom we've employed to get us access to things, and Penny, whom we've employed to stop us getting access to things.

We drive through Beijing and I'm struck by the relentlessly shiny and spectacular forest of high-rise buildings. I don't know if it's urban heaven or dystopia. It's also a mess of advertising – every spare inch of the place is covered in high-tech signage.

Our hotel turns out to be the child adoption centre of Beijing, full of Russians and Italians road-testing babies. Disconcertingly, they are in the lifts all the time (maybe it's a way of getting the kids off to sleep). The parents gaze with newfound love at their little babies who are busy

IDEOLOGICAL FOOD

screaming their heads off, whilst a Chinese person explains, through a bouffant-haired interpreter, that everything is going to be fine.

My first taste of food in a new place is invariably at breakfast time, when I'm feeling least adventurous. Luckily, breakfast in the hotel is a festival of dull stodge: congee (a sort of steamed rice porridge), steamed dumplings, fried noodles and lots of doughnutty-looking things.

I venture out and visit the Kung Fu fast food joint, which sits right next door to one of the hundreds of McDonalds in Beijing. Kung Fu uses exactly the same colours as Maccy D's for itd sign, but with the additional image of a fighter taking a boot at the Americans. It's one of China's relatively few successful attempts at brand-building, and it's a marvel of capitalist modelling. This is slightly disconcerting: I wanted to see a bit of communism.

As I walk through the door of Kung Fu the entire staff – about 30 people – yell at me and raise their right arms in a scary fascist salute. For a nanosecond I wonder if Beijing has been experiencing a spiritual crisis and they think that I'm their Messiah – I always wondered if there was something special about me. Then someone else walks in and they do the same thing. Apparently, much to my disappointment, they are just saying 'Welcome to the Kung Fu restaurant'.

I'm surprised at this Japanese-style zeal for service. During my visits to the former Soviet Union it seemed that service was a dirty word, and customers were treated like muck, so I was expecting the same from the Chinese, but these guys are as eager as a bunch of puppies. The childishly enthusiastic manager fits me out with a polyester polo shirt in the team colours, a polyester Kung Fu baseball cap and relieves me of my wedding ring and watch.

He shows me everything in his cramped high-tech kitchen – his cupboards, steamers, temperature gauges (his fascination for temperature regulation borders on the psychotic), trays, taps, and lord knows what else. After half an hour of inspecting catering equipment, I put a stop to it, much to his dismay, and ask him to teach me how to cook their most popular dish.

He shows me the mixture of MSG, salt and sugar that flavours the food. I throw half a teaspoonful in my mouth, and it explodes in a cloud of non-specific flavour. I can't speak properly for the next hour as my mouth tries to cope with an extended gauge of tongue.

We boil a large handful of lettuce with 50 ml of oil, garlic and soy, rendering it into a slimy but extraordinarily tasty salad. Never before has a lettuce contained so many calories. We also cook pork custard, which tastes infinitely better than it sounds. It's a simple steamed egg, water and pork mixture that's delicately flavoured (then boosted with a hefty whack of MSG) and wobbly, a cross between custard and set yoghurt. The food in Kung Fu is cooked to a precise formula of sizes and flavours and, as with McDonalds, consistency is everything.

The team shows me how to greet customers: as soon as someone walks through the door, elevate your arm to 30 degrees above horizontal, palms outwards to point the customers' eyes towards the menu, and shout at the top of your voice: '*Hwan ying guang lin zhen kung fu*'. I like this aggressive approach to hospitality – it shows who's boss, whilst giving a cursory nod to servility. The Russians could learn a lot from these guys.

The boss of the whole company turns up to be interviewed, which is a bit of a coup, although, oddly, he brings his own film crew. They interview me about my experience here, but I don't have that much to offer as I have no frame of reference yet – it's my first lunch in China – but I tell them that it's very nice. They seem tremendously pleased with this.

Then I get a chance to interview the boss. I ask him how private businesses like this can exist in a communist country. He flinches at the word 'communist', as though I've insulted him. He says that this is part of the new era of private and public ownership.

'So how can two opposing economic ideologies like capitalism and communism coexist?' I ask.

He's dismayed – he wanted to tell the BBC about how cheap, popular and nutritious his food is, and how he's ripe for inward investment; he did not expect some fella in a polyester polo shirt to be asking all this difficult stuff. His PR lady huffs and harrumphs, and the boss flails and flannels at my questions until I finally give up.

After the interview Penny, our CCTV minder, is angry – she thought the programme was about food, not politics. I tell her that it's about the politics of food, and the colour drains from her face. She clearly thought that this was going to be a cushy gig.

'What's wrong with asking someone about communism?' I ask.

'People don't like to discuss communism – they don't know anything about it'.

Eh? How can they not know anything about it – they are living in a communist country that's been run by the Communist party for 57 years.

I presume that they are highly likely to be communists, and they must have some kind of view on the matter.

Penny shakes her head.

I don't understand what's going on. I'm not *accusing* people of being communist – I'm in China, for crying out loud; surely they're proud of communism, and can tell me all about it.

Penny looks to the skies.

I wander into McDonald's next door to have a nose around.

'No, you can't film in here,' the manager says.

'Is the food in here healthy?' I ask.

'No, not really,' says the girl on the till, with a friendly smile.

Carrefour

I visit Carrefour, one of the French supermarket chain's 78 Chinese stores. It's now the ninth biggest retailer in the country with sales of £1.3 billion. It's an odd thing, seeing the familiar European approach to flogging food, and it would feel like home if the place didn't have tanks of live carp to buy and a deli counter full of ducks' heads. The mall outside is full of Benetton, KFC, Sephora and the like. This place feels so capitalist, I just can't work out how the Communist party keeps going in this country.

I try some Great Wall red wine. It's awful.

That night I walk around the largest square in the world, and it sends shivers down my spine. Tiananmen Square is vast – 440,000 square metres to be precise. The exact number of people who died during the 1989 protests and its immediate aftermath ranges from 200 to 3,000 depending on whether you ask the government or the student associations. I'd assume a figure somewhere in between. Discussion about the protests is taboo in China (like discussion about the Cultural Revolution) and the news media is forbidden to report anything about it. And now I can't ask people about their fast-food business without terrifying the boss. What is all this about? I'm not even asking tricky questions about whether communism is right or wrong.

These people are terrified and I can't help thinking that a grown-up, responsible world superpower shouldn't be paranoid about free speech and political comment. Is China really ready to be the most powerful country in the world?

I visit one of China's largest dumpling factories and again, it's privately owned (I still don't understand how private ownership works within communism, but no one seems able to explain it to me). The dumpling factory is a little like visiting a battery chicken farm – from the calm, quiet exterior it's hard to imagine the horrors within.

I pull on a pair of white wellies, don a white jacket and face-mask, and walk into one of the vast work halls. Inside is a scene from Fritz Lang's *Metropolis*, with rows of identical workers (wearing identical clothing and masks, all individuality stripped away) lined along the tables, heads bowed and hands a blur of dumpling and fingers. All the sitting workers are female, but male supervisors stomp up and down the gaps between them, inspecting the dumplings for uniformity. It's a disconcerting but mesmerizing scene.

The workers take a dumpling wrapper (similar to a square of pasta but made with rice flour), put a spoonful of filling in the middle, then wrap it tight using their fingers and palms to make a distinctive shape. They do this over and over, for hours, weeks on end. The mundanity and repetition must be brain-rotting. They fill a tray of dumplings, put an identifying sticker on it, then place it on the conveyor belt in front of them, which takes it down to the quick-freezing plant at the far end of the factory. There's absolutely no talking, and the only noise is the rumble of the conveyor belts. This is a perfect dystopian image of the future.

The women are paid per dumpling, and in a ten-hour shift an average worker can expect to earn just under £3. Despite this, it's a sought-after job. I sit next to the factory's fastest worker who tells me that she makes around 7,000 dumplings a day. I ask if she gets bored, but she doesn't understand the question. I try a different tack: 'What do you think about when you're making dumplings?'

'I think about how to make dumplings faster and better.'

It's not surprising that she says this – I'm sitting with the boss of the company, and you wouldn't be seen dead in China saying anything that might make your boss look bad.

Chateau Zhang Lafitte

An hour outside Beijing lies one of the most extraordinary sights in China. After meandering through tumbledown villages (which Penny won't let us stop in) and filthy peasant street markets (which Penny ...), I'm suddenly hit by the ludicrous sight of a vast, disconcertingly shiny Renaissance French chateau looming out of the paddy fields. This is Chateau Zhang Lafitte: a £40 million copy of the original 1642 masterpiece built near

Paris by François Masart, and Penny is very keen that we stop here. The middle name gives the game away – it's owned by Zhang Yuchun, an influential member of the Communist party who somehow found some communal farming land that his party was happy to redesignate as private land to benefit … himself. It will come as no surprise that he's a former senior official at Beijing's municipal construction bureau.

The chateau is set in hundreds of acres of very immature landscaped gardens that used to be farmland but has now been rezoned as land for private housing. It's difficult to describe quite how out of place it looks. Imagine seeing a streaker at the Communist Party Congress. Yup, it's about that weird.

It's an authentic Disney French-Chinese folly full of cheesy baroque statues and lots of shiny faux-gold light fittings. As I enter this ersatz Disneyland version of France, I'm struck by the acres of expensive marble and chintz.

China's President Hu Jintao has spoken of social inequality and corruption as the biggest threats to one-party rule. He is particularly nervous about unrest over the financial relationship between business and party officials, but that don't cut no ice with Zhang who asserts that, 'You can't receive high-profile guests in two-star hotels.' Quite so.

The hotel rooms in this weird place are vast and implausibly opulent – so implausibly opulent that the BBC budgets don't stretch to a night here (although I'm disheartened to learn that Channel Five were happy to pay for Paul Merton to stay here some time later). I wonder how on earth such a massive waste of cash has landed here somewhere north of the capital.

I wander around until I stumble across the back lobby, where three huge model villages are laid out, with a frightening crew of estate agents showing baseball-cap-wearing octogenarian Chinese couples and their sunglass-wearing brats around.

And then it all falls into place. The chateau is basically a white elephant that serves as the venue for gruesome weddings, corporate gigs and product launches for big, often Western, firms. Also, it serves as the centrepiece for a massive development of houses for the new rich of China. The models show a scary, Stepfordesque world of perfectly manicured lawns and closely packed mansions with tiny gardens. The brochure screams 'Find your Dream'.

These are homes for the burgeoning middle classes of China. Now, I wouldn't deny a bit of prosperity to anyone, let alone the previously desperate Chinese peasantry, but it just seems odd when the government of this bizarre country hangs onto the ideological label (and excuse for totalitarianism) of communism. This isn't politics any longer – it's hegemony, a way for the elite to assert control and retain power through patronage. This could be modern Russia, with its Tatchell-beating, ridiculously partisan appliance of justice and economic patriarchy. This, together with Penny's constant needling not to film or say anything even vaguely negative, is making me start to dislike China, and that wasn't the plan at all.

Zhang himself isn't in when I call at the chateau, so I meet his assistant, a lovely young lady by the name of Nancy. After a great deal of haggling she reluctantly lets me drive around the estate in the company golf cart (I've always loved driving electric vehicles). We fizz around the grounds chatting away, and Nancy is very happy to talk until I ask her if the land that the chateau is built on had been taken away from the peasantry, at which point her understanding of English suddenly collapses. This was just farmland, she says, as if that means it was wasteland.

Questions such as 'How does this extreme of wealth fit in with the principles of communism?' and 'How have people's lives changed over the last 20 years?' all fly into the ether, accompanied by the bad smell of political intransigence.

This might sound like an isolated case – there really aren't that many exact copies of French chateaux lying about the Chinese countryside – but it does highlight a huge, devastating problem for the majority of Chinese – the confiscation or rezoning of agricultural land to make way for development, industry or simply private ownership. Twenty per cent of agricultural land has been lost since 1949 due to soil erosion and economic development, which is catastrophic for ordinary people. Sadly, Penny and her Communist party friends didn't allow me to meet many ordinary people, so I can only imagine the worst for them. However, we do know that 70 million farmers have lost their land in the last decade and unemployment in the countryside has reached a staggering 130 million.

And as with many of these great leaps forward, there appears to be collateral damage here at the Chateau Zhang Lafitte. In the nearby village I find a chap called Li Chang who used to farm the land that the gaudy chateau now sits on. Penny is not happy about the meeting, but I somehow bully her into letting me speak to him. Li's a fabulous bloke, with eyebrows of such magnificent bushiness that he could compete at international level. He was kicked off his land to make way for the chateau and is clearly angry. He expects to be punished for speaking out against party-sponsored development, but says he is too old to care about the consequences.

In China, land has never been owned – at least not until now. Farmers would lease it from the state for 30 years at a time, with pretty much automatic renewal as long as you hadn't pissed off the party. Now, farmers are finding that they can't renew the lease, and that it's being handed over to business-minded party members or their friends. It's a woefully unfair system of patronage that smacks of widescale corruption.

Mr Li is angry that all the farmers in the village have lost their land, although as this is a high-profile rezoning, they have all been given some sort of compensation to try to avoid any unnecessary publicity, and the elderly residents receive $45 a month, which has left them much worse off as they now can't grow their own food and have to spend most of the money at the market. Li isn't happy with the money, or the way the state has treated him and his friends, and is one of the only people I meet in China willing to say so.

On the road behind the chateau I find a vast hoarding surrounding the building sites, covered in pictures of dreamy Barratt homes with neat grass and an SUV outside every door. And although it looks ridiculous, I feel mean criticizing it. We like to think that peasant farmers live in bucolic bliss, but that's a Wordsworthian Western ideal that none of the people here wants. They are desperate that their kids don't have to destroy their lives and their health farming and can instead have some level of prosperity. Few people in China want to be small-scale rice paddy workers for the simple reason that although it looks pretty to us, it's a shit life. It's no wonder that they aspire to cars, central heating and running water.

Do Not Speak to the Locals

My guidebook to Beijing leads me to the legendary Quanjude. Abandon hope all ducks who enter here. This place is a veritable temple to roast Peking duck. Sadly, it's also a temple to tourism that's both a marvel and a travesty, an ersatz version of China – a vast corporate slice of tacky pseudoculture done up in revolutionary red, with crap chandeliers, golden swathes of polyester curtains, gaudy gold fittings, glowing lanterns, women in polyestered traditional costume (offset by wireless order pads) and more roasted ducks than you can shake a chopper at.

I open the menu and morph into Everytourist, squealing with delight at duck foot webs, grilled duck hearts and 'Authentic Whole Peking Duck'. My heart leaps with joy when I spot braised camel hump. I've never eaten camel's hump before.

The duck is theatrically carved at our table by a chef/waiter in an absurdly tall chef's hat and a face-mask. He's taciturn and wearily familiar with Western tourists' wide-eyed inquisitiveness, but he's an expert carver, and he chops our duck into the traditional (or so he tells us) 60 individual pieces. It's predictably sweet and crispy for the first few slices, then cloying after that. The fat is great but so rich that it's hard to taste anything else. Luckily I've also ordered a wickedly harsh rice liquor that strips the fat (and a fair portion of epidermis) from my palate so that I can try the duck webs and hearts. The webs are the size of butterflies, slightly rubbery and very cold, as though they've come straight from the fridge, hence they taste of nothing, although the texture is interesting – like edible Marigold gloves. Someone must have had a beast of a time stripping the webs from the legs, and it's a shame because their time seems to have been wasted.

The braised camel hump comes in chip-sized strips that have been slow-cooked then deep-fried in an eggy batter. They are delicious, a little like Spam, but in a good way. Less delicious are the gelatinous, braised mushrooms served, apparently, in a pond of frog vomit. Yuk.

Yan Yan and Penny get tipsy on a single beer, while I sink half a bottle of the vicious rice liquor. It's only on the way back to the hotel that I realize what happened to the other half, as Mr Hoo, our driver, hoons down the highways.

In a spirit of optimism I visit a vegetable market on the outskirts of the city to speak to some of the peasant farmers who drive in overnight with their produce, sleep in the city with their load until it's all sold, then drive home again. I should have known better, though, because when I get there I'm banned from talking to any truck drivers. It wouldn't paint China in a good light, apparently. Why can't I just go and speak to people? I ask Penny.

'You can't do that in China. It's just not the way it works and we don't want you painting a bad picture of our country.'

'But it would be a lie to show a sanitized version, wouldn't it? Come on, Penny, this is just a market and a bunch of farmers. You can come to my country and talk to anyone you want.'

But Penny doesn't get it. This is a country that's hosting the Olympics next year – what are they going to do when a million visitors wander around with their video cameras? What is wrong with these people? It's a f***ing vegetable market, not a military installation.

We persevere and meet up with the head of the market who, to Penny's exasperation, thinks it's a good chance to shake some hands. He takes us around to see a couple of new market buildings, and I try to speak to a couple of people selling their produce. I ask them where they've come from but the market head stops me and tells the people not to talk to me. 'I was only asking him about his bloody cauliflowers,' I say. But I'm not allowed to film.

This is ridiculous. I throw a journalist's pointless hissy fit at the market manager, who's bewildered but unimpressed, so I leave. I drop into the fish market, where I can film at will, but no one comes from rural China. I do get the chance to see carp being filleted, though. As soon as they are cut open, their float bladders balloon up and sit there like little fishy inflatables. Interesting, but hardly cutting edge.

I wander back to the city centre irritable and frustrated. It's not as though I'm asking particularly tricky questions or expecting to see the worst aspects of society – and I'm paying this annoying woman to be with me, so surely she could help me get to a story occasionally rather than just hinder me.

That night we all visit Little World hotpot restaurant. The system of eating in China is, unlike journalism, very interactive and inclusive, and the hotpot is the perfect example of this. We sit at a table and select from a menu that lists ingredients rather than dishes. We choose a variety of the stranger ones, and the waiter brings a large stockpot divided into two chambers, each filled with a different stock: one chilli hot and the other fragrant. This stockpot is set in a hole in the table, with a gas ring below that will keep it simmering throughout the meal. Into these stocks we throw a handful at a time of chicken gizzards, squid, chrysanthemum stalks, thin-sliced beef, water spinach, shiitake mushrooms, mutton – lettuce, dried bean curd skin, fried bean curd, aubergine with garlic, fish balls and tomatoes. We poach the ingredients to our liking, and scoff them down. Then we throw noodles into the pot to make noodle soup, and by the end of the meal we are stuffed to bursting.

Mr Hwong

I fly to Henan Province to try to get a feel for what's happening in rural communities. I hope that I'll be given a freer rein there, away from the power-base of Beijing.

Oh, how wrong I am.

I am met almost immediately by Mr Hwong and another minder who have been tasked with ensuring that we don't speak to … well, anyone really. It's additionally galling that I have to pay him as well as Penny – I've had to bring her with me and pay for her flights. Hwong drives us to our hotel, but Yan Yan whispers that he's taking us on a roundabout route to make sure that we don't see any poor parts of the city.

Hwong is good, blaming bureaucracy, shyness of the peasants, and all manner of delays, sudden sicknesses and interference from above for why we can't film … anything. Despite holding his arms out wide and claiming we can film anything we want, Hwong's basic attitude is to bore us into submission with red tape so that we just find it easier not to bother. That night I get slaughtered on strong rice liquor with him, and even though my glasses steam up with the liquor fumes, I never lose sight of my new-found enemy.

It takes quite a while to leave the hotel in the morning – our posse of minders have to bundle into separate cars, swap maps and lay down plans to avoid taking us anywhere that the party deems unacceptable for foreigners to see. The modern façade of prosperous China starts to crack the minute we leave the metropolis and we begin to take in the poverty of rural areas, but filming becomes unpleasant and desperately frustrating. The frustration is orchestrated by Hwong, who has an interesting approach to censorship: whenever I ask him anything he really doesn't like, he ignores me.

Hwong's task is to stop us filming anything that doesn't fit in with the Party image of a perfect, happy, wealthy country, and the fact that this sort of clumsy censorship makes China look ludicrous simply never occurs to him. Despite taking long, circuitous routes to try to avoid poor neighbourhoods, we spot lots of grim peasant shacks set back from the road, and each time I ask Hwong if we can stop, he doesn't even bother to reply.

Months before, Yan Yan had set off around Henan finding rural farmers that we could talk to, but she was accompanied throughout by local Communist party officials – and whenever she found someone talkative and interesting, the officials said 'No'. Instead Hwong and his cronies claim to have decided that we can visit a farmer that they've chosen.

This farmer must be very special because finding him is exceedingly difficult. We meet up with another carload of Communist party officials and everyone consults maps and haggles about exactly where he lives. There are now about 12 minders and officials with us. Eventually we arrive at a laughably cheesy Communist party-run model village. I am unsure why we're here, and my confusion deepens when Hwong drags us off to meet the official in charge of the village, who, for no apparent reason, takes me into a meeting-room filled with photos of him shaking hands with various higher-ranking party members.

I ask Hwong what we're doing here, irritated that we've used up most of a day from our tight schedule, but he assures me we're going to meet a farmer and we're dragged around the ridiculous village, despite my protests. It's a lavish, brutally symmetrical estate of marble-lined houses, and we are led into one particularly smart number where I'm finally introduced to a sweet, smiling lady. I tell her how nice her house is, and how unusual it is for a farmer to live on a smart estate but she looks confused. I ask her what sort of farming she does and she tells me that she works in the office of a state-owned oil company. Aaaargh!

My head minder doesn't bat an eyelid when I tell him that in Britain, farmers don't usually work in oil companies. Again, I ask Hwong why on earth we are here – we'd asked to meet a farmer. And he mumbles that he thought maybe she used to be a farmer. Then his friend says that people who live outside the cities are all farmers in a funny sort of way. Aaaargh and more aaaargh!

I am furious. I tell Hwong that he's wasting my time and money and lying to me. He knows damn well that this woman isn't a farmer. He looks at me haughtily, knowing that he is in complete control of the situation and that he can do whatever he likes – can't we see that it's his job to hinder us? My impotent rage isn't helping so I take a breath and try another tack. I'm going to report you to your superiors. He smiles – they will clearly be very pleased at his hampering of our plans. Then I hit on the one thing that makes him quake in his boots: 'You're making yourself look ridiculous – can't you see that we're filming this charade, and we'll go home and make a film about how silly and deceiving you look?'

That does the trick: his attitude suddenly shifts and he becomes both angry and scared. His official smiling and bureaucratic gerrymandering end abruptly and he finally agrees to take us to a real village the next day.

On the way back, we visit a restaurant in Henan for some local food. Hwong tries to drag us off to a private room so that we don't see anyone eating, but I insist on sitting in the huge main dining room. We eat sharks' lungs (I didn't realize that they had lungs, but there you go), which are like crispy sponges, and sea slugs, which are so slimy that it's impossible to pick them up with chopsticks, and chicken heads, which are poached and gruesome, but interesting.

The Great Escape

Hwong is in a bad mood today, which is fine by me. Again, I am driven on an absurdly long detour through pretty orchards and smartly planted fields. Eventually we arrive at a small village surrounded by rice paddies and fish-farming ponds. I'm dragged straight off to visit the wealthiest family here, and Hwong urges me to cook with them. I politely decline. We are taken to meet someone else – a man who owns a vast picture of Mao. He knows nothing about food, but says that his daughter-in-law is a good cook, and that she could cook for us, but our minder takes him aside and forces him to retract his offer.

'Why are you stopping us from talking to people?' I ask.

Hwong says that I can't just stop and talk to anyone.

'Why not?' I ask – on the first day here he had specifically said we could talk to anyone we want.

He refuses to discuss it further.

On the way back to the car I meet a woman walking along the street with a bag of flower buds and ask her what she's doing with them. Hwong tries to stop me from talking to her, but I ignore him and we carry on filming. She's a gorgeous, proud and friendly woman and she says that she's going to cook them for supper. I plead with her to show us how to cook them, drowning out Hwong's objections, and then I practically drag her away from the crowd. She makes the mistake of pointing out where she lives, so I march her across the rice paddies – if Hwong wants to stop us now, he's going to have to physically manhandle me.

This woman is as close as I'm going to get to meeting a farmer – she has a fish-farming pond and lives in a grimy little shack next to it, although she has another house in the village too. She's the sweetest, loveliest lady, and inside her house I discover her ancient mother and aunt, both of them also beaming with joy and oozing hospitality. Fantastic.

'Let's cook your flowers,' I say, as Hwong and his cronies arrive to try to stop us. I ignore him and urge her to persevere. The house is dark and ragged, and the kitchen a picture of peasantly poverty, but the women are wonderful and friendly. We wash the blossoms in water, scatter them in rice flour, then steam the whole lot, wrapped in a cotton cloth. After ten minutes, we turn it through to make sure it cooks evenly.

The event is soured only by the presence of Hwong and his gang. I tell them to go away, but they don't, so I begin to yell at them to leave us alone. They finally retreat when the camera is pointed at them as I'm telling them to stop intimidating the women. They eventually storm back off to the van in a fury. I don't care any more – I am paying them $200 a day to *help* us. The women are great. I ask them if they would like to move to the model village we saw yesterday. They say no, they want to live here in the countryside.

The flowers are delicious, like eating steamed jasmine, and our lovely lady packs me off with a huge carrier bag full of them. It's an uplifting moment for me – finally I've seen a tiny bit of rural life – albeit in a pretty wealthy village, and I feel a wave of relief that subdues the rising anger in my gut.

Hwong is furious, and he tells me that I shouldn't just talk to anyone I want to. 'Why can't I talk to people?' I ask.

'Because they don't give a fair picture of China.'

'Why not? They are real people – you just want me to interview the wealthiest party members – what kind of reality is that?'

I'm feeling mischievous now, so as all the minders stomp off towards the cars, I ask Ruhi to hang back, and when they all round a corner, we both leg it up a side road like little kids, excited at the inevitable prospect of being caught. We spot a woman in a run-down house surrounded by goats – she waves at us. Then we are beckoned over by another woman who is feeding her kids outside a little shack by the road. We're hampered by our lack of a translator, but she offers us tea and proudly shows off her two boys, then takes us into her kitchen to offer us some of the dumplings she's steaming for supper. At this point, our minders find us and storm into the room, yelling that we can't just enter anyone's kitchen.

'Why?' I ask.

'Because the woman might be offended.'

I explain that she had invited us in, and Hwong is speechless. He marches us back to the car. On the way, I pass a group of beautiful, ancient men sitting smoking outside a house, and try to speak to them.

'No!' shouts Hwong.

I decide not to pursue this last one in case Hwong tries to confiscate our tapes.

The drive back to the hotel is gloriously tortuous, and Hwong's anger is written all over his irritating face. I feel jubilant.

When we get back to the hotel, the two local minders take Yan Yan and Penny aside and give them a thorough roasting, saying that we were being rude by running away from them. You bet we were. Yan Yan is scared – they have clearly threatened her in some way. She says that she's worried because she has to come back to work in China, and these Party members are powerful people – they could cause big problems for her. It's a dilemma – I don't want anyone to get in trouble but on the other hand I'm spending a large amount of the BBC's money to give a fair, unbiased view of modern China, and these people are stopping me. I can't just let myself be dragged around the show homes of China.

When the time comes to leave for our flight back to Beijing, Hwong is terrified that I will try to cut loose and film something I shouldn't, so he insists on escorting us to the airport. I interview him in the van, asking why he wouldn't let us film anything in Henan. He says he wants to make sure we showed the best of it. I ask why he's so scared of us filming the place on our own, and he says that if he came to London as a friend, we would want to show him our hospitality. I say that although I wouldn't class him as a friend, if he came to London I'd show him around, and then he can go off and see whatever he wants – there's nothing to hide. He ignores me.

Just before we check in, I find an extraordinary cartoon in the government-controlled *China Daily*, which shows a party official putting a smart new model of a house over a peasant's shack. It couldn't have been a more perfect parody of what Hwong had tried to do. I show him the cartoon and I ask if it reminds him of anything. A look of terror crosses his face and he backs away from me. His stumble turns into a run, and eventually he dashes right out of the airport, with me running after him, demanding to know what the cartoon means. He gets into the van and drives off, with a rictus grin still spread across his face.

Meat and Two Veg

Back in Beijing I visit Guo-li-zhuang restaurant. There's no point beating about the bush: this place is a cock-and-bollock joint, a specialist penis and testicle emporium that caters mainly to wealthy businessmen and Communist party officials (who are often one and the same, truth be told). It offers every conceivable John Thomas you could ever want, which probably isn't very many, but nonetheless, their menu is extensive and impressive. The place looks like a smart *kaiseki ryori* (Japanese haute cuisine) formal restaurant, complete with underfloor stream, secluded separate dining rooms and hushed, discreet staff. I have come determined to avoid euphemisms – we're making a current affairs programme after all – but I'll admit the temptation is strong.

I ask a chef to show us the preparation of a penis first so that I can get a feel for the process. He enters holding aloft an eye-wateringly large yak's knob. It's about 45cm long, but thin, so thin. It's been boiled gently and – I can't believe I'm writing this – peeled, except for a hunk of foreskin still clinging on to the end. He cuts the thing in half lengthways with a pair of scissors. As he chops through the very tip of this impressive member, I get an undeniable empathy twitch in my own penis and a bizarre feeling of nausea in my groin (I didn't think that groins could experience nausea). I can't help myself yelping in sympathy. He then uses a knife to make hundreds of little snips along the side of the penis and chops these into 5-cm long pieces. When these are dropped into boiling stock they curl up into little flower shapes that are so incongruous, I can barely believe my eyes.

I ask the chef if he thinks it strange to deal exclusively in genitalia, but he shrugs and doesn't know what to say. He's just happy to have a good job, really. His friends don't take the mickey, his parents are proud of him, and he does what he's told. OK.

Less taciturn is the female manager of the place, who says that Chinese history is one of famine, poverty, drought and disaster, which is why the Chinese have become used to eating every part of the animal – they have to extract every edible morsel from the food they have. I ask if this is good communist food, and she proudly says that most of her customers are male Communist party members. Their meal costs an average of two months' wages for a dumpling factory worker, and I ask how a conscientious communist can be seen here (up to £250 for the rarer penises) when the average peasant is on the poverty line. She holds her hands up in the air and tells me that they come for the virility benefits that genital-eating offers. Apparently you can go for hours after eating a good portion of penis.

We try the water buffalo penis first, in thin shavings. It started long and thin, but someone has shredded this noble old chap on a mandolin.

It has the texture of squid, and tastes of the mild chilli stock it's been poached in. We are given three sauces to dip the penis into – lemon and soy, chilli and soy and a sesame seed paste. It's good, and the penile nature of the meat lends an undeniable frisson of excitement to the meal. I tell the boss that 'it's the first time I've had penis in my mouth, but I like it and I'm going to do more of it'. Well, someone had to say it.

She seems pleased and pours me some deer penis juice, which I'm delighted to say is the vilest concoction I've ever had the privilege to imbibe. It's as sour as a smacked lemon and as bitter as neat quinine. My face freezes in an agonizing spasm and Lord knows how I manage to keep from throwing up. Mr Hoo, the driver, asks if I want any more, and when I shake my spasming head, he grins and downs it in one. I pity Mrs Hoo – she's going to have a busy night.

We try goat's penis, chicken feet, bull's penis tip (that'll keep you up all night too, the boss warns), terrapin leg and all manner of radishes. I'm offered dog's penis ('the only one with a bone in it'), and served with a glacé cherry placed pointlessly on the tip, but decline. All the knobs have intriguing, delicate and bizarre textures, although the flavour is mainly of pork braised in hot stock. But my favourite dish of all is undoubtedly the bull's perineum, which is a delicate piece of flesh the size of a chicken oyster that's been poached then slow-fried. It's sweet and crispy, with a deep taste of soy and honey. Fabulous stuff.

Yan Yan isn't too keen on penis, but she's adventurous in the face of adversity, and tries most things with a curled lip.

Just before we go, I ask why the girls get off lightly. Why don't they serve any female genitalia?

The boss bursts into giggly embarrassed laughter. 'That's a crazy idea – why would anyone want to do that?'

'Well, because it's protein and you Chinese are renowned for eating everything.'

'Don't be insane,' she says. Then she remembers that she's heard of a dish of donkey vulva but she's not sure where. She thinks it's a disgusting idea.

The Night Market

The next day I manage to stagger out of bed at first light in time to watch the legendary Chinese early morning workout in the park – accompanied, of course, by another two minders. Mr Chen, a local t'ai

IDEOLOGICAL FOOD

chi master, gets me up in front of hundreds of onlookers to show me some moves. Obviously I look like a tool, but doing the moves does make me feel calm and poised. As soon as I'm finished, a handsome old gent called Mr Huang comes up to practise his English on me. I tell him that I'm here to make a film about food in China and he tells me that he's a great cook, and invites me for lunch: 'I cook good Chinese food for you.' I gladly accept, take his phone number and arrange to meet him later that day.

When my minders find out, they tell me that it can't be organized. I say that it already has been, and refuse to take no for an answer.

Inevitably, the party minders have got to Mr Huang and grilled him before I arrive (Penny had demanded that Yan Yan give her the phone number, and then passed it onto them), although they don't risk my wrath by trying to stop me, and I refuse to let them stay inside with me whilst I'm there – they've given up on us now, which is a great relief. Mr Huang lives in a small, four-roomed worker's flat that exhibits the kind of ingrained filth that comes with decades of poverty, the kind of squalor that looks disconcertingly beautiful. He tells me he had been an important crane engineer during the early development of Beijing, and although he's an old man now (he's 75), he's fit as a fiddle, getting up at 6 a.m. every morning to do t'ai chi in the park. He's also very proud of his cooking.

Mr Huang shows me how to make a strong, pungent fish-head soup ('good for your brains and nervous system'), stir-fried peas (sadly, not very good), rice, pork stew and stir-fried fish. We have a rare old time. His kitchen is cramped but adequate, with a two-ring gas hob, a few pots and pans and one small, very dim light bulb. Every wall has a patina of filth that must have taken years to get to this perfect art director's vision of urban grime. The house has no carpets, and no unnecessary luxuries other than a few calligraphy banners drawn by Mr Huang's brother.

Mr Huang doesn't need any more than he has (or at least, if he does, he isn't saying) and seems pretty happy with his life. This is the right kind of place for a retired couple, he insists. Our talk turns to communism, and although he seems happy to talk about it, his wife tells him sharply not to reveal anything to me. Oh, come on. Although he has been a party member for 50 years, he won't be drawn on what communism means to him, what modern communism is, or whether China is going through fundamental changes. It transpires that both of his daughters are now in the United States, and one is a US citizen. Hmm.

'OK,' I say, 'if you won't talk about communism, can you tell me what being a party member means to you?'

'You should serve the people with your heart and soul; whatever you do must conform to the wish of the people.'

'And has communism changed, do you think?'

'I think our main goal hasn't changed in terms of the policies. I feel it is like people walking. The destination is always the same but the style and speed of walking is different. The speed it is walking now is suitable for our development.'

And that is as far as he would go. Shame really – he was a lovely bloke, but clearly my minders had got to him. It seems odd that they wouldn't talk about communism – presumably they are proud of China's immense achievements – the millions of people who were persecuted and slaughtered along the way shouldn't have died for nothing.

Later that night we decide to have some fun and visit the Beijing night market where we find all manner of scorpions, squabs, weird bivalves and cockroaches. This is your basic extreme eating experience, similar to a rough sex one-night stand: unedifying and ultimately unsatisfying in retrospect but bloody great at the time. I try most things on offer: scorpions that are skewered alive and dispatched instantly in boiling oil (crispy on the outside, smooth in the middle).

'Deleeeshoush! Very healfy,' yells the theatrical stall owner, who's clearly seen a few camera crews and tourists in his time.

I agree; slightly disturbing, but delicious nonetheless. And as I gingerly eat its poisonous tail, I feel like I'm eating a large and dangerous Walkers crisp.

I try all manner of bugs, kebabs and weird fish, most of which I never find out the names of. It's all fun, icky, spine-tingling and exhilarating. Tiny squabs are the only real revelation – eaten whole, heads, wings and all. They have been lightly grilled and are a remarkable combination of delicate poultry flavour and crunchy texture.

I go on to eat, for no good reason other than a frisson of adventure, snake skin, grubs and erm … lamb kebab. Snake skin is a little reminiscent of crocodile: like fishy pork, pleasantly fatty.

And then we film a beggar who happens to be going through a bin in front of us, and Penny goes nuts and stops us. 'Why are you filming him? He has nothing to do with food.'

I am bewildered – I'm making a documentary, and if something happens in front of us, isn't it reflective of modern China? They've stopped me from meeting any of the hundreds of millions of rural poor, so they've already made sure China is depicted infinitely better than it really is.

She goes on complaining bitterly about it until we arrive at the hotel.

On my last day I take a deep breath and visit China's greatest, biggest, hairiest tourist fleshpot. I walk up a path of several thousand steps to get to it, which after the first kilometre, I realize is perhaps a mistake, what with the rucksacks of camera kit that I, as sole bloke on hand, foolishly offer to carry.

When I finally get there, the Great Wall of China is many things: naff, cheesy, extraordinary and impressive, which is probably why it appears on Chinese visa stamps. It is, like many great things, a wild folly that could only be built in a country where rulers can force grand and utterly imbecilic gestures like these to be built at the cost of thousands of lives. It's also a bit of a metaphor for modern China: impressive, bold, paranoid and obstructive. As a defence mechanism, it was crap, and never stopped any invasions (Genghis Khan is said to have simply bribed the guards to let him in). The fact that a tool to stop people getting into China appears on my visa stamp tells you everything about modern China and its grasp of irony.

* * * * *

I'm on the plane on my way home, and it's a huge relief. My love affair never transpired, and I leave feeling angry and frustrated about China because of the paranoia and subterfuge. Despite the wealth and technology its mindset is still stuck in the dark ages. This is a paranoid, juvenile country and it seems out of place in the modern world.

I think about my next trip. The behaviour of China's officials has been laughable, but hopefully it has wiped away the growing sense of normality I've begun to feel about the abject misery and desperate poverty I've seen over the last few years. I need to start over again as a functioning, rational emotional being, with my eyes open and an ability to put what I see in some sort of context. I haven't been looking forward to my last journey because I know that where I'm going hatred is probably more highly concentrated than in any other place on earth.

ISRAEL AND
PALESTINE
God's Food

. . . .

ISRAEL

POPULATION: 7 million

PERCENTAGE LIVING BELOW THE POVERTY LINE: 22%

UNDP HUMAN DEVELOPMENT INDEX: 23/177

CORRUPTION PERCEPTIONS INDEX POSITION: 34/163

GDP (NOMINAL) PER CAPITA: $20,399 (30/179)

FOOD AID RECIPIENTS: n/a

MALNUTRITION: n/a

WEST BANK

POPULATION: 2.5 million (according to *CIA World Factbook*)

PERCENTAGE LIVING BELOW THE POVERTY LINE: 46%

UNDP HUMAN DEVELOPMENT INDEX: n/a

CORRUPTION PERCEPTIONS INDEX POSITION: n/a

GDP (NOMINAL) PER CAPITA: $1,500 (200/229)

FOOD AID RECIPIENTS: 600,000 (West Bank and Gaza)

MALNUTRITION: n/a

. . . .

Nobody tells you this before you get to the Middle East, but Israel and the Palestine territories are *tiny*. Israel is the size of Wales, the West Bank is the size of Cornwall, and the Gaza Strip is less than half the size of the Isle of Wight. Yet this dusty, rocky little patch of land has provided us with a conflict the bitterness and misery of which dwarfs all others. Some claim that its politico-religious conflict is the root cause of the gravest dangers facing the world right now. The fight between Israelis and Palestinians has been marked by years of atrocities and an ever-deepening spiral of hatred, misery and vengeance.

The situation here is so bitter and complex that any journalist hoping to report on it for the BBC has to take a special course to ensure that events here are fairly reported. Both sides have accused the BBC of being biased, and newspapers in Israel frequently criticize Europeans for being 'awful' about Israel. It's the textbook case of 'one man's terrorist is another man's freedom fighter'.

The Jerusalem Crowne Plaza

I'm soaking up the atmosphere of the Jerusalem Crowne Plaza, one of those utterly miserable hotels the BBC loves its staff to stay in. In fact the only upside to the Crowne Plaza is its peculiar and highly amusing function as an orthodox Jewish dating venue, and each night the lobby is rammed with courting couples. 'Courting' may be exaggerating matters a little – they're putative, proto-couples meeting up to find out if they are suited. The guys – young Orthodox men sporting long *pe'ote* sideburns, large black hats firmly glued above them, and their torsos wrapped in black overcoats – sit talking to earnest young women of marriageable age. Lurking a few tables away a chaperone is viewing the proceedings to ensure a complete lack of hankipankiness, although in truth there's likely to be neither hanky nor panky between these devout boys and girls.

My first conversation with an Israeli turns into a stand-up row after I tell the inquisitive hotel shop owner that I'm making a documentary for the BBC. 'Why are you so *awful* about Israel? Why do you hate us so much?'

'I don't' doesn't seem to cut it with her. I take a look at the *Jerusalem Post* (take the *Daily Mail* and turn right, and you'll find this paper somewhere around Saturn) and it contains more discussions about how the BBC and Europeans in general are 'awful' about Israel for, amongst other things, reporting the UN's view that West Bank settlements are illegal, and its view that Jerusalem isn't strictly speaking the capital of Israel. This is clearly not going to be an easy trip.

Efrat, my Israeli guide, picks me up and I drive to the BBC bureau. It's two months since Alan Johnston, the Gaza correspondent, was abducted, and he's still in captivity somewhere in Gaza, so they are on high alert.

They ask what I'm here to do, and I tell them that I'm doing a story about food and conflict. The bureau chief looks at me as though I'm insane.

We take a quick drive around Old Jerusalem: it's a truly beautiful city that oozes history. It's the holiest city in Judaism, the third holiest in Islam and one of the most important in Christianity. I think it's a little weird that there's a pecking order of holiness, being more of an omnipresence and omniscience kind of guy, but what do I know?

The Palestinians say that east Jerusalem will become the Palestinian capital (if they ever get a state), but since Israel annexed it in the 1967 Six Day War, this looks unlikely to happen. Israel calls Jerusalem its capital and has located its Supreme Court and parliament here, but the UN (along with most of the rest of the world) hasn't recognized this, saying that the final status of the city is part of future negotiations on a Palestinian state. See, nothing's easy here.

My first foray into Israel is with Gil Hovav, Israel's most famous food celebrity who's Jewish, but no BBC-hater, and who turns out to be friendly and knowledgeable. He's taking me for a guided tour of the city starting with Mahane Yehuda, the main food market. Palestinian suicide bombers have struck here six times in the last 20 years killing 24 people and wounding over 300. Yet it's your classic cultural melting pot and the range of foods on offer is extraordinary: Israel is made up of Jews from all over the world, and they have clung onto their traditional cuisines.

'Is there such a thing as Jewish food?' I ask Gil.

'Here you'll get Iraqi food, Egyptian food, Syrian food, Yemeni food. These are all the Jews who came from these countries to Israel, and they brought their food with them. Then you have the Ashkenazi food. East European food, Poland, Germany, Hungary, you find it in this market as well. And, of course, Russian, Russian, Russian. We have had about a million immigrants from Russia in less then ten years so. Russian food is very strong.

'You can buy almost everything here. You can even find non-kosher food, although it's mainly kosher. The minute you introduce a non-kosher item to a store everything in it becomes non-kosher. Since the big Russian immigration, you can even find pork and seafood in this market. It was a definite no-no before. But people demanded it so you can find it.'

I ask if traditional Jews are offended by the fact that you can buy pork in Israel. 'Every once in a while they very politely burn the store. But if the store survives then you can find pork here.'

IDEOLOGICAL FOOD

We wander towards the Orthodox areas, but Gil warns Efrat not to come. She's wearing modern, Western clothing, and this doesn't go down well around these parts. We wander into Mea Sharim, 'Eastern Europe in the 18th century. This is the main ultra-orthodox neighbourhood in Jerusalem. Its very big, very populated and very poor.'

We pass a sign addressed to women and girls saying 'Please do not pass through our neighbourhood in immodest clothes'. Gil explains that if women come dressed inappropriately, they are likely to have urine thrown at them from the nearby houses.

The residents of Mea Sharim mostly follow the strictly orthodox Haredi Jewish tradition. Men and women are often segregated, and modern technology often rejected. 'It's so poor that you won't find a lot of restaurants here, but if you find one it'll be European because traditionally the ultra-orthodox come from eastern Europe.'

We stop at a small cave-like restaurant and eat kugle – a shredded potato cake that's traditionally eaten on Saturday, the Jewish day of rest (Shabbat), when no work is allowed, including cooking.

'Kugle is baked in the oven overnight,' Gil explains. 'On Shabbat you're not supposed to operate your oven. So you can start it on Friday, and cook something in it overnight for lunch or breakfast the next day. And since on Shabbat you're supposed to eat hot food this is the best thing because it doesn't burn.'

It's filling, but not a lot else. I try to tuck into it, cheered on by Gil: 'Come on eat up, make God happy. Think of winter in Hungary or Poland.' But it's hard to swallow and I have to give up.

A few minutes walk takes us through the Ottoman defensive walls of the old city and into east Jerusalem and the Arab quarter. To the thousands of Palestinians who live here, east Jerusalem remains under occupation and over 150 Israelis have died in attacks here since 2000.

We pass from an orthodox Jewish area and suddenly stumble across an area that's completely Muslim. Gil says, 'This is Jerusalem. It's a mosaic, you really can travel in time, travel in religion, travel in space. And these places are so close to each other, and yet there's a lot of conflict around.'

I see a building covered in Israeli flags. 'They talk about Jewish settlements; well this is a synagogue in the Muslim quarter of Jerusalem. It's a mini settlement.'

'Are things like this done specifically to enrage the Arabs?' I ask.

Gil considers this, then replies, 'I think so, but they don't. I find it difficult to see their point of view. But they would say, "It's ours and we're just coming back to it".'

Just off a dusty, flagstoned alley in the middle of Old Jerusalem is an Arabic restaurant set inside a couple of dark arches that's rumoured to serve the best hummus in the Middle East. Gil tells me, 'This is a holy moment. You are going to face the hummus of your life. This is Abu Shukri, deep in the Muslim quarter of Old Jerusalem, deep within the walls. This is where you can get what is considered the best hummus in Israel. Even during the intifada years Jews would sneak into the Muslim quarter just to have a bite of this hummus. It's really hummus to die for, I mean literally, you could.'

The genesis of hummus has become a cliché to describe the Middle East divide: both sides claim it as their own, that it was originally developed as a dish by their own cultures hundreds or even thousands of years ago. Gil says it's simple: 'Hummus is Arabic. Falafel, our national dish, is completely Arabic. And this salad that we call an Israeli salad, is actually a Palestinian salad, so we sort of robbed them of everything.'

The hummus is, indeed, the best I've ever eaten – partly because it's packed full of oil and herbs but also because it's a controversial dish eaten in a hot, sweaty, troglodytic restaurant in a Muslim quarter of a Jewish conquest, dripping with history and pain, and the brain often merges psychological elements with sensory information. Alternatively, it could be that it just tastes great.

The Pig

I meet The Pig, the BBC's war zone Land-Rover. She's hewn from vast sheets of inch-thick steel, is as heavy as a tank and drives like…well…a pig. The Jerusalem Bureau has kindly lent her to me for a few days for our trips around the occupied territories. The BBC's International Man of Mystery and Risk Assessment, the lovely C____, has insisted that I travel everywhere inside the West Bank in an armoured vehicle, but the ones you hire in Israel come with Jewish drivers, and they would be torn apart if they were found in the places we're going. So we're stuck with the Pig for now.

Sadly, no one in the Jerusalem Bureau fancies giving up their weekend to drive us around, even for cash, so it has fallen to Marc to drive The Pig around the West Bank. I can't do it because I left my driving licence at home precisely so that I didn't end up driving god-awful vehicles like The Pig around war zones. Heh, heh. She is a seriously uncomfortably hunk of metal in which to travel. Her ventilation system accurately re-creates the noise of a jet engine, with none of the resulting movement of air, which is not nice when the temperature hovers around 42 degrees. It's like Hades on wheels. On the plus side, she will protect us from high-velocity rifle rounds and possibly the odd explosion.

We travel to the Palestinian village of Bil'in. Bil'in has been split in half by the 675-km long security barrier that the Israelis claim has been built to protect its citizens from suicide attacks, but which the Palestinians claim has been built to make their lives even more unbearable, and is effectively a pre-emptive land grab of West Bank territory before the real borders of a Palestinian state have been decided. The barrier (the BBC isn't allowed to call it a 'wall' as the word is too emotive) does indeed stray deep into the West Bank in many places, effectively annexing a large amount of territory, but it's also true that the number of suicide bombings has fallen in recent years.

What's certain is that here in Bil'in the barrier has made life difficult for Palestinians by separating residents from their land (about half of the village's land is now on the Israeli side), and it has also reinforced their anger: it's become a symbol of their sense of oppression and a focus for their protests. Every Friday for the last few years, there has been a violent anti-barrier demonstration.

Abu Nadir, his wife and four children have grown up in Bil'in. He greets me with a huge smile and gives us a breakfast of bread, hummus and olives. He says his family have lived off the land for centuries harvesting olives from their trees and keeping livestock. He also used to work in Israel until he was refused entry after the intifada in October 2000. The trouble is that his olive groves are on the wrong side of the barrier and he is allowed only intermittent access to them, so now his food supply and livelihood is threatened. 'The Israelis say it's for state security but it isn't. The fence is there to steal our land for the settlements, it's an occupation.'

Abu Nadir will be protesting against the barrier this afternoon after prayers, as he has done every Friday since it was built. We wander out of town to make a quick recce. A few hundred metres after we pass the town mosque, we walk up a hill and the barrier looms into view: three high fences separated by a path and a wide road wind across the land, with the occasional gate and checkpoint. I probably shouldn't say it, but it does remind me of the Berlin Wall.

I go through an open gate inside the first fence and walk along the taller fence to a checkpoint to see what will happen. A man with a herd of goats has been sitting there for some time waiting to be allowed through, but when I arrive, a soldier wanders over from a bunker on the other side. After seeing my press pass he opens the gate and lets me through, telling me to have a nice day. My Palestinian guide says that they never usually let people through on the mornings before a protest, but he probably didn't want me to film the goatherd not being allowed access to land.

I walk a few hundred metres along the barrier's central road until I come to an access gate, and suddenly I'm on the Israeli side. On the hills where the Palestinians' land used to be there are some enormous settlements being built. Some of this land may have been bought, but many of the Palestinians say that their lives were made intolerable by the Jews and they had little choice but to sell it and move away. They also claim that whilst Israelis are allowed to build on disputed land, it's almost impossible for a Palestinian to get building permission anywhere.

As I leave, four large troop carriers pull up on the Israeli side, and the drivers give me a friendly wave. Soldiers emerge and start setting up trestle tables and urns for tea and coffee as they chat with each other in the sunshine. It's like the advance team preparing for a WI meeting.

I return to the village to meet Abu Emad of Bil'in's ruling council and one of the organizers of the weekly demonstration. He's an affable, reasonable-sounding man sitting on a mountain of anger: 'The world thinks that we Palestinians live like everyone else and that we can support ourselves. But we are enclosed like a bird in a cage. Israel cages us, and now we are not allowed to travel, not allowed to build factories, we're not allowed to use the water or any basic utilities. And still they tell us we are free and to get on with our lives. But we are just prisoners in our own homes.

'For the Palestinians losing land is the same as losing food because we are traditionally subsistence farmers.' The villagers say that five existing settlements are expanding onto their land, and an entirely new one is currently being built. They say that eventually the settlements will form part of the largest Israeli settlement in the West Bank, called Modin Illit, although they can only legally do this if they buy land from the Palestinians and most settlers claim to have bought land legitimately.

IDEOLOGICAL FOOD

The call to prayers rings out and I go to wait outside the mosque for the demonstration to begin. Opposite the mosque is a house for foreign nationals who are here to monitor the Israel Defence Force (IDF) activity and offer support to the residents. It's strange waiting for a regular bout of violence to begin; I wonder if this is what a football hooligan feels like before a match. Many journalists have been injured covering this demonstration and I wonder whether I should put on my flak jacket and helmet, but decide that I will look ridiculous and possibly even draw fire.

Prayers end and the villagers emerge from the mosque chatting and joking and greeting the foreign nationals. The mayor of Bil'in, Abu Salim, has attended every protest. 'This wall is unjust,' he says. 'It strips us of our dignity and our land, and casts a shadow over all aspects of our lives. We have lived and worked on this land. It is our livelihood, and we shall never give it up no matter what. We shall continue to resist.'

The foreign nationals unfurl a banner saying 'Fuck the Occupation' and about 100 people march out of the village towards the barrier chanting, shouting and singing. I pass the hilltop again to find 20 or so photographers and cameramen filming the march, all wearing their helmets and flak jackets. I wonder if I've made a bit of a mistake. There are nearly always injuries here, and three weeks ago a protester was left with brain injuries after being shot in the head with a rubber bullet. Across the other side, below the barrier, are 50 or so IDF soldiers, all casually holding their weapons and watching us approach. There's no sense of aggression. When we get within 400 metres, though, I hear some loud bangs and the first tear-gas grenades fizz through the air. They land amongst us, and I get caught in the immediate cloud of the first gas, and get the full experience. Once you've tasted the stuff I swear you'll never look back, because it's without doubt the most powerful tear-gas around. If you've never tried tear-gas before, here's what you've been missing: it smells of spent fireworks – that acrid, slightly sulphurous, gunpowdery smell (similar to the smell of burnt-out stereo when you've been overloading the bass) – and rips my nostrils to shreds, while my eyes feel like I've bathed them in lemon juice. The sting swiftly transmogrifies into an unbearable rawness, spreading across my face, into my nose and throat. I stumble away from the gas cloud in the direction of the village but I can't really see where I'm going and my whole face is in excruciating pain. I finally manage to get out of the cloud and find Marc, who's feeling pretty grim, but doing better than me. The sensations begin to fade after about five or ten minutes, but leave me weakened and shaken.

Nonetheless, the protesters go back for gassing again and again. An ambulance turns up to help people who are really suffering, and some of the younger protesters start throwing stones using slingshots. The IDF start firing rubber bullets (these ones are like small corks and heavy with a slug of metal in the centre), and things begin to get a bit hairy, so I put on my flak jacket and helmet. A few people are hit by the bullets – one guy is hit in the leg and can't walk. He'll have one hell of a bruise tomorrow. The tear-gas is pretty effective at keeping the protesters from the fence until a gang breaks from the main group and runs off through the bushes. They make it to the fence below us, but are immediately arrested and driven off in an IDF van.

A few rubber bullets sing past me so I decide to move to the right-hand flank to see what's happening. I find Mayor Abu Salim screaming obscenities at the IDF. He's got a lot to say, and he shouts a bit fast, but his basic line appears to be this: 'You are the bastard sons of Druze Arabs, and your mothers are Druze whores. Take this to Sharon, take this to Olmert, to all the Israeli government! Get off the land! Take your fucking wall and stuff it up your fucking arse, you fuckers.' Although I'm not entirely sure about the Druze angle, the rest is clear enough, and Abu Salim appears to have taken shouting lessons because he's terrifically loud. The IDF clearly appreciate his efforts because they fire a set of rubber bullets as a thank you, one of them zipping right by me. I decide to take my leave before Abu Salim gets me killed.

Because this is a regular weekly protest, both sides know what to expect, and as a consequence it's like a terrible, vicious game. The protesters keep trying to reach the fence and the Israeli army tries to stop them. In many ways everyone's a winner here: the Israelis have the protest nicely under control with the gas and rubber bullets, and from the soldiers' body language they don't seem particularly concerned. They are probably talking about their girlfriends and their plans for the weekend as they expertly plop another tear-gas grenade in front of us. And the Bil'in villagers have done pretty well out of it too: there must be 20 international TV and photo journalists reporting the gig, so they've managed to get pretty extensive press coverage.

(Since I left the villagers have won their appeal to the Israeli Supreme Court, which has ordered the government to re-route the barrier so that the villagers can access their land properly. So far this ruling hasn't been implemented and the protests continue.)

Itamar

I am still under strict instructions from C_____ not to travel to Jewish settlements in the West Bank unless I carry a flak jacket and drive in an Israeli-owned armoured van: a Palestinian-owned car won't be allowed into the settlement, but cars with Israeli number plates are often attacked as they travel in the West Bank. So I have hired Shimon, the world's slowest driver, to drive us there in Big Momma, his tomb on wheels. One of the reasons he's so slow is the sheer weight of his truck, which is clad in thick steel as a defence against roadside bombs and gunfire, and it's dark and gloomy inside due to the lack of windows.

I'm on my way to visit Itamar, a particularly isolated Jewish settlement set deep inside the West Bank, which sits on a hilltop overlooking the 130,000-strong Palestinian city of Nablus. Established in 1984, most of Itamar's 1,000 residents are members of Gush Emunim, a messianic settler movement that believes there is a biblical imperative to inhabit the West Bank and the settlement now has around 4 square km of land to the fury of the Palestinians. They are frequently attacked and most male adults carry a gun at all times. Palestinians have killed over 15 residents of Itamar, the last attack leaving six dead, including a mother and her three children who were shot in their house and the attacker himself.

The settlements are probably the most contentious aspect of the Palestinian-Israeli conflict, and the Arabs see settlers as colonists stealing land from them (as do a fair few secular Jews who see the settlers as the main cause of attacks on Israelis). Settlers are generally Jews who inhabit land in the West Bank and Golan Heights (and more problematically, in east Jerusalem) that Israel invaded and took control of during the 1967 war and still occupies today (there were also settlements in Gaza and the Sinai Peninsula, but the Israeli government forced their closure). This is land that the Palestinians claim as theirs and that was generally expected to end up being part of Palestine, but is still under Israeli control with little movement towards resolution. The settlers are frequently attacked by Palestinian fighters, but they are well armed and protected by the IDF, who are often stationed alongside them. According to the UN, the settlements are illegal, but this is disputed by Israel.

There are currently around 460,000 Israeli settlers in the occupied territories, including around 200,000 in East Jerusalem. Settlements are started in various different ways, sometimes by groups of Jews parking caravans on hilltops in occupied territory and slowly but surely establishing a community and beginning to build proper homes. At first Israel refused to allow settlements and even forcibly disbanded them, but in the absence of peace talks to resolve the issue of a Palestinian state, and the continuing attacks in the Intifada uprisings and numerous suicide bombings, the Israeli government now rarely stops them from doing this (although building by Palestinians or the Bedouin living in Israel is strictly controlled, with houses frequently demolished because they lack permits), and instead assumes a duty to protect them as Israeli citizens and provides power and amenities.

If you're finding this confusing, I'm not surprised. Why on earth would people do something so blatantly antagonistic, and how does Israel justify it? The Palestinians claim that the settlements are there to pre-empt or sabotage any peace treaty that might give them sovereignty, and that the land belongs to them. Israel contends that this land was captured during a war against their aggressors and that the settlements are a strategically and tactically important consequence. Also, there were some Jewish communities in the West Bank before 1948 so many people see this as *re*settlement of land that originally belonged to Jews.

Much of the landscape of the West Bank is made up of parched and rocky ancient terraces that seem best suited for olive trees and bony goats. Yet on the hilltops the Jewish settlements like Itamar are surrounded by high security fences and topped with army lookout towers watching over the modern tarmac roads and the streets of homes, all built to the same modern design that wouldn't look out of place in a cul-de-sac on the outskirts of a commuter town. Around here, however they look strange: suburban Barratt Homes slap bang in the middle of the Bible.

The van makes the gate guard nervous – unfamiliar armoured vans are seen as possible terrorist vehicles around here. But after I get him to radio the head of the settlement, he lets us in. There are a few men wandering the streets with M16s hanging over their shoulders as they push prams along and they eye me with the suspicion I deserve.

I am here to meet Alon Zimmerman, an ex-surfer from California ('I'm a college drop-out, a leftover of the '60s') turned Messianic settler. He's here to retake the Promised Land on behalf of Judaism, and he rejects the term 'West Bank' in favour of the Zionist names of Judea and Samaria.

IDEOLOGICAL FOOD

I've had a lot of difficulty trying to meet settlers because they tend to dislike publicity, and they especially dislike the BBC. Alon has allowed us to come and film because he's keen to get publicity for the organic produce he grows and sells here, and for his fruit leather (like a bar of dried fruit). But it's a two-way street, because the Zimmermans are having a 'Perdion' (a ceremony to celebrate the arrival of the first male grandchild) in two days' time for their first male grandchild, and I would like to watch the ceremony, meet other settlers and try to get a sense of how the community lives.

However, Alon warns me that his wife Rachel is very orthodox and practical and has refused to talk to me because, frankly, she can't see what good will come from me being here. As for my guide Efrat, a very secular Jew from Tel Aviv, she doesn't look too kindly on the settlers – she's especially incensed that she has to wear long sleeves and trousers to avoid offending them – and she dislikes Rachel before she's even met her. This is going to be interesting.

Alon speaks with spiritual, messianic and evangelical conviction about cucumbers, bread and war; he sees food as a key building block of his faith, but also a root cause for conflict. 'If you understood Hebrew you'd know the root word of war is bread. *Lechem* is the middle word of war, so in other words all wars are basically based on bread.'

The Zimmermans have nine children who take up the vast majority of their time, and Alon's kitchen is *balagan* (a filthy mess) according to him. But the kitchen has nothing on the bathroom where their son rears chickens. The little chicks have taken over half of it, running about next to the washing machine, spreading crap around the floor and over clothes. Efrat is astounded at the squalor, and she breathes through her mouth to avoid the smell.

Rachel storms into the room. She's a ball of energy, rushing around telling us that she can't see what the point of all this is anyway, before departing abruptly. I am instantly terrified of her. Alon sighs and takes us off to see his hothouses on an edge of the settlement, where I help him pick broccoli and prepare the earth for a new crop. It's sweaty work, and my hay fever makes my throat and eyes itch like the devil's own scrofula as I try to keep up with his phenomenal speed and energy.

We yank broccoli stems for several hours and chat about land and food. 'Of course food is the source of all our conflict,' he says, 'because food equals land.'

I ask him why he's willing to put himself and his family in such danger here in this outpost, and he explains, 'We've returned home to resettle the land that God gave to the Jewish people.' As the Itamar website puts it, 'We came here to LIVE and revive the ancient earth THAT HAS ALWAYS BEEN OURS.'

Alon wishes that they could just live in peace with the Palestinians, and that the fighting would end. I mention that that's easy to say, but he is living on land that the Palestinians say is theirs. He tells me that the Bible says this isn't true.

We give up the backbreaking work because Alon has to take his father to hospital, so we say goodbye and I ask him to convince his wife to speak to me. He promises to try. In his absence Moshe, the head of the Itamar council, packs me into his van for a guided tour of the settlement. It's a poor place by Western standards, and as Moshe tells us, 'People here live simple, frugal lives'. He goes on to say that Itamar is beautiful and peaceful, and he and his fellow settlers are fulfilling their biblical destiny. This would ring a little more true if I didn't have his loaded M16 jiggling around between my legs. He is defensive about the settlements, and is adamant that, 'Anyone can open the Bible and see that this is a land given to the Jewish people by God – to the Jewish nation.'

I tactfully suggest to him that the Palestinians also claim it as their own, and he replies, 'That's a great question – you are very well prepared with your questions,' and changes the subject. I don't pursue it; it's not easy, trying to discuss the politics of land while at the same time ensuring that we aren't kicked off the settlement.

Moshe takes me to the farthest, highest point of Itamar, passing various places where attacks and deaths have occurred, and we gaze at the spectacular valleys, overlooked by ominous-looking Jewish settlements that seem to crown every single hill and mountain-top. Nearby is the city of Nablus, notorious for breeding Palestinian fighters, and I ask him if he sees enemies when he looks down onto the Palestinian homes, but he says that he sees a struggle yet to overcome.

Moshe says, 'Every step we take we try to make peace. What we get in return is war, bloodshed, killing of innocent men, women and children.' He suggests I take a look at the Itamar website later, which I do. I find this hands-across-the-water attitude to the Palestinians: 'Why do you think the Arabs are willing to blow themselves up? Because they know the end is very near, the sands in Yishmael's hourglass have just about run out …'

IDEOLOGICAL FOOD

I spend a long, hot sweaty day with Alon planting endless cucumbers. He tells me, 'If you dig in the ground deep enough, after you get below the remains of the Christian era and the Muslim era you'll find the dust of my forefathers here.' I try again to convince his wife Rachel to talk to me, and, after seeing how much I have helped her husband, she actually seems to be melting a little.

When I return to Jerusalem I call Alon again and he says that Rachel has finally agreed to talk to me.

Perdion

Rachel has suddenly become friendly and talkative, although she remains a little scary. She has a ferocious look in her eyes and a grin on her face that sits there whether she's berating her husband (she seems to do this quite a lot) or making salad.

I help her to prepare the food for tonight – chicken, cucumber salads and hummus – and she talks about food and faith. The Torah lays down strict rules for food preparation, and all manner of kosher rules 'about 20 or 30 per cent of the commandments'. I ask if she understands the rationale behind many of the rules, but she says she doesn't need rationality, 'People are always looking to explain things, but it's more important to accept the word of God.'

Rachel explains that tonight's ceremony is about redemption. I ask what the baby is guilty of, and she gives me a look, as if I've accused her grandchild of being evil. 'I don't mean that – it's just that if the child is being redeemed, it must be guilty of something. Maybe it's a symbolic guilt.'

She looks puzzled. 'Yes, I suppose so. Maybe there's a lot of sadness at the root of it all. In fact, there is. A lot of sadness.'

I ask if it's really worth living somewhere this dangerous. 'My children have been through one terrorist attack after another. I've got one daughter who's been in two terrorist attacks. She's had her face sewn up, she's had plastic surgery. This son has been in two terrorist attacks. All my children have had close friends killed, and that's how they live, they live here, they live deep in the ground.'

Her son is helping us cook, but he says that he doesn't like settlers and he doesn't like Arabs 'because both sides fight, both sides are extreme. Each side comes with hatred, you can see it in their faces. I don't like living like that.'

That night I join in the ceremony and eat some of the food we've prepared. There's a disappointingly low turnout – Alon had laid on an armoured bus to ship people in, but few people are brave enough to make it all the way out here into no man's land. A large, sweaty guy who's the spitting image of Borat's fat producer sings and plays the Bontempi keyboard at a quite remarkable volume, whipping the assembled throng into a fair old lather. There's much drinking, singing and dancing, and although the scholarly orthodox men drag me onto the dance floor, few people want to talk to me.

When the party ends, I help clear up into the small hours and then spend the night in a mildewed Portakabin, grateful that I've managed to spend three whole days with the settlers without being kicked out, but I must admit I've been disturbed by the experience.

Yanun

I head into the West Bank again, this time accompanied by the World Food Programme, to stay in Yanun, a Palestinian village just below the Jewish Itamar settlement. Most people in this village rely partly on food aid to survive. I am with a Mehjdi, a fast-talking Palestinian WFP employee who has drawn the short straw of accompanying me on an overnight trip.

Yanun is a poor farming community made up of subsistence farmers, mostly goatherds, who own olive trees, and who say they've been forced off a great deal of their land by local settlers. The houses are rudimentary but they have some electricity and running water. Yanun is at the head of a set of valleys that stretches out deep towards Jordan, and when the sun shines, the view is a stunning vista of ancient olive terraces flanking biblical hillsides (I know, I've used the biblical analogy a lot so far, but it just works around here).

Our contact isn't there when I arrive so I sit under a tree to wait. Someone spots me and brings me a cup of wickedly strong coffee, then another family sends a pot of delicious sweet tea. It's a very different welcome from the one I got in Itamar.

After a short while Abu Nasim arrives. He's the head of the family that's agreed to show us around and put us up for the night. He's a smiling, furry-faced villager with a deep tan and wrinkled skin from years spent working outside, but there's a world-weariness about him, despite the smiles. He's just arrived back from Nablus in his illegal unregistered car, having taken his son to see a doctor about an infected eye.

Abu Nasim (which means 'Father of Nasim' – Nasim being his eldest son) welcomes us into his house and he and his wife Om ('Mother') ply us with tea and coffee. They introduce us to their two giggling daughters, then Abu Nasim takes us and his small herd of goats and sheep for a walk around his village. It's poor but beautiful and peaceful, and again there's a real sense that biblical tales were played out on this earth although the effect is spoiled by the army watchtowers that look down on Yanun. Abu Nasim says he has the feeling that he is always being watched. Halfway up a hillside, he stops us and says that if we walk any further we are likely to get shot by the settlers. He points to his olive trees that cover the hillside beyond. 'I can't harvest the olives from those, so they rot on the trees and go to waste.'

The settlers around here don't just protect their land: they also stop the locals from coming anywhere near them. I guess it's for security, and they have every reason to be nervous as they've often been attacked in the past, but it means that Abu Nasim and his family go hungry, and creates a huge amount of resentment. Whilst the settlers are bristling with weaponry, the Palestinian villagers aren't allowed to own guns, so they're easily bullied. It's no surprise, then, that they turn to militancy.

He tells me that the settlers make pre-emptive forays into the villages around here to frighten and threaten Palestinians. They particularly enjoy pointing their guns at the village kids to terrify them. At one point, two years ago, the entire village moved out after attacks and intimidation by the settlers became intolerable, but after a while they and a few other families moved back, defying the settlers. Four years ago a shepherd was stabbed to death while out herding his sheep and there have been many documented attacks by settlers. Abu says that the Israelis never bother to investigate the murders of Palestinians, but if a settler is attacked, countless Arabs are made to suffer.

We go to the highest house in the village and I want to go to the top of the hillside so I can see down to the valley, but Abu Nasim says, 'Why? You'll just get shot.' Call me sentimental, but I find it depressing that Abu's kids will never see the top of their own hillside.

We return to Abu Nasim's house for a lunch of hummus, flatbreads, goat's cheese and olive oil. He tells me that being unable to harvest their olives has made them poorer, and the lack of grazing area means they have to buy feed for their goats. 'We have shortages of cornflour, rice and sugar,' he says, and they can't afford to buy fresh vegetables or meat. His sons all suffer from mineral and vitamin deficiencies and they are constantly ill.

'Look at my daughters. They don't have any teeth. When my daughter comes home from school she says, "Mother, the girls at school keep asking me what's wrong with my teeth." Sometimes I just burst into tears because I don't know what to say. There's nothing I can do.'

I ask how they feel about living on food aid from the WFP. 'I am not comfortable getting it, but look at our situation: we cannot farm, we cannot have lots of livestock. We used to grow our own chickpeas and store them in large amounts; now we are given only a few kilos by humanitarian organizations. The main reason for our terrible situation is the settlement behind us. We are in a small jail like Abu Graib. The only way out is towards the front of the town. The rest of the land has been seized. We are now living on a little over 1 square kilometre. In my father's day we had 300 goats and grazed them around the village.'

His words sound angry but he has a shrugging, disbelieving demeanour rather than a militant one. During lunch, the boys cough constantly, and curl up on their mother's lap. She strokes them gently throughout the meal. After we've finished a boy comes running in to tell us that the WFP aid truck has arrived. The villagers get a delivery of CSB, fortified flour and sugar. Around 40 men and boys stand in the sunshine chatting and drinking tea and coffee as the rations are sorted, then they help each other carry the sacks to their houses.

I help to milk the family goats, much to the amusement of Abu Nasim's children. When you milk a goat, you have to remember that neither the delicacy nor the love that you show to your main squeeze's nipples are of any use to a sheep, goat or water-buffalo. These girls sport industrial-quality tits. Grasp the teat with confidence and use your palm to manoeuvre the milk from the udder into the teat itself, and then imagine that you're trying to get the last bit of toothpaste our of a nearly-empty tube. Squeeze hard, but not aggressively and out should squirt a gratifying burst of milk. Abu Nasim is watching and he tells me that he borrowed money to buy his flock of goats but now that the settlers have taken away grazing land he has to buy animal feed to keep them alive, and the only way to pay for it is by selling the cheese and milk to animal feed salesmen. He's stuck with a flock of goats that makes almost no money, and a loan that he may never be able to repay. He is distraught at his inability to make enough money to feed his children but at least they have cheese and milk, so they get enough calcium.

IDEOLOGICAL FOOD

Om Nasim shows me how to make goat's cheese: after boiling the milk she adds a couple of drops of rennet, stirs it and leaves it for 15 minutes until it has taken on the consistency of set yoghurt. We take some small squares of muslin, wrap fistfuls of the nascent cheese in them and twist gently to squeeze out a little of the whey. The cheeses are laid on a board set at an angle, and more whey slowly drips down it into a bowl. We make about 20 wraps, and once they're done we immediately unwrap and rewrap them all, tightening them with a couple of extra turns as whey drips down our wrists. These are left for an hour, then we unwrap them once more. They now have the consistency of mozzarella. We unwrap and rewrap them again, checking that they are all exactly the same size, then cover them with another board and weigh it down. A couple of hours later, the cheeses are firm and tight, about the size of a packet of cigarettes, and ready to store away. We roll them in salt and put them in a bucket. The salt will remove more whey by osmosis and flavour the cheeses.

We eat some of the cheese that night for dinner. It is rich but blandly flavoured – like a good mozzarella but a little firmer. The mature ones are too dry and salty for me, but the ones we've just made are delicious and creamy inside. Abu and Om Nasim had wanted to cook me a special feast, but I ask them not to – I want to experience their normal life and eat the food that they normally eat, and I certainly don't want them to spend money on food that they can barely afford. Abu Nasim's clearly a bit miffed about this – his code of hospitality means he ought to treat me as an honoured guest – but he reluctantly agrees. So I eat the cheese, with hummus, some olives from his trees, bread and more olive oil.

After dinner we are joined by two young Polish men from a Christian ecumenical organization that helps keep an international presence in the village in an attempt to discourage the settlers from attacking Yanun or forcing the villagers out again. I make some balloon animals for the kids – I'm the world's worst balloon modeller, but they don't seem to mind.

Abu Nasim pulls out an ancient TV but can only manage to find one very fuzzy channel. It's running repeats of WWF wrestling, complete with maniacal voiceovers and ridiculous costumes. We sit in this ancient house drinking Arabic coffee and sprawling on cushions as the sun sets on the most fought-over, holiest land on the planet, whilst on the telly a man who looks like a pig on steroids appears to be smashing seven shades of shit out of what I can only describe as a spandex bat.

We bed down for the night in the room we ate in – Marc, Mehjdi Nadir (our WFP driver) and myself – all sprawled out on cushions. Throughout the night the sons cough and splutter, and none of us gets much sleep.

By dawn the room smells pretty rank – the only thing for it is to go for an early walk, so I'm sitting writing this under an olive tree on a Palestinian hillside, shaded from the brutally clear morning sunshine. Whatever religion you are, I defy you to sit here on these crumbling olive grove terraces and not feel some sense of awe and history. Although there's a brief but palpable serenity, looking down towards the Great Rift Valley and across to Jordan you do get a sense, though it troubles me to admit it, that this land has been fertilized with blood, and that perhaps peace doesn't really belong here

The valley is beautiful, bathed in a sharp sunlight and hissing gently with insect life. The ancient terraces ring the hills and there's no movement or sound except for rustling leaves in the trees – until I hear the pop of a distant gunshot ringing out from one from somewhere above. Then, on the hill opposite me, a settler's JCB starts work pounding rocks on the scrubland and digging next to a watchtower. It looks from here as though they are laying out a new cul-de-sac of houses.

A man shouts at me. It's Rashid, the village mayor who's just back from taking his sheep grazing. He's waving at me and shouting 'Salaam', but he doesn't have time to stop. He warns me (using the international language of finger drawn across throat) not to go any further up the hill or I'll be shot.

I return to the house to help Om Nasim cook bread in her *taboohn*, a goat-dung fired oven. A deep hole has been filled with broken stones and floor tiles, then covered with a steel lid, on top of which is what looks like a pile of ash, but is actually a deep fire of goats' dung smouldering away. She tells me that it never goes out. She wipes away the surface ash, and underneath it's a furnace of bright red embers. Within this has been set a large iron pot half-filled with stones, and this is the oven. She lifts the lid and lays a piece of dough about 60 cm in diameter straight onto the stones, then replaces the lid. After four or five minutes, the bread is baked a deep, mottled brown, marked in places with a little charring, and smelling damn fine. She grabs it out with her bare hands despite the heat, and lays it down to cool, a few stones still sticking to the bread. It has a slight taste of goat's dung which I rather like.

IDEOLOGICAL FOOD

It's time to leave. I have listened to two sets of people who have wildly differing views on the conflict over these hills, and it's difficult to know who's right and who's wrong, and even harder to see how a resolution to this conflict can ever be found.

Nablus

I'm heading for one of the unhappiest places on the planet: Nablus, the biggest Palestinian city in the West Bank, next to both Itamar and Yanun. It's a renowned centre for Palestinian militants, entirely surrounded by the Israeli army, and inside it's awash with weaponry, frustration and anger. Six Israeli checkpoints control all access for people and goods in and out of the city and many people haven't been able to leave since the second intifada in 2001 because of the number of suicide bombers who came from there.

The drive is tense. I get through the checkpoint with just a few cursory frowns from the soldiers, and a few hundred metres inside I pick up my guide, Alaa (who has great difficulty getting through checkpoints) and he takes over the driving. He tells me that there's a rally going on in the old city for a militant who died recently and suggests that we go along. I'm a little wary, but he assures me that it'll be safe.

In a small central square, three or four hundred men and boys have gathered to listen to men reading out speeches. The atmosphere is bitter, angry and violent. On the back of a truck about 30 men stand in military clothing, each holds an M16, and they fire into the air after every few sentences to show their appreciation, deafening everyone around them. I worry for the hundred or so young boys sitting on top of the adjacent buildings and Alaa says that every now and then people get shot by mistake at these rallies. There are other gunmen scattered around the square who occasionally get so worked up by the speeches that they, too, start firing into the air, at which point everyone starts panicking in case it's the Israelis trying to snatch the militants. 'The men on the truck are all wanted men,' says Alaa, 'but they don't care if anyone sees them – they are dead already and it's just a matter of time.'

The kids on the rooftops are clearly in awe of the militants, and it's not hard to see why. In a city where children have bleak futures and little cause for optimism, a life as a famous fugitive followed by a blaze-of-glory ending is as much as they can hope for. And quite apart from the sense of retribution, anger and religious zeal, to these boys, being a militant is *cool*. The guys with guns command respect that they're unlikely to find any other way.

I stick out a mile, but Alaa has warned people that I'd be here, so they tolerate my presence. I am invited up onto the truck to get a better view, and they fire their guns very close to my ears, so that I'm soon rendered entirely deaf. When a man starts singing a song to the dead militant, Alaa suggests we leave.

You can sense the pressure in this city, and although the Palestinian Authority has nominal control here, Nablus's main police station has been hit repeatedly in Israeli air strikes. That night, there's sporadic gunfire, including a startling burst as I'm on the phone to my daughter. I speak up and talk nonsensically to try to cover up the noise. Later, I'm woken by more gunfire, but I'm getting used to it now, and I go back to sleep.

Nablus Bakery

I get up at dawn and head for the old city. This place is classically beautiful in the mould of Damascus or Istanbul, all white stone and paved streets swarming with old gents smoking and drinking tiny glasses of sweet tea. But when you take a closer look, the walls are covered in flyposters of militants wielding guns, and the occasional outline of Israel, depicted dripping with blood. Alaa says that they are pictures of dead 'martyrs' Some of them look as young as 16.

It's a while before I notice that sitting in the alleys I stroll past are men holding M16 rifles and eyeing me with suspicion. 'There are a lot of wanted men here,' says Alaa, 'militants who would be shot on sight by the Israelis.'

I ask why they are sitting openly on the streets. 'It's OK; the Israelis can't operate in the middle of the old town, it's too dangerous for them.'

I wander down tiny alleys, along cobbled walkways and up precipitous staircases until we find Abu Sharif, a gently spoken one-armed baker in his 60s who works with two of his brothers. He lives with seven of his family in a small second-floor set of rooms with a view out towards the hills ringing Nablus. He agrees to let me help him for the day and we head off to the bakery.

His two brothers and one of his sons have got there before us and the wood-fired oven is nearly up to temperature. They make four different types of bread – mainly wholemeal pittas and flatbreads made from flour (only Palestinian flour), water and salt – no yeast. I offer to help. 'You can try, but you'll only slow us down,' they say. I manage to bake the simpler breads easily enough, sliding them into the inferno with a flat paddle, and yanking out the cooked ones so they are just about marketable. But when it comes to spreading the dough to make wider ones, I am clearly a shambles, turning perfectly good balls of dough into Munch grotesques. I try to lay out the dough balls for proving instead, but I'm just as cack-handed at that, and the brothers are soon cackling with laughter.

Despite my ineptitude, the bread tastes wonderful. I pull loaves out and drop them onto a stone ledge where they sit sighing steam. They cool for a minute, then I rip them apart and the wonderful smell wafts into my nose. They are browned and slightly charred in places, and the taste of the charred bits is sublime. We start by making a few brown pittas and then we churn out hundreds of flatbreads of all shapes and sizes. Abu Sharif's brother Keza makes a batch of white flour breads for his family who won't eat anything else, much to his dismay, but the breads that sell on the ramshackle stall outside are the wholemeal ones.

As they teach me, we talk about the situation in Nablus. They tell me that food has doubled in price since the second intifada. 'There's food in the streets, but no one can afford it, so about half of the city goes hungry.' Abu Sharif says that women go to the market, pick up food to look, then simply hand it back again because they don't have any money.

The IDF often blocks access to the city and sometimes doesn't allow food supplies in or out, so their bakery doesn't always have flour to bake with. 'Often we can only work two days a week because there's no flour, or there are incursions by the army. The IDF come, demolish houses and arrest people, usually relatives of wanted militants, and then leave again.' In the past, it was rumoured that Saddam Hussein's regime would pay huge sums of cash – in the region of $20,000 – to the families of the suicide bombers. It was taken as read that the Israelis would swiftly arrive to demolish their houses, so Iraq would pay to have them rebuilt again. This is no longer the case.

We hang out with Abu Sharif and chat some more as he sells his bread on the street corner. 'The Israelis are trying to strangle us,' he says, shrugging his shoulders as though there's nothing that anyone can do about it. Suddenly he lunges at a thin man who passes by muttering to himself and wallops him across the head, sending him wailing up a side alley. 'He keeps trying to steal my bread,' says Abu Sharif. Alaa tells me that there's a high level of psychological problems amongst

Palestinians, exacerbated by the pressures they face. But there's little sympathy around here, and I spot the mutterer being abused by various different people throughout the afternoon.

I wander the streets of Nablus again, stopping to drink hot minty tea every so often. Drinking tea and coffee is an art-form here. The tea is called *shai* and they drink it black and sweet, sometimes minty and sometimes not, but invariably served in small glasses that are too hot to hold, and a glass of water served alongside. The coffee is a different matter: it's mixed with a touch of cardamom and unfiltered. Each potent little cup is topped with a scum of bitter coffee dust I like the cardamom and the hefty whack of coffee in the first few sips, but if you suck the grounds up by mistake they're pretty unpleasant.

That night I have supper with Abu the baker and his family. His apartment is in the centre of the old town and from his window the hilly skyline is covered in Israeli army observation posts. Behind the tree line is an Israeli settlement. He says, 'There isn't as much food around because of the economic situation. The way people eat has changed. They are eating less meat and cutting down on costly foods.'

'How does it feel to have the Israelis always looking down on you?' I ask.

'Neighbours never like their neighbours. So if neighbours don't like each other what am I to think about those settlements over there? They are monitoring me in my own home.'

'What do you think of the settlers?'

'I consider them enemies, enemies to my people, to my homeland. They are like a cancer. It starts small then spreads everywhere, exactly like the settlers.'

That evening I hear that there's an Israeli army raid into the city. In the firefight that followed a stray Israeli bullet hit a pregnant woman, killing her unborn child.

Hedera

I visit Aron, an Israeli stallholder in Hedera where, on 26 October 2005, a Palestinian militant detonated a bomb outside his falafel stall. Aron had just taken over the shift from his brother and was busy serving customers when the bomb went off killing five people and injuring 28, including Aron. 'There weren't that many people killed, but they were people I knew. Especially an old lady, a regular customer, came here every day to eat while her husband did the shopping and she was killed.'

I ask him how he feels about the bomber and he's remarkably calm about it, reminding me of the Palestinians I met in Yanun: 'Look, I'm 60 years old. I know about Arab living conditions, why the bombers are being sent and who is sending them. They have been taught to have a certain mentality, and I can't change that. But I hope the next generation won't study it, and will move towards peace.'

Tel Aviv

I'm back in Tel Aviv and the difference is astonishing. This place is as laid back, secular, friendly and architecturally ugly as Jerusalem is uptight, religiously strict, rude and beautiful. It's all concrete blocks and apartments, but there are cool restaurants and a clear vibrancy to the place. Streets are full of cafés and gorgeous people, and although the beaches are dominated by gargantuan 1970s' era hotels and acres of concrete, there's a palpable relaxed atmosphere. As if to prove the point about Tel Aviv's coolness, Gay Pride day is drawing to a close as we arrive. On the beach below my hotel room, lots of people in shorts and bikinis are dancing in the sunset.

The next day I go to the Old Port, an area full of restaurants and overpriced surfing shops, and visit a restaurant called Beny the Fisherman. The owner, Beny (a fisherman, as it happens), looks like a very naughty ex-rock star. He's dressed all in white, with a lion's mane of curly Brylcreemed locks tumbling down his back, and a smile that makes him look like Jack Nicholson on heat. He's also a major player on the Tel Aviv scene, and as if to prove the point, his mobile phone rings constantly and customers in the restaurant drop by to pay their respects, Godfather-style.

He tells me that he used to be a fisherman, but set up this place after blowing a fortune on gambling. His wife now holds the purse strings, and by the wry smile on her face, she had to fight to get him on the straight and narrow. The restaurant, however, is bursting with customers, with people queuing up along the quayside to get in (to the irritation of the neighbouring restaurants). It's hugely successful, but non-kosher, serving shellfish *and* opening on the Shabbat (bang out of order for kosher observers). The Torah explicitly bans shellfish or any fish that don't have scales.

Beny cooks my lunch himself, talking as he cooks: 'I've been a fisherman all my life. In the last 20 years things have changed. You couldn't sell seafood before. People wouldn't buy it. Then young guys started going abroad and developed a taste for it. Before, Israel wasn't that cosmopolitan, then everything changed. People came back with a new take on stuff like seafood and other things.'

I say that Tel Aviv seems to be on a different planet from Jerusalem and Beny explains, 'They don't have sea in Jerusalem. Here there is the beach, it's summer. Summer, sailing and fun, that's Tel Aviv. Jerusalem is the holy city. People there are a bit different. You go there to pray, to visit. People who come here from Jerusalem don't want to go back.'

I'm slightly confused about secular Jews, though. Lapsed Christians I know back home tend to say they are no longer Christian, but here in Israel, people can be totally secular, yet totally Jewish. Do people come to terms with levels of spirituality or do they just ignore the issue?

Beny is a case in point: as well as this cheeky non-kosher joint, he also owns Beny Hadayg, apparently one of the strictest kosher restaurants in the city (double-kosher or kosher kosher, as they call it). I visit the restaurant to meet a kosher cop and try to work out this culinary/spiritual relativity. A kosher cop is someone who makes sure that all the food in a restaurant is prepared to kosher rules laid down in the Torah, so he should know what it's all about.

In Beny Hadayg I meet Raffi, an orthodox Jew complete with *pe'otes* tucked into a skullcap and dressed in thick black clothing that shows up all the flour, sweat and assorted greasy detritus of a working kitchen. The roaring fires and hissing grills make it too hot for me in here so Raffi must be boiling underneath all those clothes.

Raffi scuttles about the kitchen sifting the flour for bugs, salting meat to remove the blood, slapping chops on the grill, fish in the oven, and livers on the rotisserie. He blesses the meals, blesses the bread and checks everything for provenance and kosher authenticity. There are hundreds of specific food rules, but the main ones are: no pork or shellfish, no mixing of meat and dairy produce and no bugs. As he potters through the lunchtime prep, Raffi tells me he's 'looking for cockroaches or worms or any other bugs'.

Raffi is not, however, the chef. The chef is a small, cheerful Arab bloke by the name of Malik who looks on bemused as Raffi runs about doing his kosher thing. Malik says, 'We also have our religion and we have to follow its law so I respect any other religion.' But I get the sense that he thinks this is all a bit silly. He and Raffi have to perform an elaborate dance around each other, with Malik preparing and seasoning

IDEOLOGICAL FOOD

all the food, then Raffi checking it and placing it on the grill, then Malik stirring, fiddling and plating everything before Raffi checks it again. It looks suspiciously like me meddling with the food on the rare occasions that my wife does the cooking. Malik concedes that there were lots of arguments to begin with, but they are now a good team.

I ask Raffi what kosher rules are meant to achieve, and he tells me 'We are commanded by God, who told us what we can and cannot eat. By eating only kosher food I fulfil God's will.'

I'm still confused about *why*. 'So if someone doesn't eat kosher food is it possible they'll go to hell rather then heaven?'

'It's not for me to judge. But foodwise, I feel that by keeping kosher I improve my chances. It's not automatic that if you eat non-kosher food you'll go to hell.'

I confess to him that I'm still confused, and ask what spiritual difference there is between kosher and non kosher food, but he doesn't understand   he just says that the rules are there and if you don't obey them, you might go to hell.

'I can understand that, but *why*?'

He thinks my question is absurd. 'You don't ask what the rules are for – you obey them.'

Beny sits at a nearby table and says, 'I opened this place because my daughter eats kosher and I love my daughter very much and I eat kosher but sometimes, you know ...'

Now I'm completely baffled, so I drag Raffi over to try to sort out this kosher thing once and for all. I ask him, 'Is Beny going to heaven or is Beny going to hell?' He says, 'I can't tell. But sorry to say this, according to religious law a man that opens a non-kosher restaurant is responsible for leading people astray. But if a man opens a kosher place, he is helping people to do a good deed.'

Beny is sanguine: 'Everything is weighed. How much good and how much bad. That's how you are judged.'

I take a long look at him, and suggest, 'You've been bad, haven't you?'

He laughs with a Cheshire cat grin. 'Maybe,' he says. 'Look at Raffi's phone,' he says, 'that's kosher too.'

Raffi shows me the orthodoxy approval stamp on his mobile. 'Approved! Some one has checked it that there is no SMS, and no way to access unsuitable things. You can't do anything with it. No Internet, no camera. It's good for the spirituality of kids and parents not to expose them to bad things.'

After I leave the restaurant, I confess to Efrat that I still haven't got to grips with the issues of kosher, orthodoxy and secularism. She says, 'I am very secular.'

'Does that mean you're less Jewish?'

'Don't be insane,' she says. 'You're either Jewish or you're not.' She just doesn't believe that she's going to hell for observing fewer of the rules.

Haifa

The ancient port of Haifa is a ghastly sight: a concrete rash that spills inland from the Mediterranean, crowned by a vast oil refinery. I presume that everything in Israel was built in a blinding hurry after the state of Israel was established in 1948. You can imagine the panic: 'Oh, my God, the cousins are coming, and there's nowhere for them to stay.'

I drive to an immigrant dormitory town with row upon row of crumbling concrete apartment blocks, all ugly, functional, but gratefully received by the newly arrived diaspora. Aviva is one of approximately 53,000 Ethiopian Jews who were airlifted from Ethiopia in two secretive and controversial operations in 1984 and 1991. Back in Israel there was much debate over whether the Ethiopians were really Jews at all, or just freeloading, welfare-seeking migrants. It certainly wasn't easy for them to leave their homeland and all their possessions behind, and integration into Israeli life for Aviva has been difficult.

She takes me to her local shop to buy food, and I ask her if it's anything like the shops back home in Ethiopia. She laughs and explains that when she first arrived, she burst into tears at all the food on the shelves after a lifetime of struggling to feed her family. 'I took armfuls of food, but the shop owner had to explain that I should come back when I had some money.' The food was unusual too: 'We didn't know how to eat things like pasta or lentils, let alone digest them, and many of us had malnutrition problems to begin with, but we soon learnt.'

Aviva remembers the traumas of the five-day journey from her home to the airlift points: 'We were hunted and intimidated along the way – my father was an important man so the authorities imprisoned him for some time to stop him from leaving, but eventually we managed to get out. We couldn't bring anything with us – we lost it all.' She arrived at the airstrip and remembers seeing the huge white bird for the first time. She didn't know what to think, but it had always been her dream to come to Israel.

IDEOLOGICAL FOOD

These days Aviva makes Israeli staples such as hummus, bread, pizza and chicken nuggets, but today she wants to make some of her traditional food for us. She cooks injera, made entirely of fermenting yeast, poured out from huge bags of Dutch-produced dried yeast. They look like oddly honeycombed crêpes and taste only of yeast unlike the ones I ate in Ethiopia itself. They're not entirely pleasant, but they are fun to eat. Aviva's parents, her absurdly beautiful daughters and some old friends from Ethiopia join us and we all cram into the sitting room to eat. I ask them about the old times in Ethiopia and how their lives must have changed, but they prefer not to talk about the past. She cries when she remembers the journey she's had and their hard life in Ethiopia.

Aviva gives me some traditional beer to drink. It has the consistency of mud, a taste of salt and a flavour of yeast. It must be extremely alcoholic to be this disgusting, so I drink a huge slug of it. But when Aviva tells me that it's not alcoholic, it's just a traditional drink, I give up. Eventually her eldest daughter puts on some traditional music and we all get up to dance around the coffee table to Ethiopian drum-and-wail. Her daughters teach me how to dance: it's all about the shoulders, apparently. Everyone, including the grandparents, looks funky and cool as their shoulders float around as if they aren't actually part of their bodies, but I just look like Vicky Pollard, shrugging manically. It helps clear the air of sorrow, however, and by the time I leave I am sweaty and exhausted.

The Bedouin

I head into the baking hot, bone-dry Negev desert in the south of Israel to a village called Tel Arad. About 140,000 Bedouin live in the Negev and they were incorporated into the Israeli state and offered citizenship when it was set up, but their lifestyle has made the transformation difficult. And, as they point out, they are Arabs in a new Jewish state.

The Bedouin have lived here for centuries, but their nomadic methods of subsistence, and ancient systems of traditional land ownership (usually lacking any sort of formalized documentation), have made them a thorn in the side of the Israeli authorities eager for land for the continuing influx of Jews from around the world, even in the relatively difficult environment of the desert. Under pressure from the government to become house-dwelling citizens, about half the Bedouin have now sold their land and moved into government housing. Many more, however, have refused to sell and live in what are called unrecognized villages, like Tel Arad.

I'll be honest – I wasn't expecting anything like this. My romantic idea of tents and wandering nomads haven't turns out to be just that – an idea. The reality is a messy wreck of a village, desperately poor and crumbling. The only clues as to its inhabitants are a few raggedy, filthy-tempered camels.

I meet one of the village elders, Hajj Audeh Abu Khaled, who's lived here since he was a boy. Many of the Bedouin are refusing to move from the land they're on until their claims are met. They've been refused access to basic amenities by the Israeli government, and their houses are under threat of being demolished because they either won't move off, or because they've been built without permits (which they say are almost impossible to obtain). It's a stalemate that has been going on for decades.

Abu Khaled says, 'I am an Israeli citizen, but only on paper. They bring in people from all over the world, from Russia, from Britain. Me, whose people have been living here for centuries, since the time of Abraham, I don't have the right to live on my own land or build a house.'

The Bedouin of Tel Arad try to maintain aspects of their traditional culture, hence the presence of camels, which aren't a whole lot of use for anything else. I ask to meet one of the women in the village in order to find out about food supplies, but the Bedouin are very wary of letting strangers meet their women. I persevere and I'm eventually introduced to an elderly aunt called Hajjah Eidah Omm Mohammad who is making the flatbread that's a staple of the Bedouin diet. She rails about Bedouin men: 'They don't get involved at all; they don't touch one single thing. They just bring in the money and everything else is done by the women. Even to do the housework, we wait for them to go out, and then we do everything. They could be dying from hunger and they still wouldn't do anything. Women do everything.

'Life is tough for Bedouin women. I would like to see men share some of the burden.' Blimey, I wasn't expecting that.

Later over dinner (no women allowed), I ask the men what they think the future holds. Abu Khaled says, 'Our future is full of problems, and if the policy of our government doesn't change, it will be even more difficult. Every day that passes is more difficult then the day before.

'What are my dreams? I don't want much. I'm like a hungry man. First of all I have to feed myself. If I'm thirsty then I have to drink. Only then can I have bigger dreams.'

IDEOLOGICAL FOOD

How to Milk a Camel

Abu Khaled shows me the village's illegal water supply – the Israeli authorities have banned water supplies into unauthorized villages, so an enterprising bloke has laid down a pipe and pumps in water and charges for it. Even when people are this deprived, they find a way of making cash. Then I am taken off to find a camel.

Camels used to be the main transport and food supply for the Bedouin, but now they're mostly status symbols. A good young camel can cost the same as a second-hand car. They do provide some milk, however, and it's very high in vitamin C and richer than either cow's or goat's milk so it is often used to nurse very young babies.

We find an exceedingly grumpy camel, and Abu Khaled's cousin shows me how to milk her. The technique seems to be to grab one of her vast teats, and to employ much the same hand action as used with a goat, but all the time, dodging its flailing legs and snapping teeth.

When a camel has a calf, the Bedouin traditionally reserve one row of teats for the calf and one row for themselves, although no one seems to have discussed the tradition with this particular camel. I finally manage to get one enormous gushing squirt of milk into a cup and take a good swig. It has a deep, gutsy smell to it but a surprisingly clean taste, like cow's milk.

Gaza

Sderot is the closest major Israeli town to the Gaza Strip and for the last six years its residents have been the target for Kassam missiles – home-made rockets that the Palestinians regularly fire over the border. Since the intifada ended, they are the Palestinians' main weapon of attack on Israelis, and also Israel's current main cause of bitterness towards the Arabs. Whilst I'm here, they are frequently mentioned in the papers as a reason not to negotiate with the Palestinians. Most Kassams land in open ground, and are simply a psychological weapon, but they do also kill.

I meet Avi, the head of an ambulance unit that's deployed whenever a missile lands. His home has been hit twice by missiles and he's lost a good friend in one attack. We drive around the town in his ambulance, and he shows me where rockets have landed and where people have died. He then takes us to a hill from which we can see Gaza.

The boundary fences are a kilometre away and the army patrols them, but Kassams can travel up to 16 km, says Avi. The missiles are just lobbed over, really, and there's no telling where they might land: Avi's kids' school was hit that morning. The trouble is that access to Gaza (and hence all trade) is completely controlled by Israel, and since Hamas started to take control (refusing to recognize the right of Israel to exist), all payments to the Palestinian Authority have been halted, causing horrible hardship in the tiny Gaza Strip. The Kassams are terrible, random weapons, but many people see them as an expression of frustration and humiliation as much as violence.

I have a chat to Kirsty Campbell, the spokesperson for the World Food Programme in Israel. She also seems to be in charge of security, love and affection for the WFP's embattled staff around here. She's a welcome relief from the usual official in Israel – she's friendly, frank and reasonable, happy to tell us her feelings off the record, as well as the official UN line.

We're standing about a kilometre from Karni, the main crossing for all the goods that keep Gaza alive. This is effectively Gaza's main artery, and the only way that its residents can sell goods to Israel and vice versa. It's also the only route for food aid into the strip and today, as on many days, it's firmly closed. This is nothing short of disastrous. Eighty-five per cent of Gaza's population relies on food aid.

'There are around 850 million people around the world who are hungry, meaning that they can't get a nutritional meal on a daily basis (on average most people need around 2,100 calories a day to function properly). It's actually a bit more complicated than that – as well as macronutrients such as carbohydrates, you need micronutrients like vitamins and minerals,' says Kirsty. She tells us that although some Palestinian women may look fat, it is often because they have a terrible carbohydrate-only diet, and they are actually malnourished because they can't afford fruit or vegetables, and suffer from vitamin deficiencies.

Out of these 850 million, the WFP help about 80 million through school food projects (a free meal at school is often enough to get kids into schools and out of the fields), work-for-food projects and, where absolutely necessary, simple food-aid handouts. The trouble about food deliveries, though, is that they create dependency and destroy local farmers' ability to sell any produce. Gaza, with few jobs, little land and a large refugee community is heavily dependent on WFP help.

IDEOLOGICAL FOOD

As we talk, we hear the constant rattle of machine-gun fire, and the sounds of rocket-propelled grenades and explosions. Just over the fence Gaza is disintegrating as Hamas blast their arch rivals Fatah out of the few buildings that they still hold. The viciousness of the rout is fuelled by the fact that Fatah is itself accused of staging a similar coup against Hamas in the 1990s, so vengeance is sweet and bloody.

We look over at Gaza City from the perimeter fence of the kibbutz. It's a pile of crumbling concrete buildings over there, and I can't imagine what misery and terror the people must be feeling. Our news correspondents say that the only people on the streets are gunmen, that there's no food and much fear. I can't help wondering how Alan Johnston must feel (it's now 95 days since he was kidnapped) to hear all the shooting and explosions around him; he must be wondering if the worst is about to happen.

Right now, there appears to be a meltdown in Gaza with factional war between Fatah and Hamas causing mayhem and reports of 40 dead on some days, up to 65 on others, and hundreds of wounded. Today Hamas has taken control of most of the Gaza Strip, wiping out a large proportion of the militia belonging to the more moderate Fatah.

It's hard not to feel exasperation at the chaos here. The last Israeli settlers were evicted from the Gaza Strip in 2005, but instead of a rebuilding of the Palestinian territories and an improvement in living conditions and Palestinian pride, the place has descended into internecine chaos, nasty politics and violence aimed at Israel.

Kirsty is equally frustrated with the situation. The WFP simply carries on sending food over, watching conditions deteriorate. Chaos gets worse, and everyone throws their hands in the air. Then everyone starts sorting out the mess all over again.

Suddenly a Kassam rocket whizzes close above our heads. I'm shocked – I thought they were too busy shooting at each other in there – and I decide to leave.

So that's it, is it?

I've had a warped view of the world over the last two years. I've poked my nose into its grimmest, poorest, most miserable and damaged corners. At first I worried that I would lose empathy, become desensitized by what I saw and pessimistic for the future. I worried that I was a poverty tourist, a disaster entertainer, and that meeting people living such difficult lives would be patronizing and insulting, but everywhere I went people wanted me to tell their stories, to show me their homes and meet their families. And when I came face to face with the worst deprivation imaginable it had the strange effect of making me certain, deep down, that life for these people *will* get better. Because when we learn about real people rather than just the politics, the disasters, the ideology or the oppression that symbolizes them, we begin to care a little bit more and eventually that care will lead to change. I also realized that pessimism is an admission of defeat, a self-fulfilling prophecy, and a luxury that we mustn't choose. We have to believe that the people of Cité Soleil will emerge from hell, that democracy will re-emerge in Burma, that refugees in Uganda will return home, that the corrupt will be destroyed by their own rottenness and that eventually … eventually, some wealth will filter down from the rich to the poor. If we are defeatist about these things, we do people an injustice.

It is generally agreed that the planet will need to produce more food over the next 50 years than it did over the last 10,000 years combined due to population growth, industrialization and medical advances. The pressure that this puts on people and the environment is going to cause food and water-related wars, environmental degradation, widespread hunger and a desperate need for solutions, all of which will be compounded by unsustainable soil management and an agricultural switch from food production to ethanol production. The world and its people need our help, our concern and, hell, even our fascination if that's what it takes.

For me, that fascination came when I saw myself reflected in the people I met: I saw my weaknesses, my sense of humour, my aspirations, my frustrations and my love for my family reflected in Odwa, Anna, Theo, Sabra, Maye and Faté. I am deeply sad that I may not see some of them again, and I know that my life will be the poorer for it.

A note on sources

Population: the national statistics bureaux for each nation, or, in their absence, the UN Department of Economic and Social Affairs 2007 mid-year estimate.

Percentage living on less than $2/day according to Purchasing Power Parity, the International Monetary Fund's *World Economic Outlook Database April 2007*. (N.B. this is calculated by taking into account the differing cost of living in different countries. However, because many chapters are concerned with issues of international trade (which PPP does not help with), the nominal GDP is also given – see below.)

Percentage living below the poverty line: the *CIA World Factbook*. This is a relatively unreliable figure, as all countries judge their poverty line differently (rich countries tend to offer a more generous definition), but in the absence of better statistics, I've had to use these.

UNDP Human Development Index position: the UN Development Programme's *Human Development Report 2006*. This looks at three basic dimensions of human development: 'a long and healthy life, knowledge and a decent standard of living'.

Corruption Perceptions Index position: from Transparency International's *Corruption Perceptions Index 2006*.

GDP (nominal) per capita: International Monetary Fund's *World Economic Outlook Database April 2007*.

Malnutrition: percentage of population suffering from under-nourishment in 2001–3 as stated in the UN's *The State of Food Insecurity in the World 2006* report.

Thanks to

Marc Perkins: brilliant series producer, stress-bearing girder, drinking buddy and great friend. Thanks for bringing me back alive, if a little hungover.

Everyone at BBC Current Affairs who worked on the TV series, yet is criminally under-acknowledged in the book, especially the eminently huggable Will Daws, Karen O'Connor (still got those pictures of you frying my testicles), Alex Mackintosh, Colin Pereira, James Jones, Nadia Beginin, Mark Collins, Ruhi Hamid, Chris Alcock, Olly Bootle, Julie Noon, Callum McRae, Susan Crighton, Jane Willey, Nigel Read, plus many more too numerous to mention.

The fixers who sorted and translated and calmed us down when things were getting hairy: Dawit Nida (Ethiopia), Aleem Agha (Afghanistan), Yoon-jung Seo (South Korea), Mario Delatour (Haiti), Efrat Suzin (Israel), Alaa T. Badarneh (West Bank), Yan Yan (China), Louis Fon and Joseph Danjie (Cameroon), Bitek Oketch (Uganda), Ilyena (Ukraine), Black Tom (Burma), Louise Murray (Arctic), Luisa Ortiz Perez (Mexico), Sandra La Fuente (Venezuela), Richard Broadbridge (Fiji), Ralph Steele (Tonga) and Anuj Chopra (India).

The many organisations and charities who helped and protected us, and especially the World Food Programme in Afghanistan, Uganda, Haiti, Israel/ Occupied territories and Ethiopia, MINUSTAH forces in Haiti, the US army in Kabul and the Karen National Liberation Army.

For this book, thanks to Nicky Ross, Christopher Tinker, Gillian Holmes and everyone at Random House, as well as Borra Garson and Michelle Kass.

Thanks also to Mimi, Erica Sutton, Eliza Hazlewood, Loris, Eve Perkins, Tom, Stephan & Sylvie and Joseph Mitchell-Krafchenko for the armbands thing – a debt I can never repay.

And of course, thanks to my long-suffering family, who had to endure sixteen versions of the phrase, 'Now listen, Daddy's got to go away again tomorrow ...' To my magical, gorgeous nymphs Georgia, Daisy and Poppy. Thanks for letting me go, and for making me feel so desperately, unbearably homesick whilst I was gone.

A dedication

I'd like to dedicate this book to the people across the world – refugees, babushkas, hunters, herders, soldiers, farmers, mothers, fathers and cooks – who opened up their hearts and thoughts to me, shared their food with me, told me jokes as well as tales of unbearable tragedy, and took me into their families and homes with generosity and good grace despite poverty, hunger, oppression and disenfranchisement.

It's also for my mum, Jean Gates, who helped me realize that food is a brilliant way to understand the world.